DAKOTA DAYS

DAKOTA DAYS

JOHN GREEN

St. Martin's Press   New York

Design by Lee Wade

Library of Congress Cataloging in Publication Data

Green, John, 1947–
    Dakota days.

    1. Lennon, John, 1940–80.   2. Singers—Biography.
I. Title.
'ML420.L38G7 1983   784.5'4'00924   [B]   83-2881
ISBN 0-312-18176-0

To Baba Lu Aiya et Yemáya

Contents

Introduction

My name is John Green, and I am among other things a professional tarot card reader. I have been reading tarot for some seventeen years now. For those of you who are not familiar with the art of tarot, there are some things you should know. Tarot cards are a wonderful device for seeing into people and the situations in which they find themselves. Clients tell their card readers things that they wouldn't tell anyone else —their lovers, their spouses, their families, or their friends. As a student of mine put it wonderingly, "People unzip themselves!" So a reader has an excellent opportunity to see into his fellow man in a way that is denied to others.

Ordinarily a reader would never write about a client. We are, by both preference and necessity, a discreet lot. But the case of John Lennon, I think, represents an appropriate exception to that rule. Much has been written about him since his death that has been so utterly adulatory as to flatten this protean, antic soul into a two-dimensional tin god, more to be hero-worshiped than loved or understood. Having known the man intimately for the last five years of his life, I don't believe that that is what he would have wanted. During his life John was seldom shy about sharing his fears and faults with the world. Indeed, that was much of his art and appeal.

One of John's favorite references was to the story of the six blind Hindus describing an elephant. One would hold the ear and say that the elephant was like a leaf. Another would press against the side and say, "No, no, the elephant is like a wall." Each in turn touched a different part of the elephant and assumed that that part was the whole. So do we all when we attempt to describe the truth.

I do not claim here that this book is the whole story of John's last years, for that would be false. This is the part of the story that I saw and shared, day by day, year by year.

In telling this story I have used several literary devices that I hope will help convey the atmosphere of those years. Most obvious of these is the extensive use of dialogue. Some of the conversations are in fact quoted verbatim, but others are reconstructions and condensations of often very lengthy conversations, recorded in the style of the speakers and using their particular idiolects.

You may well ask how this card reader remembered all this information. In response, let me say that, first, I have a fine memory and, second, working with John was a decidedly memorable experience. But again, I only claim to have a hold on our elephant's tail. I am sure that John did not tell me everything that went on in his mind and I am just as sure that he told others different things than he told me.

There are certain elements of the story that I have left out because they do not belong in print. After all, even public figures deserve their share of privacy. Some references to the darker side of John's personality, however, have been included here to give the reader a clearer understanding of the man and the trials he endured. They have not been included to demean him—quite the reverse. How could anyone believe in or admire a man who appears to have no faults? Such references are there simply to give the reader a more complete picture of a very complicated man.

So what we have here is not John Lennon's whole story. It is instead that part of the story that *I* know and thought important to share. This is the card reader's story, told through reconstructed conversations, of the man's inner thoughts and feelings on the events that influenced his last years.

The man I knew was not the Beatle, not the performer or the rock star. I met him when his muse had abandoned him, leaving him unable to write, a calamity that drove him into isolation and despair. Since we had to tell the press something, we concocted the story that John was being a "househusband." But I think that the real story is far more interesting. It is the story of an artist's heroic journey down to the bottom of himself and his triumphant return.

That is a story worth knowing—the story of a man who did not desert his fans, but was afraid they would desert him if they knew that he could no longer write the songs they craved. In his lifetime I helped keep his secret for him. But now, more than two years have passed since his death. It is time to look at another part of John Lennon's life and to see the man whole.

· 1 ·

KING JOHN
CONSULTS THE
ORACLE

I first met John Lennon on Ground Hog Day of 1975. I had been lured out of my Fifth Avenue burrow for the occasion by Yoko. It was, she said, an emergency.

I was used to Yoko's emergencies. They happened day and night. They came in two varieties: routine and titanic. "The cat is under the sofa and what should we do?" was a routine emergency. A 60-million-dollar lawsuit was the other kind.

The phone call came at an atypically civilized hour: 6:47 P.M. I immediately assumed the worst. Having been conditioned by long months of 2:00 A.M. calls waking me from a dead sleep to ask if I "had some time," I instinctively mistrusted the convenience of the hour. Convenient emergencies are generally the worst kind.

"John's home!" Yoko rasped.

1

This might not qualify as an "emergency," but it certainly qualified as news. Fifteen months earlier, in October 1973, John had walked out the front door saying he was going for a paper. There had been a few phone calls since then, but for the most part his exact whereabouts during that time had been more or less a mystery. According to Yoko, his return was as sudden and unexpected as his departure. Apparently he simply showed up at the door and said, "No papers!"

"And . . . ?" I urged, bracing myself.

"And I think he's been poisoned!"

"And . . . ?"

"And you have to read for him right away. It's an emergency."

"I'll be right there," I answered, but Yoko had already hung up. She knew I would come. I was paid for this sort of thing. I was Yoko Ono's grand exalted number-one wizard, tarot card reader, and all-around panjandrum, on call all day, every day, and every night as well.

It's a living.

A half an hour later I was sitting with Yoko in the White Room, one of the ten large rooms in the Lennons' apartment in that grand old New York landmark building, the Dakota. The White Room, so called because every last thing in it was white—walls, ceiling, blinds, rug, piano, and the two large sofas that filled the corner of the room nearest the door—was the apartment's formal living room. The fact that I was to read tarot cards there, rather than in the bedroom or the kitchen, indicated the seriousness of the moment.

I lowered my considerable bulk carefully into one of the big white sofas, compressing the foam rubber until my knees were in my armpits. Yoko settled lightly on the sofa to my right. Her long jet-black hair and signature black sweater were in sharp contrast to the all-white backdrop. She took a deep breath and reached for a cigarette, which I lit for her, and began briefing me for my official meeting with John.

"John's here," she said, as if that explained everything.

"You said that."

"You have to read for him." She blew out the smoke and the words with the same breath.

"You said that too."

"But he doesn't know who you are."

"Tell him," I suggested.

"You don't understand! If he thinks you have the same name as he does, he will be jealous."

"I'll leave," I volunteered.

"No, no! You have to read for him." This was going to be difficult. "Remember when John was in Florida and you kept giving me information from the cards about what he was feeling and where he was so I could always find him?"

I nodded. Guessing which motel your client's husband is holed up in that day is a neat trick. I was rather proud of our success. Yoko would collect the names of every likely motel in the area and then we would read cards on each one of them in succession to see where John was most likely to be. Our success rate had been good, which was important because a call to the wrong place asking for John Lennon could easily start undesirable rumors as to why he was there and with whom. As pleased as I had been at our success, however, I was unsure as to why Yoko was referring to it now. She explained.

"Well, he asked me how I could always find him because he thought I was having him followed and I wasn't, you know. I told him that it was my new psychic because he likes psychics too and he asked what your name was and I told him and he said, 'You know if we ever get back together again I want you to get rid of that psychic.' So now we're back together and I told him I did—get rid of you, you know—so now I can't tell him who you are, so you're Charlie Swan, that's what I told him, see?"

"I'm Charlie?"

"Yes, you have to do it. I told him, you see? No, promise!

I'll get him now." So saying, she launched herself from the sofa, snubbed her cigarette half out, and raced toward the door. Pausing briefly, she turned to warn me—"Remember, you're Charlie Swan, Charlie"—and then she was gone.

She was gone only a few minutes. When she returned she was leading John like a prize Holstein-Friesian. There he was, John Lennon, somehow larger than life. There were the famous little round glasses, bent nose, and tight smile. Less expected was the curious visual impact he made: He radiated. He stood in that stark-white room and gathered light as if a follow spot was on him. Fascinating effect. I've since come to think of it as the mark of a true performer. But it was his voice that struck me most. Although I had never met the man before, he sounded so familiar.

"Hello, Charlie," he chimed as he stuck out his hand in his best hail-fellow manner. Somehow I managed to lumber to my feet and shake his hand. He looked up at me. "God, yer a big one, aren't ya?" he gasped in mock awe.

"Only sometimes," I responded in a tone of grave politeness, although he was quite right. I am six feet six and 250 pounds after a bit of serious dieting.

We clasped hands while Yoko smiled on with motherly pride. Looking straight at me, she asked, "Would you like to come to the kitchen for some coffee, John?" Then she sucked in her breath a little to underscore her error.

"John?" whooped John. "You call ol' Charles here John, Yoko? He's not John, *I* am! He's Charles. Aren't you, Charles?"

"So I'm told."

As we silently made the mile-long trek to the kitchen, I observed that the signs of John's presence were already apparent: a shirt here, a magazine there, little plates for snacks everywhere. John and Yoko walked ahead of me, arms around each other in the attitude of lovers reunited. It was going to be a long evening.

At the end of the hall we turned left, passed through the white door with its stained-glass insert, and entered the spacious kitchen. It had a desk and a small work space, more foam rubber sofas, beige this time, set in a conversation pit in front of the video and stereo center, which was built into the wall. At the far end of the room, across a terra-cotta tile floor, a plain wood table was set against the window. John and I drew up chairs while Yoko got the coffee. No one spoke.

I was more than a little nervous. This was, of course, John Lennon, megacelebrity, and I was going to read his future with seventy-eight little pieces of cardboard—the tarot deck. In such circumstances, I always have a moment of thinking what an ass I might make of myself. But more than that, I was pondering this man in the light of the image I'd built up in months of readings for Yoko. All that time, she had primed me to regard him as dangerous, unpredictable, and downright brutal. This image sorted oddly with the hugely charming fellow John was projecting. The result was to make me ready for anything.

The nervousness was making my hand shake enough to rattle my coffee mug ferociously as I set it down. I felt obliged to explain.

"You know I'm jittery."

"Why should *you* be scared?" asked John. "*I'm* the one who's scared of *you*. It's *my* future, you know!" Mr. Lennon was being charming. It was working.

I took my tarot card box from my briefcase. The cards were inside, wrapped in a purple silk scarf—a touch of showmanship. I unwrapped the deck with elaborate slowness. With a tinkle and clatter, the coffee cups were whisked away to make room for the cards. I looked at Yoko.

"This is John's reading," I said. Yoko knew spectators weren't allowed at tarot readings. "Perhaps you'd excuse us?" It wasn't really a question.

"Oh, it's all right," she said, smiling brightly.

I swung around to John. "Usually readings are totally private," I explained. "That way, you can feel freer in what you ask and I can be freer in the way I answer."

"It's all right, John," Yoko insisted. "I know what you are going to ask about: being poisoned."

This had the effect of suddenly reminding John that he was supposedly poisoned, and that his previously buoyant demeanor was perhaps not quite the best impression to convey under the circumstances. He promptly slumped in his chair, trying to look pale, with the identifiably sickly expression of a man who had been off with his mistress for a year and was wise enough on his return not to appear too happy too soon. All was *not* forgiven.

"It's all right, John," pressed Yoko. "You can ask anything. We don't have any secrets, do we?"

"Okay," he answered. By now, he looked genuinely ill.

I suspected that as Yoko had more than a few secrets, her husband might just have a few of his own. This reading was going to be like trying not to step on anyone's toes in a rush-hour subway.

Nevertheless, I shuffled the cards and laid each with care in its proper position. The result looked something like a cross between a stained-glass window and the molecular structure of a compound salt. "You'll have to give me a minute to read this," I said to John. "They're not in English."

"We think May did it," volunteered Yoko. May was the mistress in question.

I squirmed and twitched in deliberation, following the map of cards. "Well," I said, heaving a sigh and dragging lengthily on my cigarette for effect, "you haven't been poisoned."

Yoko, used to more elaborate answers, wanted more. "What else does it say? We think she put it in John's tea."

But there was nothing in the cards that said poison and I

always trust the cards, so I chose to stand pat. John looked down at the twenty-two cards laid out on the table and I could see he wanted more. I suspected that the poison story was a ruse to get sympathy. I had read *on* him for Yoko long enough to know that he was not above a fib or two to deflect any stormy recriminations upon his return. I think also that he suspected that any self-respecting commercial occultist would jump at the chance to declare him deathly ill in order to perform a spontaneous (and lucrative) cure. He stared at me mistrustfully.

"How do you know I haven't been poisoned?"

I turned toward him so that Yoko couldn't see my face and said with a smile but in a very grave tone, "The same way I know it was jasmine tea." I had made that up. No one had mentioned jasmine tea, but playing the hunch that the story was fake I used it as an opening to show John that I had found him out and wasn't going to betray him.

His eyes grew wide with understanding. "That's amazing," he cooed, echoing one of Yoko's favorite expressions. The pact was formed. "How did you know it was jasmine tea?"

"I'm psychic."

"It's good you weren't poisoned," said Yoko, a little disappointed by the anticlimax.

"A great relief," agreed John. Then he seemed to fall to musing, his gaze roving about the room patiently, whistling under his breath.

"I get it," snapped Yoko. "You want me to leave the room."

John folded his face into an engaging smile and fluttered his eyelids at her.

"I'll be in the White Room if you need me," she huffed, and left.

"Good night, dear," he called after her.

John held his expression fixedly on the closed door, waiting for her reentry until experience told him she had passed the point of no return. Then he turned his attention toward me.

Drawing a breath and brightening, he said, "You know, Charles, this is a historical occasion. King John comes to the Oracle. You *are* an oracle, aren't you?"

I nodded, not wanting to interrupt the performance, knowing that it would give me time to study him.

"It's timeless. All through history people like me have come to people like you, afraid you're not real and more afraid you are. You *are* real, aren't you, Charles?"

"It comes and goes."

"It's the classic horror-movie plot. The wife drags Dad to the fortune-teller and the fortune-teller turns out to be a bona fide seer from Seers and Roebuck. Very scary, what?"

"Is it?"

He pouted and tried a new approach. I could tell he was curious. I could also tell that he had a real question for me in there. He danced around it so nimbly that I knew it had to be important. Still, he wasn't ready to ask it. Instead, he told me hours of stories, defining himself with little tales and parables, creating for me the impression he wanted me to have. A great many of his stories were about people ripping him off. He knew they did and boasted that he didn't care.

"Legal eagles, laundry ladies, it's all the same to me," he said, waving his hand airily. "Everybody knows who I am, knows I'm rich. I go down to the corner to buy a pair of socks and all of a sudden it's a fifteen-dollar pair of socks. If I buy a dozen, I'm Mr. Lennon, the hero, or at least a . . ." he groped for the right term.

"Rich dupe?" I volunteered.

"Good loser," he continued firmly. "If I say, 'Fifteen dollars for a pair of socks is too fuckin' much,' then I'm a heel. And as we all know, time wounds all heels." He recited the last in a menacing singsong. "I like that line: 'Time wounds all heels.' Don't you? You can have it. It's not mine. The rich gotta pay

8

too much for everything, because they're rich. I call it the poor people's tax. I've stopped fighting it. Anyway, the money goes to a better class of people that way."

"Have you considered that by not fighting, you're encouraging people to rip you off?"

"Yeah, I thought about it and I decided that it was bullshit. I make a record; I gotta pay the guy in the studio; the guy in the studio's gotta pay the grocer; the grocer's gotta pay his shopclerk; and she goes out and buys my record . . . hopefully. Everybody's gotta pay too much for everything, and the more you got the more you gotta pay pay pay." His tone had become contemptuous. Then he seemed to decide that he didn't want to do that rap, so he changed direction again.

"You know, I've met a lot of psychics." He proceeded to tell me of a card reader he had met who had to look up the meanings of the cards in a book. Then there was a girl in India who could tell how much change you had in your pocket just by looking at you. Mystics and magicians, Lennon had met them all.

"And they don't fool me, you know. I can see right through an act when I see one. So if you've got any plans about being the next Maharishi, I'd just forget it."

"If I wanted followers I would have incarnated as a mother duck," I assured him.

He smirked and was off again. "Do you believe in UFOs? I saw one, you know!"

"This is a test, this is a test. Do you believe what I say I saw?" I announced in a mechanical voice.

"Well, do you? I mean, do you think it's crazy?"

"Listen. I'm a tarot card reader. I believe that I can see the future with a fistful of cards and you're asking *me* what's crazy?"

"Right," he went on obliviously. "I was on the roof, about nine in the morning, doing my usual, watching the people go to work, when I saw this thing, this ship. It wasn't much of a ship, maybe big enough to hold two people. It didn't make any noise, just glided along above the East River, heading downtown." I could tell that he enjoyed this story. It was another test, a different mesh through which to sift me.

"Were there any reported sightings that day?" I asked when he had finished.

"How the hell should I know? I'm not an enthusiast, you know. I don't go following this sort of thing. I just saw it. I sure as hell wasn't going to report it. Headline: 'Ex-Beatle Sees Saucer.' Oh, that's good, what was he on? Soooo, what's your opinion, dear witch doctor?"

"You see a saucer, I see a ghost, and somebody else sees a bird, a plane, or Superman—or nothing at all. What you see depends directly upon what you're looking for. It's called selective perception. You see what you choose."

"But what was really there?"

"Beats me, I didn't see it."

"Do you ever give a straight answer to anything?"

That was my opening. I picked up the cards. "Questions?"

"Yeah, okay. What about career?"

"What about it? The more specific the question, the more specific the answer."

"Okay." He seemed to be warming to the reading a little. "I've got a record I'm going to release. I want to know how it's going to do." He explained that he was talking about an album to be called *Rock 'n' Roll.* It was a collection of classic songs from the early days of rock.

So I spread and read the cards, spread after spread, hour after hour. I read on the record's distribution, its promotion, its radio support, and anything and everything else I could think of. Each time I spread the cards on a new topic, I'd ask him questions that the cards suggested, then spread the cards yet again on the new subjects that emerged. As he answered, he was first agitated, then defensive.

"I thought you were supposed to *answer* questions, not *ask* them."

"When I don't know, I ask. You wouldn't want a half-asked answer, would you?"

"How do you expect me to know about this stuff? My manager handles this sort of thing."

"Apparently not."

"What d'you mean?" he asked, curious now. "What does it say?"

It didn't look good, so I tried to be as succinct as possible. "It says you got the three of shit, the four of nothing, and the five of get out of town. You're unsure about distribution and there's no organized promotion. You mistrust half the people you're working with and aren't even sure who the other half are. The timing of the release is nowhere near what you want it to be, and if you want a prediction about sales, it looks as if the whole thing is going to get deadlocked in the courts. You have created a series of events through calculated neglect that will cause the ruin of the project that you claim to love." This was the first warning of trouble with this album, which a year later would have John facing a lawsuit for $42 million.

"Christ, don't spare my feelings." He stood and walked around the back of his chair, wrestling with the information and resenting it. Finally he asked, "And what do you suggest I do about it?"

"Correct it, change it."

"How?"

"Well, I'd start out by remembering that you're John Lennon."

"Not anymore, I'm not."

"Then who are you?"

"Oh, right, sure, I'm John Lennon, all right. But it's not what you think. I'm not the heavyweight rock star anymore. You think, sure, go make a record, sell a billion copies, just like that. But it's not like that; the record companies don't care that much anymore. The quote fans unquote, don't care that much either." He wasn't spinning UFO stories now. He meant it.

"But you care. You love it, right?"

"Love? I hate it! I hate the whole damn business."

"So quit," I suggested. "Why bother? You've made it. In a business where almost everyone washes out, you won, and won bigger and better than anyone else . . ."

"You don't understand. It's expected of me."

"By whom?"

"By me, and fuck you very much!"

"So, do it."

"So, do it, says Little Mystic Sunshine." He mimicked my tone sarcastically. "Well, I can't do it. I don't know how anymore. It's gone. My muse is gone. Poof! Up the chimney. Up your ass. Gone. You got any answers for that, Oracle?"

"Is that a question? Do you want me to read on it?"

He sighed and sat down. "No, I'm tired. I don't want to play anymore."

"Next time."

"You wish." He smiled thinly.

He sat beside me, looking magnetic no longer. I waited, and in a moment he changed again.

"You know, Charles, of all the mystics and psychics or seers or whatever it is you people call yourselves . . ." He paused, " 'Sensitives!' I guess that's the word that sums you all up. I think you're the best I've met so far." He meant it as a compliment, showing he wasn't angry with me.

"A card reader's first obligation is to get your attention. At least I managed that."

"Well, you know, Charles," he intoned playfully, "anyone can go out and buy a deck of cards and call themselves a reader, but that doesn't make them one."

"And anyone can go out and buy a guitar and call themselves a rock star, but that doesn't make them one either."

He snorted, even laughing a little. The reading over, I swept up the cards. "I always like this part. It makes me feel like a croupier in the Twilight Zone."

Yoko burst into the room. "Oh, Charlie," she called, "before you go I have a few questions that I need to ask you."

"I bet," said John in an exaggerated stage whisper. Then with great formality, he rose and turned to me. "Well, Charles, it certainly has been an unpleasant experience. I hope we don't have to repeat it."

Back inside the White Room and resubmerged in the sofa, Yoko zeroed in on me.

"What did he say?"

"About what?" I was determined to play dumb.

"About me, to start with."

"Well"—I thought about it—"I don't recall that he said anything about you at all."

"You recall very well. You have a perfect memory."

"You wouldn't want me to betray a confidence, would you?"

"Yes. I pay you, don't I?"

I shuffled the cards. "Perhaps it would help if you asked specific questions."

I was baiting her and she knew it. "I want to know how John feels about me. She spoke slowly with exasperated care.

I laid the cards. "I'd say he loves you."

And he did. Over the next five years I was to have the opportunity of seeing John demonstrate that love in many ways.

Yoko and I finished our reading and I wrapped up the cards in their purple silk. She escorted me back down the hall to the door, where we were met by John.

"I'll be seeing ya. Or will I? Perhaps you should read on that," he quipped with a mischievous grin.

They closed the door behind me and I stepped into the hallway to wait for the elevator (an Otis, said to be the second oldest in New York and in my opinion definitely the slowest). After more than six hours of being "on," I had a chance to review my meeting with the famous John Lennon. He was, I decided, an antic soul, filled with laughter, variety, and mischief, with a shrewd intelligence just beneath the swiftly changing surface. Through the relative quiet of New York City's streets at 2:00 A.M. I went home to bed—and found myself dreaming of him. Later John reported to me that he too had dreamed that night—of tarot cards. He told me that in his dream he was in a train station and that his ticket to ride was a tarot card—except that he didn't know which one to use because he had the whole pack in his hand.

"But I took it to be a good omen," he concluded. "At least I was playing with a full deck."

· 2 ·

DIAL M
FOR MYSTIFICATION

The morning after my first meeting with John, I pulled the phone out of the freezer and readied myself for another day of urgent queries from Yoko. Not owning a phone I could unplug, I had hit on the technique of stowing the receiver in the freezer to wrench some time free from her incessant phone calls. It irked Yoko that I did this, but the alternative was a cauliflower ear from unremitting telephone readings, and so I continued perforce. The moment I replaced the receiver in its cradle, the phone began ringing vigorously. So began a series of mystifying conversations lasting several days.

"He's behaving verrry badly," she would begin. "I want to see you, but I don't think it's the right time. We have to be careful." Then suddenly, she would put me on hold, coming back moments later to say, "It's okay to talk now, I think, but

15

maybe you had better check." That meant, "read on it," so I would spread the cards to see if the phone was tapped or there was a spy in my apartment or the room was bugged or whatever. Invariably, these dangers were found to be lacking and it was "okay" to talk. This introduction done, we began on the main theme:

"I have to know what he's thinking. I have to know what he's going to do!" Presumably it never occurred to her to *ask* him what he was thinking. I did my best. Reading for Yoko, however, often required that I give clear answers to singularly obscure questions. There was, for example, the following peculiar colloquy in the first week of John's return:

"Hello, Charlie? I had a talk with my friend, Mr. K——, last night and he says that my number is in a very bad position with John." Mr. K—— was another of Yoko's extensive stable of readers, psychics, and miscellaneous miracle workers. He was a gentle Japanese restaurateur who was a student of the Japanese system of numerology.

"Charlie, listen. My friend says that I should do nothing about 'the problem' until after the fifth of next month—that's when the new Japanese month starts—and I checked the numbers myself and I think he's right, but I just want to check with you. What do you think?"

"Yoko . . ."

"No, no, don't use names, we may be being bugged. Maybe you should read on that first."

"It's very early for this sort of thing."

"It's seven A.M."

"You did call at four."

"I know, I let you sleep. I've been waiting. What do you think?"

"About what?"

"You know! About 'the problem' and this month."

"Which problem?"

"Listen to me, 'the,' that one!"

16

"You mean, 'the king' or 'the people'?"

These were code names respectively for John and Apple Records.

"No names! Listen, I'll concentrate on 'the problem' and you read. Just tell me what it says."

I can read cards in my sleep. It was a skill that came in handy at times like these. "Your friend says no action, huh?" I asked, shuffling the cards. I still had no idea what "the problem" was.

"Yes, and I agree." She was usually confident about inaction.

Here's the answer, I thought. What's the question?

"If you believe in your heart that it is not the time to act, then the actions you take are likely to be less successful. In that I see his point. It is not necessarily action, however, to reconsider the issue with new mental action. You may find it particularly useful to consider the problem without as a symbol and the problem within as the real issue." How could I go wrong with an answer like that? I thought.

"Is that for the bugging or 'the problem'?"

"That's the problem."

"Okay, I'll check that with him and the High Priestess, and call you right back. Don't put the phone in the freezer." Click.

"Who's the High Priestess? Hello? . . . Helloooo? . . ."

I hung up the phone and went back to sleep. She might call again in ten minutes, or an hour, or a day. Or not. I learned from her numerologist that they even had these cryptic conversations in Japanese.

After several days of such largely incomprehensible communications from Yoko, I was finally summoned back to the Dakota. Yoko met me at the oak front doors and led me quickly to the kitchen where we sat down to a long reading, spending hours on various subjects—none of which was John. Finally, my perplexity got the better of me.

"Yoko, I have to ask. What's been going on here? What caused the turnabout?"

"What turnabout?"

"You call me several times a day for several days and say you're living in a state of siege. Then you say you need to see me and that it's 'gravely important.' I arrive and it's business as usual. That's a turnabout."

She seemed puzzled, then brightened. "It worked out!"

"What did?"

"Everything. Isn't it amazing?"

At length I pieced together the story. She had thought John was placing a curse on her.

"John was spending a lot of time in the library, you know, and that's where the magic books are. He told me he was reading them and I noticed that the energy was getting a little funny, you know. I didn't want to say it over the phone because I was afraid of him overhearing or reading my mind maybe—we're very close mentally, you know. Then he was sending out all the assistants to buy him books and even wanted to talk to you, but I worked it out."

"How?" This I had to hear.

"Well, he still wants to learn about magic, so I am going to teach him."

"And the teacher always knows more than the student?"

"Yes, exactly. I'll call him and see if he has anything to ask you." Thrilled with the cleverness of it all, she reached for the phone.

A minute later John marched in. "Well, Charles, long time no seer," he greeted me. "Nothing today, Charles, but something for tonight. We're having a séance, and you ought to come."

"Why?"

"Why? Because the very air around here abounds with occult doings and we're going to talk to the dearly departed."

"Don't you think you should wait till they talk to you first?"

"Come on, as chief headhaunter you should be here to protect us from evil spirits and the like."

The séance was to be Yoko's first installment in John's occult education. Yoko had put out the word that she was looking for miracles. An aging couple had contacted her, presenting themselves as mediums, whom John had immediately nicknamed the Rabbits. According to the Rabbits, the Lennons had many friends "on the other side" who wished to communicate. So that night John and Yoko sat watching the aging male Rabbit, whom John dubbed Peter, act as medium, while his wife, "Bunny" (according to John), served as his assistant. John had fully expected that I would be there, but I decided to play hooky. Yoko was sure my hesitancy was due to professional jealousy and would not take no from me as an answer, so I simply said I would probably arrive a bit late—say two or three days.

She hadn't told John any of this, and it was in midsession that John asked, with idle curiosity, "I wonder what happened to Charles Swan?"

"Ooooooh," moaned Peter Rabbit in the high, strained, nasal tone of his "spirit guide," "there was an . . . accident . . . on the astral planes of the time-space continuum. Charles was taken . . . before his time. It was an accident . . . a miscalculation . . . of the cosmic Lords of Karma." John was tickled. Earlier references to various friends had been vague but accurate enough to leave John unsure as to the authenticity of this encounter with the unknown. The reference to me made up his mind. John was possessed by the spirit of mirth. "But why, why was he taken away before his work was finished?" he cried.

"It is not for poor mortals to judge . . . the Judges of the Universe. Charles's work . . . on the earth plane . . . was completed . . . now he continues in the time-space continuum . . . with his tasks."

"Could we talk to him please? Just a few words please?" John was enjoying himself thoroughly.

"Ah . . . ah . . . there is . . . a great deal of interference with the spirit entity you knew on earth as . . . Charles Swan . . . However . . . we will try. . . ." There was a long pause, punctuated with suitable grunts and ahhhhhs, during which John's excitement grew. "Yes . . . yes . . . ah! I can see him now . . . he is working . . . he is happy . . . he wants you to know that he is . . . happy. . . ."

"Charlie!" called John in a plaintive voice. "Why did you do it? How could you? I could have believed it of anybody but you, Charlie. Tell me why, please! Just tell me why!"

Old Peter Rabbit never turned a whisker. "He says . . . he says . . . that he had to do what he did. He hopes that you will forgive and understand . . . there will be a reunion between you later . . . all will be made clear in the great continuum of time and space . . . there are many things which . . . must be . . . things which we cannot understand . . . until later."

John was hot for the game. He invented more and more preposterous names and circumstances. He hoped that he could force Peter to break character. Instead, Peter simply claimed to grow weary under the strain. So the veil to the other world was lowered once more. The graying Rabbit rose from his chair and, calling for lights, asked if it had been a successful contact. John pumped Peter's paw and claimed that it was a most rewarding experience, then rewarded him with a fattish check.

According to both John's and Yoko's versions of story, John thanked the old couple graciously and led them to the door, which he closed behind them. Turning to Yoko he said softly in answer to her unspoken question, "They put on a good show, tried hard. That old guy stayed on his toes. They're old, they need the money, I don't, so why not?"

She did not have time to respond before John turned away. He walked to his room and called me.

"Hello, Charles?" he gloated. "I'm afraid that I have a bit of bad news for you. It seems you've passed away. My condolences!" I could hear him chuckling before he hung up.

The day after the séance Yoko called me and said that John "needed to talk to me." As usual she met me at the door. "He's in the Black Room," she said. John was currently using the Black Room as his room. Since his return had been so sudden, the couple had decided that it would be best if they maintained separate bedrooms for the time being.

I tapped on the door. In a portentous tone, John called "Enter." I did and found him sitting in a T-shirt and faded jeans in the middle of a mattress on the floor. He looked up as in mock surprise.

"A visitation! A wandering spirit from the time-space continuum!" He motioned for me to sit in one of the two black lacquer chairs to his left, which, along with the black carpet, black upright piano, and black writing desk, gave the room its name.

John sat cross-legged on his mattress, his longish hair bound up into a topknot, a wicked gleam in his eye. Slipping his hand under his pillow, he produced a cassette player and punched the "play" button with a ceremonious flourish. The room was filled with the sounds of strange moans and wheezes. It was a tape John had made of the previous evening's meeting with the Rabbits. Then he studied my face for reactions. John had a way of studying you so intently that he seemed to be a camera. I wasn't quite sure what reactions he was looking for, especially since the earlier parts of the tape were pretty straightforward. But then we got to the part about me, and my reactions took care of themselves. We went from smiles to chuckles, from laughter to belly laughs, and finally to howls of delight. It was one of our finest moments.

"I have a surprise for you," he said at length when we had recovered. "A new project."

"Another séance?"

"That was yesterday. No, we three are going to embark upon an adventure. Do you think you could find the Spear of Destiny?"

For those of you who don't know, the Spear of Destiny is the legendary weapon that is said to have pierced the side of Jesus of Nazareth during the Crucifixion. A companion piece to the Holy Grail, the spear too is reputed to have great magical power. A common belief, where such beliefs are common, holds that the owner of the spear will rule the world.

Again his hand slipped under the pillow and produced a paperback book. It was clear by its rumpled condition that he had read it thoroughly.

"We could find it, you know," he said, weighing the book in his hand. "It wouldn't be so very, very hard. We've got the advantages, you know. Who's looked for it before? Armies. The Church. We'll be adventurers, but adventurers with enough money and time. That's an advantage. And, we know where it isn't."

"Really, where isn't it?"

"Logically, it can't be in the hands of anyone who knows what it is. The spear has tremendous power. If someone had it and knew that he had it, then he *would* be in the news, wouldn't he?"

"Presuming, one, that that person wanted the power, and, two, that if he had it, he wanted to be public."

"Come on, can you imagine turning down power like that or keeping it a secret?" To John the idea was incredible.

"Yes." I was serious.

"No! It's got to be in the hands of some monastery or something. Somewhere in a place so small that no one would believe that it was the real thing. They probably take it out once a year or so, Good Friday maybe, and show it to the locals. Everybody in a hundred-mile radius would know about it, but to them it's a relic, see? They worship it, look, say 'gee,' and that's it. The

people know it's there, but everyone else just says 'local legend, local legend' and dismisses it. God, there you go making
your patient face again."

"What makes you think it exists?"

"Okay, they got everything else, don't they? The shroud He
was buried in, the True Cross, the towel He wiped His face
with, the robe, so why not the spear? You don't think that the
hard-core following was going to let a treasure like that get
away, do you? It's all there, all the pieces, it makes sense that
it exists."

"Existed."

"Oh, no. There have been regular reports about it ever since.
Just like all the other relics."

"So where is it?"

"Somewhere in southeastern Europe."

"That's a sizable area."

"That's where you come in. Psychics are supposed to be
good at finding things."

"I'm a card reader, not a psychic."

"Whatever." He had a plan. "We'll organize a tour, travel by
bus, keep away from large cities, and keep our ears open. We'll
say we're making a film and record the whole process."

"What is it you really want out of this, John?"

"Power."

"To do what?"

"Whatever I want, change the world, whatever. I always had
the plan, but I never had the power. I thought I did. Big star,
big deal. No one listens when they don't have to; it's too much
work."

"So you'll make them listen? That's why Hitler wanted the
spear, isn't it?"

"Well, I'm no Hitler, and don't give me that ol' 'absolute
power corrupts absolutely' shit either."

"I wouldn't dream of it."

"Good! Are you in or out?"

"If you leave the country before you settle with Immigration, you'll be out and have to stay out."

Almost exactly three years earlier, at the end of February 1972, the Immigration Service had refused to renew John's visa, on the grounds that he had an arrest record in London dating from October 1968. That had begun a legal struggle that remained unresolved as of early 1975, and so long as it was, John could not leave the country without forfeiting any hope of getting back in.

"So? We'll have to solve that first, right? Then we go."

"Well, maybe you go, but I have a few other things to do first."

"Such as?" he leered.

"When Immigration is solved, I'll still have five more little jobs to do to fulfill my agreement with Yoko."

"What agreement? What things?"

"Ah. Early last November when Yoko put me on retainer, she said that she had seven things that she wanted accomplished. If I could help her achieve these ends then I got a lifetime contract. Food, clothing, shelter, and all the readings I can eat."

"So what are these things?"

"You're the first. Yoko wanted to get back together with you."

"And you did that?" he said, patronizingly.

"I helped."

"How?"

"By telling her the right attitude to take toward you. When you first met her, she paid you total attention, wrote you daily, and won you over. Courtship over, you, my dear, were the ignored groom while the bride busied herself with the world you opened up for her. As you had less to do, you again needed attention; hence, May. While away with May you were bound to have the natural reaction of wondering what things might be like back home. All Yoko had to do was stop waiting around believing that it was a 'loss of face' to chase after you and chase after you. Catching you was easy."

"Don't you think I had any part in the decision?" John was irked.

"Of course you did. It's what you basically wanted, but emotionally you are not an aggressor. You need the other person to commit themselves first. So, every time she spoke to you, she was positive instead of being full of crises. Nothing to scare off the game, as it were."

"But how did you get her to change? She's always got an emergency."

"I didn't change her. I simply told her that you didn't want to hear it."

"You were right."

"You were more eager to carry on with an old commitment than to start all over again with a new one. She is, in many ways, the only doorway that you have left open to a past that can only become more important to you as you get older."

"I've thought of that. If I started a new life, I'd just come to the same crossroads ten or fifteen years down the line. What else were you supposed to do for her?"

"As I said, you were the first. Second is Immigration, which will settle itself out in time anyway . . ."

"You're sure of that, are you?" He seemed dubious.

"If the government wanted you out, you'd be out. But here you are. You're just on a short leash, and that is where they want you."

"Why? At least, why do you think?"

"Because you are an unknown quantity. Unpredictable and powerful. If you wanted, you could go to any city in the U.S. and attract thousands of people just by announcing a concert. Out of thousands, it is not unlikely to suppose that you could

motivate hundreds. Add to this some onetime antiestablish-
ment public statements, a few million dollars, some left-wing
connections, and presto, you're a weapon."

"Don't tell my wily Immigration lawyer that it's all so simple. He's working round the clock on this."

"Is he?"

"What are the other five?"

"Three, to stop the barrage of lawsuits against you. Four—"

"And how do you propose to do that?" he laughed.

"No idea! Four, to establish an income for the two of you
which is independent of the record industry—and I have no
ideas about that one yet either. Five, to create a new and
favorable public image for Yoko—"

"Now *that* doesn't surprise me," he said softly.

". . . which will come from achieving the first four. Six, to
return you to the music industry, which I can't do but you can
and I suspect will . . ."

I hesitated because the seventh of Yoko's goals wasn't really
something I thought I should mention: a child.

"And . . . ah . . . seven, greater spiritual awareness for the
two of you," I lied. "So the story ends that we all live happily
ever after."

John wrinkled his brow and took a deep breath.

"You're not in the least bit ambitious, are you, Charles?"

"Me? Don't be silly!"

The plan to find the lost Spear of Destiny was neither long-
lived nor long remembered. John, at a loss for what to do with
his boundless energies, created one scheme after another in the
following weeks, all short-lived. What he wanted above all
was to create songs again, but that, unhappily, he could not do.
The artistic block that had paralyzed his creative energies for
the past several months and that would bring him close to
despair some three years later, debarred him from his heart's

desire. So he sought distraction in lesser pursuits. A few weeks after the spear, it was "I'm writing a book!"

"John Lennon's Guide to Bisexual Gardening?" I suggested.

"I like that, I'm going to use it. I won't credit you for it, of course, but I'll use it."

"Feel free . . ."

"It's going to be a journal: observations, commentary, humorous mostly. Want to hear some?" Everyone who passed within arm's reach of him had to hear some, even the "servants," as Yoko called them. And everyone said that what they'd heard was very good. That kept him happy. Encouragement was all he was after.

Eventually, the journal went the way of the other projects. At first he wrote every day and then every few days. Finally, the little collection of pages disappeared.

He fought the boredom creeping into his life with bold attention-getting moves. His celebration of Yoko's birthday on February 18, 1975, became a display of material splendor. This, he hoped, would wash away any remaining black marks against him caused by his absence. The Lennons' anniversary on March 20 supplied him with yet another distraction.

About a week before this event, Yoko ushered me into the kitchen, where we found John standing proudly, all smiles.

"We want to get married," he beamed as we walked in.

"High time you made an honest woman of her again."

"But I'm serious!" he glowed, elongating the word.

"Okay. But I thought you were married."

"We are, but we want to reaffirm our vows. I mean, with the separation, it's a good time, don't you think?"

"That's nice," I said, and meant it.

"And we want you to perform the ceremony."

"Mind if I sit down?"

"It will be beautiful," smiled Yoko.

John's voice took on its official tone. "In celebration and

commemoration of our happily reunited union and on the occasion of the anniversary of our nuptials, it is our wish to retrowel our troth and retie the knot. It is our further wish that you, our dear Charles, perform the necessary necessities."

"Surely you jest."

"Charles," warned John, "this is definitely not the laughing part. You had your chance before, but now . . ." He held his finger to his lips. "You can do that, can't you? With all your occult whatever, you ought to be able to marry two people."

"It's a beautiful idea," smiled Yoko, seemingly still a little wary of John and not wanting to interrupt him while he was performing.

"Well," I said, stalling for time, "it's very flattering, of course, but . . ."

"Is there always a 'but,' Charles?"

"There sure is this time."

"Make it good."

"I'm trying. You see, there is no 'occult' ceremony for marriage that I know of."

"Our anniversary is on the equinox," said Yoko.

"Surely you can make something out of that!" John was in full swing. "Something Celtic, you know, a good old-fashioned Druid wedding feast. You'll love it. Now you make something up and tell us what you'll need. Make sure you have lots of things for us to do, okay?" The matter was settled.

The following week was full of excitement and confusion. John called me daily for instructions.

"What do you want me to dooo?" he cooed. "There must be some sort of ritual preparation for this sort of thing."

"Of course there is." I took a deep breath and winged it. "First, baths. Every morning. Hot water and the heads of a dozen carnations. White ones are best."

"Then what?"

"Bathe first. Then call me back." That bought some time.

Basically the problem was a theatrical one. If John wanted a diversion to keep his spirits up, then I was determined to keep him busier than an electric muskrat. The only occult consideration was not to go about offending any of the powers that be.

"You need to build an altar," I instructed. "It is to be constructed of two cubes of white wood. The measure of the cubes to be one cubit on each side."

"What's a cubit, Charles?"

"Call it eighteen inches."

He had the job finished by the next day.

"What's next?" (What indeed?)

"Supplies! Silver chalice, unused knife, two jade rings, white candles—plenty of them—and you'll need spring wine . . . May wine will do nicely. And, let's see"—I consulted my list—"yes, purest sea salt, lamp oil, tons of flowers. You'll both need to wear white . . ."

John went foraging.

A few days before the "ceremony," Yoko and I sat in the kitchen of apartment 72 toiling over tarot cards. Suddenly, John burst into the room.

"You should have seen their faces!" he whooped, setting down an armload of required props for the intended ritual. "I went into this shop and I think they were devil worshipers or something. You would have loved it, Yoko, everything was white . . . white white white and glass shelves everywhere. They had all their crap laid out perfectly, what a joke." To John, a satanist was an object of ridicule. He had no sympathy for the devil.

"Well, it was so clean! Magicians are never that clean, are they, Charles? I was the only one there, so I thought, What the hell, if you'll pardon the expression, have a bit of fun. Why not? You gotta picture this: There are two clerks, a guy and a girl, both kids, and both wearing these priest T-shirts. They were sooo serious.

29

"So the guy says, 'What do you wissshhh?' Like that." He began to mimic the clerk's mannered sibilance. "So I say, 'Candlllesss.' Doing him, having him on, you know. So he points his finger like he's giving directions to Hades and gives me his 'look,' great tourist stuff. I say, 'Let there be light,' and wink at him. So there I am on my knees looking through the stock, and they got everything, all wrapped in cellophane like a Long Island supermarket with very hair-raising prices. They had candles in the shape of men and women, black ones, red ones, brown ones, but no white candles. I look up"—he acted out the gesture—"and the girl is leaning over the counter, long blond hair, not bad, with this devil head hanging on a chain around her neck. She's giving me the glare too. 'What are these?' I ask her all wonder and innocence. 'Curssssing candllessss,' says she. 'Do you have any white onessss?' I ask and she shakes her head, no. 'What'sss the matter?' I say. 'Do you only curssse minoritiesss?' She had to think about that. But, what I really wanted to do was break her up. It's a contest with me. When someone's running a number on me, I always try to break them up. But she's good, you know, very straight face. She asks me if there will be anything 'elssssssse.' And I think, so that's how it is. So, I stand up very slowly looking straight in her eyes. 'Chalissssss,' I say and pull a face." He demonstrated a prune face. "That got a bit of a smile out of her. She had to look away when she said, 'Over here,' but she was losing it. I could tell. 'GREAT!' I shout, loud enough to make her jump. Run their trip on me, will they? I'll give them a nut case to deal with. I was a little afraid I'd get a ceremonial dagger in the back, but I really wanted to out-creepycrawly them. So there are the chalices, all of them with inverted crosses, goat's heads, topsy-turvy pentagrams, the business. Looking them over, I say, 'No, no, not quite right, not the thing.' Then I ask, whispering, 'You wouldn't happen to have . . .' looking around and getting confidential so she'll lean over to get my secret

'. . . any statues of . . . Saint Margaret?' She lost it, giggled. I loved it. You should've been there." He leaned back in the chair laughing, then regained his composure slightly. "When I left, I said, 'May the good Lord bless and keep you.' God, got them fuming. I loved it. Just what the assholes deserve. Maybe you should check and see if they cursed me, Charles." Then using a Yoko voice, "You never know." He chuckled merrily.

By the time the twentieth arrived, John had managed to collect all the necessary paraphernalia for the ceremony that I had designed at his request. I spent the day in the White Room dressing it up like a store window, while John and Yoko attempted to spend the day at opposite ends of the apartment so that John would not see his intended before the "marriage." This, however, proved too difficult a constraint and we all agreed that it was too much of a "Christian restriction for a 'Druid' rite."

As the hour of the ceremony approached, Yoko seemed just a trifle nervous. John reassured her and teased smiles out of her with little "I love yous" and smiles of his own.

At the stroke of nine all was in readiness. John and Yoko, dressed entirely in white, entered the White Room, which was filled with white carnations and softly lit with white candles. They walked the width of the room, turned right, and approached the altar, which was near the piano in the far corner. The couple came to a halt in front of a small silver dish of burning oil. They looked lovely.

Despite the whimsical origin of the event, the aura of genuine warmth and affection between the two lent an air of quiet solemnity to the room.

"It's just like the first time," John quipped at the altar, "except we've got ol' Charles here instead of the British consul."

I was too nervous about my duties as priest to respond. I began my patter, saluting the Gatekeeper and the compass points with as much theatric intonation as embarrassment would allow. I don't think John ever noticed that the names of the "Druid" deities being called upon were in fact the familar names of Christian angels. If he did, he never commented and I never asked.

After some fifteen minutes of "ceremony," John and Yoko placed jade rings on each other's fingers and promised that at some point in the near future, they would take them to the seashore and dip them in the surf as a symbol of their tie with the sea eternal and the life-force. They pledged their troth and drank a toast of white wine to themselves from a silver chalice.

Later in the kitchen we finished off the "sacramental" wine. John told me that after I left he officially moved back into the bedroom.

· 3 ·

"WE'RE PREGNANT!"

On a fine April afternoon, about a month after the Lennons' curious occult remarriage, I got a phone call from Yoko.

"Guess what?" she teased happily.

"I wouldn't dare," I said seriously.

"We're pregnant! Isn't it amazing? Now, I have to see you right away. I haven't told John yet because I need to know how he's going to take this. I'm in a phone booth on the street outside the doctor's office. I'll be right over to see you." Click.

Visits from Yoko were rare, and my apartment was hardly in shape to receive a client. Quickly I folded up the bed, picked up socks and other flotsam, and attempted to create at least some illusion of order. I was so engaged when I heard her knock at the door.

I let her in and she went directly to the reading table, settling herself into one of the director's chairs and hugging herself in her mink jacket while I got out the cards.

"Okay, we're pregnant and we're going to have the baby, understood?" she announced as the consultation began. Then came the inevitable barrage of questions. Will it miscarry? Boy or girl? Retarded? Deformed? She puffed furiously at her cigarettes. Most importantly, how was John going to take the news?

"He'll be thrilled," I predicted. And he was, as I learned the following evening when I went to read for him.

"Have you heard the good news, Charles?" he said as he walked into the White Room. "We're pregnant!" He sat down across from me on the sofa, obviously in a serious mood. "I'm going to be a father again, Charles," he began, "and I'm not prepared for this new beginning. I've got too many ends, too much unfinished business. Particularly with May. You know, I never really settled things with her. I don't see her anymore, but she's still around. She calls sometimes, but I don't talk to her. Even so, it makes Yoko crazy. I guess you've heard *all* about that from her, haven't you?" I nodded. "I'm not being fair to May. I know it and it bothers me. She didn't do anything wrong."

"So . . . talk to her. The silent treatment is probably hurting her more than anything you could say."

"I can't. I'm afraid. If I called, she'd ask me to come and see her. I can't say no, can I? I can never say no. So I'd go see her, and even if I didn't sleep with her, it would ruin things here . . . this life, this marriage. I can't risk that. There's going to be a baby. I have to straighten things out. I mean, I don't know if May is waiting for me or wants to tell me to go fuck myself, which she certainly has the right to do, or what."

"What did you tell her when you went away?"

"Didn't. I didn't really know I was leaving. I never do. I mean it was in the air. 'Someday he'll go back to his wife.' But we didn't talk about it because that was always something that was going to happen 'someday,' not Tuesday or the twenty-eighth or a time we could plan for. Then one day I realized that someday was today and I was here.

"I never really go *away* from things, you know. I go *to* things. I never realize that I've left till I get where I'm going. I've always been that way, always coming to something new. If I thought about what I'd have to leave I probably wouldn't."

"You left Yoko," I interjected.

"No, not really, and she didn't throw me out either. I'd been doing my *Mind Games* album and it really had me going. I was *going* to put in all these great ideas, and I was *going* to finish it. I was *going* all the time. Yoko and I were bothering each other, but I was on the go and didn't notice how much. So one night I was just *going* to get a paper. Then I realized what I was actually doing was *going* for a walk. Then while I was walking, I realized what I was really doing was *going* to see May. I was seeing May and that was *going* on till I realized that I was *going* to stay with her awhile. That's how I realized I'd left Yoko and that's when I realized that I was *going* to get back together with her . . . 'someday.'

"Now I'm back, and I'm *going* to stay, I'm *going* to not call, write, or otherwise do anything to upset this particular apple cart, as it were. May wasn't just a bit of fun on the side, you know. She knows Yoko too. It was Yoko's idea to hire her.

"Like I said, Yoko and I were having our problems, sexual among others. So Yoko suggested a mistress, because she didn't want to deal with me in bed. It seemed reasonable that if we got the sex barrier out of the way, the rest of it could work. So she came up with May and laid everything out for her. May would work for me, and if anything went on between the boss and the secretary (and knowing the boss there would be!), well, that was all right with the boss's wife. That is, as long as the boss's wife was kept informed.

"Originally, we all agreed. It sounded like a good idea. The marriage had its problems and May was an answer. But as always happens, it got involved. May got involved with me and started feeling loyal and protective toward me, which I love. She stopped her reports to the wife, for which I will be eternally grateful. That's when it stopped being a good idea. I couldn't be married to one woman and sleeping with another. I was fragmented as it was. I needed a whole something in my life."

"And do you have that whole something now?" I asked.

"Well, three quarters of a something maybe. But as the baby proves, Yoko and I do sleep together, sometimes. Besides, I'm not convinced that a perfect relationship is a whole one. To be perfect it has to have a few holes, doesn't it? But that still leaves us with May."

As he talked I sorted and shuffled the cards. When he finished I laid them out in a spread that was designed to answer a "how-to" question. "You said that she was hired. That means you paid her?"

"Yes."

"And what you want to do is communicate to her without writing or talking to her that you are not going to see her again?"

"Exactly."

"You're still paying her, aren't you?"

"Well, the office is."

"As long as you continue to pay her, she has to expect that you want something. If you don't want anything from her, stop paying her."

"You mean fire her?"

" 'Lay off' might be a better phrase," I answered, unsure how he would respond to the idea.

"That's brilliant! Fire her! That's fuckin' brilliant! That tells

May it's over, it makes Yoko feel secure, and it lets me off the guilty hook! That's great!"

This was the first step in what emerged as John's determined effort to reorder his life and affairs in honor of the coming child. We spent the rest of that evening and several to come going over every aspect of his life as he saw it, assessing and reassessing friends, business, his relationship with his as-yet-unborn child, sifting and winnowing the fragments of a chaotic-seeming past in an effort to construct a better, somehow purer, future.

His business was particularly in need of ordering. In a complex and byzantine set of maneuvers, Capitol Records had forced his *Rock 'n' Roll* album, originally released under the title *Roots,* off the market. Now a legal battle loomed. There were queries about accountants, lawyers, and a horde of others. I kept trying to drive home to John the extent and importance of his own power and authority—both of which he habitually squandered, evaded, or simply ignored. I tried to show him that these were in fact his child's real heritage.

"You have to take possession of your own power," I told him a few weeks later as we sat together at the kitchen table over a late-evening reading of cards. "If you are serious about preparing your life for your child, then you are going to have to stop abdicating your power and the responsibilities that go with it. You must learn to delegate authority without dispersing it."

John disliked hearing this. The idea that he had power and that power entailed responsibility made him uncomfortable. He preferred to romanticize his problem.

"Preparing for the baby, well, there's more to that than Xeroxes and bank accounts, you know. There's heritage to consider." He thumped a book lying on the kitchen table. "Yoko has a real family history to offer. Samurai and Shinto priests stretching back a thousand years or more. What have I got? Me! I'm the biggest thing that ever happened in my family. You know, Yoko's family supplied the first Japanese in Harvard, the first Japanese in Washington. They've got major banking interests. That's something to offer a kid. Me, ha! I got nothing."

I was sobered to realize that he was genuinely depressed by this idea. In John's eyes, it seemed, it counted for naught to have bewitched the souls of millions and to have utterly changed the face of popular music for an entire generation.

"Is that why the Celtic lore?" I pointed to the book on the table.

"Yeah. Hunting up a little history, racial if not family."

"So? History is what happened and you are what's happening. Your children are what will happen."

"Happening? Not anymore. Even in the old days I wasn't really important. Do you know that when I met Yoko she didn't even know what a 'Beatle' was?"

I had heard this story several times both from Yoko and other sources. It seems that in November of 1966, Yoko was having an exhibition of her work at the Indica Gallery in London. John apparently wandered in out of curiosity. The manager of the gallery pointed him out to Yoko as a millionaire and encouraged her to introduce herself to him because it might help boost sales. Introduce herself she did, and the two found that they had an immediate rapport. It was then that Yoko claimed not to know who either John Lennon or the Beatles were.

Over the next eighteen months and much to the discomfort of John's wife, Cynthia, Yoko sent John daily messages. These ranged from long typewritten letters to one-sentence telegrams saying, "Look in the sky, I'm there." John reassured Cyn that the relationship was strictly business and sought to prove it by occasionally funding one of Yoko's art projects. It wasn't until the late spring of 1968 that John and Yoko began their affair. Cyn was out of town with their son, Julian, and John invited Yoko to his home in London to show her his studio. They talked all night and made love at sunrise. To celebrate their union they recorded *Two Virgins,* their first album together.

"Yes," I said, "I've heard that story, but I never believed it. I know men who were cloistered monks at that time, and even they knew who the Beatles were. I think that that was just Yoko's way of telling you that she was so busy with 'real' art and 'real' culture that she never noticed your scene. I think you believed her because under all your bravado and surface confidence, you have a very poor sense of self-worth. She told you that you were unimportant and you accepted it because you secretly believed it, so much so that you gave away half your hard-earned position in pop music to someone whose major talent was giving you her undivided attention."

"I just love the way you reduce everything to simple statements," he sniped.

"And I love the way you go hunting after your 'racial' roots and ignore your own feelings. A curious way to prepare for a child, that."

"Been talking to the wife, have we?" he leered.

"Every day."

"And does dear, sweet Yoko tell you what to tell me, my dear?" His voice had an edge to it.

"No, Yoko tells me what to ask, the same way you do. Tarot cards tell me what to say."

"She's been complaining?" He sounded genuinely concerned.

"Since the first day I met her."

"She told you I go out once in a while?"

"I've heard rumors to that effect."

"Oh well"—he was in a temper—"Father Charles, the spiritual master, doesn't approve, does he? And Machiavellian

Charlie doesn't want King John to have any vulnerabilities. And Amy Van der Charles the Third doesn't want a dog's breath of scandal, does he now? Do you have an answer for that, Witch Doctor Sigmund Swan?"

"Do you want the truth or an honest lie?"

"Oh, yeah, I missed that one: the unshockable Swannie. Try the truth for a change."

"I think you ought to give yourself a break. Go out and party more."

"More?"

"Sure. You've committed yourself to what you *think* is the right way to be, not the right way for *you*. You're gonna have a family again. You don't want to fuck up again. You think you blew it once because of your 'bad' side. So you fight it. The pressure builds and builds and finally Lord Lennon goes out and ties one on just like all the rest of the husbands in the world. And then, just as predictably, you feel guilty. You don't like the way *that* feels, so you build a wall around *that* feeling. But it's gotta come out somehow, so you end up calling *me* a lot of names. Me! Chuck, your friendly neighborhood mercenary, just doing the most good for the highest bidder. You've got months before the baby comes. Relax!"

"Is that what *you* think, or Yoko thinks?"

"If you want to know what Yoko thinks, ask her. As for me, I think of you as a potential, a plot to be farmed. My tools are cards and my goal is harvest. See? I make everything sound simple, right?"

"The only thing simple about you is your name," he was smiling again.

"Only because I didn't get to pick it myself."

As the weeks wore on, John's flare-ups grew more frequent during readings. Anger became his only weapon against boredom. When he wasn't in a temper he was being the righteous

• • •

proponent of pure living—Yoko's pure living—and this was telling on the couple's relationship, as I could tell in my readings with Yoko.

"He's impossible," she confided one sunny afternoon in late June, as we sat at the kitchen table for one of our frequent sessions. "He watches me all the time. If I go to the toilet, he follows me. He's afraid I'm stuffing myself with garbage, but I'm not. I just need to eat more now." She was eating a fistful of chocolate.

"But you're the one who insisted that you keep a strict macrobiotic diet."

"I know, I know, but every once in a while I need a little change." I lit her cigarette. "I think it's healthy to have a little variety. Besides, even the doctor said that I have a tendency to be too strict on myself. I think John is just trying to upset me because he doesn't want the baby." This was a constant theme.

"He wants the baby, he wants the baby, he wants the baby, and you know it. Why are you investing so much negativity in this event? Be joyous!"

"You know very well why. It's because this baby has to be perfect. This baby is going to change the world. If a messiah were going to be reborn today, he would choose rock stars as parents so he could have access to the media. Everything is perfect for a new prophet. It's the right time and *we* are the right parents. Everything we are doing is perfect: exercises, meditation, diet. I just hope the baby isn't retarded. You want to read on that again?"

"Yoko, we always read on that! There is no reason to suspect that you will have anything other than a perfectly normal baby."

"Normal?" She sounded hurt. "Our baby can't be normal! We would hate a normal baby! No, she has to be perfect."

"She?"

"Now don't be stubborn, Charlie. I know that you said 'a

boy,' but this time the Messiah has to be a woman. It makes sense, doesn't it? Last time a man, this time a woman. That's the economy of the universe."

"A retarded lady messiah?"

"It's nothing to joke about, think of the karma involved. I don't think that is anything to laugh about."

"You have been tested by your doctor and you passed."

"I'm getting another doctor."

"Why? He even makes house calls! What more do you want?"

"He won't believe me about the baby. He insists that there is nothing wrong. And he humiliates me! He says I have to be careful because of my age! That's very insulting. I only hope he didn't say anything like that to John. Besides, he's against the idea of natural childbirth. He wants me to have the baby in a hospital. I can't go to a hospital, that would be too humiliating. I want another doctor. That way I can tell the new one that the old doctor was worried about retardation."

"But that's not true, Yoko."

"Whose side are you on? If I say I'm concerned, then any doctor will just pat me on the head and say, 'There, there, don't be a foolish woman.' "

"Then why not try a woman doctor?"

"Because they're no good. Now I have some names I want you to check so we will get a good doctor this time." She reached for the phone. "Yes, I want you to bring me some tea, and some noodles, and an orange . . . What? . . . No! No honey, sugar is bad for you, you know." Then she had some chocolate while she waited for her snack.

As the summer of 1975 progressed, pregnancy inflated Yoko, increasing her concern for her own health and that of her coming child. Each day brought a new diet, a new phobia. She consumed packs of cigarettes and kilos of chocolate. In her seventh month she simply took to her bed. John's reaction to her became increasingly hostile.

"Man your harpoons!" he howled as he ushered me into the bedroom one night in late September for what had become our daily meeting. "Thar she blows off the starboard bow, Moby's Mommie!"

"Hello, Charlie," Yoko whispered, choosing to ignore John's introductory salvo. "I just have a few little questions." She was doing her best Camille.

"Then," sneered John, "I'll be back for what's left of you in a few hours, Charles. Perhaps you'd care to join me later in vast quantities of cheap booze. We'll get disgusting and abuse the wife a bit." There was no veil on his contempt.

"Sure thing, see you under the table." My chief function in this household these days seemed to be making weak jokes and playing DMZ between them, so that she could eat and he could drink. It was definitely not fun.

Yoko lay in bed, wearing what had become her only garb, a particularly unflattering puce muumuu. She waited the customary interval until she heard the rattle of the bead curtain that hung at the entrance to the bedroom hallway.

"You see how he is? He's like this all the time. I get no rest at all, I think he's trying to kill me." With spiteful triumph, she retrieved her chocolates from hiding.

"He has a point, you know, not that he is expressing it well. You *are* heavier than necessary and that is *not* healthy."

"Heavy? I'm pregnant! What's *your* excuse?" (I was a tad plump at 293 pounds.) "Besides, it's the way he puts things. It makes me nervous and that makes me want to eat. Thank God you talked him into going to Long Island, at least for the weekends; it's the only peace I get."

Talking John into giving up his oppressively watchful guard over his coming child was one of the easier tasks I had performed for the Lennons. All it took was the lure of the first rays of the summer sun. John, a passionate sun-worshiper, was more than ready to get out of the city and bask at the shore. I had an easy task convincing him that time apart was as important as time together for a budding family. It was agreed that he would spend the weekends out of town. The arrangement seemed to give everyone some much-needed breathing space. But even this had failed to calm Yoko's irritated spirits.

"He hates the baby! He's trying to kill her! He can be very cruel, you know. Once he and Julian and Kyoko and I were in a car and . . ." she began to repeat a story she had told me several times before. It seems that Julian, John's son by his first wife, Cynthia, Kyoko, Yoko's daughter, and Yoko were motoring through the Scottish countryside when John, never a good driver, lost control of the car and the family went off the road. The car was damaged, but the family escaped unscathed, save Yoko, who suffered a cut on the forehead. Each time Yoko told me the story her injury became more grievous.

She pointed out the famous scar yet again. She had repeated and embellished this story many times. "I was bleeding, it was terrible, and all he could do was dance around the car with Julian singing, 'We're all right! We're all right!' What kind of man do you think would do that?"

"A frightened man who was glad he was alive and who felt that death had passed over with no more serious damage than a superficial laceration on his beloved's forehead," I answered honestly. In all retellings, I noted, she never mentioned that Kyoko had been endangered too.

"You'd better be careful, you know. He doesn't like you, he thinks you're stupid. If I didn't fight so hard to keep you, you'd be out in a minute. Now I have to know about this doctor *you* selected. He's no better than the last one; I think I need another man. You know what he did? He sent for my medical file! He didn't *trust* me! That's no good. I think he's trying to scare me so he can get a bigger fee. He doesn't even want me to have the baby here, what do you think about that?"

"I think he's right."

"Who cares what you think? Tell me what the cards say, and don't lie just because John told you to. John believes in doctors and not in the powers of the mind."

I laid the cards. "I understand your desire for natural childbirth, but you can do that in a hospital just as well as at home. And *if,* mind you I said 'if,' there are any complications, then a hospital would have the equipment and staff that you might need."

"So you're changing your mind again. You read before in the cards that there would be no problems; now you are talking about needing special equipment. Be honest with me. What will go wrong?"

At that moment there was a knock at the door. I swept up the cards. It was not for anyone else to know what I was doing for the Lennons.

"Yes?" Yoko called faintly. "Come in."

Mrs. Jones (not her real name), a woman with the unique ability to serve the Lennons without being dominated by them, entered with tea.

"Where's Charlie's coffee?" demanded Yoko. "Why didn't you bring coffee for my guest? Run and get some!"

"I don't care for any coffee, Yoko," I said.

"You always like coffee! Now stop trying to be nice to the servants." Mrs. Jones disappeared. "You're such a socialist, Charlie, always defending the working class. That kind of person needs orders. If you weren't so poor you'd understand that."

"Make me rich and then we'll see," I offered.

"Besides, she isn't working out as well as you said. She steals things, you know. I should be in bed, and instead I have to go around checking up on the servants, and then I find that she is taking food home and doing her wash with ours. You know what that means, don't you?"

"It means she's taking home scraps and saving some laundromat money. She's loyal, she works hard, keeps her mouth shut about your private life, and puts up with a lot of crap."

"You're just defending her because you read on her and said she'd be good."

"What about the numbers you had Mr. K—— read on her?"

"I think she lied about her name. That makes a bit of a difference, you know. Besides, I was desperate. All the assistants were young and skinny. I didn't want John to start an affair with one of them while I was pregnant. He would, you know; he's done that sort of thing before. I have to be very careful. It's bad enough he goes to whorehouses when he's out, but if it were an assistant, then she would write a book or something. I had to take Mrs. Jones."

There was a tap at the door and Mrs. Jones reentered. "Thank you, Mrs. Jones," I said as she handed me my coffee.

"We need a little snack," insisted Yoko. "Noodles with eggs, right away." Mrs. Jones left without comment. "You see that?" complained Yoko. "How rude. You don't know how it is to suffer with servants."

"I can't imagine."

This was, of course, lost on Yoko. She was already fixated on her next concern, which was, as always, John. "I want to know about John. I think he's coming on to the woman who's doing the natural childbirth classes. He seems very happy while he's there. I don't trust him when he's being happy."

"You don't trust him when he's not either."

"You stop that."

"Yoko, John is a man who loves his wife. I've read for a lot of husbands, I'm an expert. If he wanted another woman, he could have one. If he wanted to hurt you or the baby, it would already have happened. He holds on to you like a talisman because he wants your relationship to work. If you don't want him, divorce him and you will still be rich. If you *do* want him, then you'd better start loving him."

"I do love him!" she seemed injured. "I love him, I'm the only one who protects him, I'm his only friend."

"Then act like it. I read for him and he says he loves you and you hate him. I read for you and you say that you love him and he hates you. Wake up! If you *can* love, do it, for yourself, for John, for the baby in your womb."

A little later, a little wearier, I ambled into the kitchen to find John. "Well, what about that drink you promised?" I asked.

"Sorry, Charlie." He was imitating a well-known TV commercial. "I'm afraid that I wasn't really being serious. I don't keep any booze in the house these days. Bothers the wife. We could go out for some if you like."

"No thanks."

"Have you got us all patched up for another night?"

"I'm working on it."

"Must be hard on you. Is this the first time you've been pregnant?"

"Nah. I've read on a legion of babies and yours is typical of the breed."

"Liar. I've done this myself, probably more times than even I'll ever know. There was a time when 'Having John Lennon's Baby' was a desirable thing to do."

"Still is."

"Is that what you told the wife?"

"No," I lied, "that's what she tells me."

"Yes, she probably did. Women are very strong, you know. Why, did you know that the Celtic women used to ride and fight in the chariots with the men? Sometimes they led them. There was this one queen, Boadicea, and she led an army against the Romans. Scared them to death."

"Still looking for history?"

"What's wrong with that? I have to have something to give the kid. What have I got? Money? Fame? Myself? What's that? I need something that is important. I need something a child can be proud of."

Mrs. Jones entered quietly. "Can I get you something, Mr. Lennon?"

"No, that's okay, dear. It's late. Why don't you call it a night? You too, Charles. I'll see you tomorrow and thanks."

"But what if Mrs. Lennon needs something?" objected Mrs. Jones.

"Thanks," he smiled, "I'll take care of Mrs. Lennon."

· 4 ·

AND BABY
MAKES THREE

The Lennons' son was born on John's thirty-fifth birthday, October 9, 1975. Later John would claim with a smile that he had actually planned it that way. But that was later. In the days immediately following the birth John was not in the mood for humor. The child had had to be delivered by Caesarean section and Yoko was required to stay in the hospital some two weeks to recuperate. John haunted the hospital during visiting hours and banged around his ten-room apartment the rest of the time.

Late one night during this period, John called me. In the wee small hours I listened to him relate how the event could have been happier as far as he was concerned.

"It's not as though I've gained a son. It's more like I've lost a wife!" he complained. "Nothing's worked out the way it was

49

supposed to, you know. We had it all planned out. We'd have the baby at home, we said. I would be there for the delivery, we said. Natural birth, no problems, we said. So what happens? Off she goes to the hospital, telling me she doesn't want me there, and the doctors perform a Caesarean section. Now they're keeping her for observation because of 'complications.' It's good we planned everything so carefully. Birth classes and health foods, and now they're shooting her full of some damned drug. What was it all about, all the talk, all the plans? What did we get out of it?"

"A healthy son."

"That I can't have with me till some man in a white coat says I can. It's like the doctors own my family."

"When a forty-two-year-old woman—"

"Don't start that. You sound like one of the white coats. Age has nothing to do with it. It's all a matter of condition. Yoko is in a lot younger condition than her age."

"Have it your way. When a woman of any age goes about having a baby by eating a ton of chocolate, then fasting and going on radical diets, smokes like a fiend, and keeps herself in a state of constant agitation, she's lucky if she doesn't miscarry."

"My, aren't you full of compassion and understanding."

"Not when it isn't needed, John, and not at three in the morning."

"All right, I'm sorry about the hour, but I'm lonely, and when I get lonely I get scared. When all I've got to talk to is me I tell myself bad things, like maybe the baby wasn't such a good idea."

"Too late."

"I know, but it's all so different from what I expected. I knew how everything was going to be. I had it all rehearsed. I even rehearsed what I was going to say when the hospital called to tell me that I was a father again. Then I waited and waited and started to tell myself bad shit. So I rehearsed what I would say if they called to say the baby died . . . or worse."

"So when they called and it was good news, what did you say?"

"Nothing. I just listened while they told me Yoko had had the baby and I should come right down. Then I said 'Thanks.' Not much of a speech."

"It was all that was required."

"When I went down to see her there was the usual gaggle of press. They all wanted to know how she was and how I felt. But I put them off. I told them that I just got there, but I'd heard Yoko was pregnant. Lennon wit, they liked that. The press probably knew more about the situation than I did. That's why I read the papers, you know. It lets me know what's happened to me.

"So I went in to see her," he continued. "At first they wouldn't let me. This doctor stood there telling me that he always admired my work. Just what I needed, a fan. There's my wife locked away somewhere in the bowels of that place and *our* doctor is getting his rocks and rolls off on the ex-Beatle.

"Well, I made it *graphically* clear that I wanted to see *my wife* and he goes into his hoodoo about 'complications.' He tells me how Yoko's tubes are all screwed up, so they had to go in after the baby with a knife. Of course, he didn't bother to mention that it was the likes of him that screwed up her tubes in the first place. Fuckin' mechanics. Then he wants to know if Yoko's on drugs. Well, right there, that let me know that he couldn't have taken any blood tests!"

"Was she?" I tried to be gentle as I probed.

"No! Of course not! I *doo* do things once in a while, but I wouldn't let her touch anything while she was pregnant. Cigarettes were bad enough. And for your information I wasn't doing anything either.

"So this *doctor* explains to me that the reason why he asked is that the baby was trembling when he was born. 'Well,' I said 'perhaps he was trembling because you scared him when you cut his mother open and dragged him out!' So he takes me to see the baby. All the time, mind you, I've been asking to see my wife, but he takes me to see the baby anyway."

"And how did he look?"

"He looked like a red raisin. How does any baby look? Oh sure, fatherly pride being what it is, my baby always looks beautiful. But really, there's nothing to see, just a red, wrinkled kid. It was Yoko I wanted to see. I wanted to *see* if she was okay. I can tell by looking at her. But the doctor said she was sleeping. I told him that I wanted to *see* not *talk* to her. I didn't mind if she was sleeping. I *had* seen her sleep before. That's when he finally took me to her."

"And how did she look?"

"Awful. God. You know she always looks so good, young, strong. She has a very strong face. But when she's really sick or scared she looks awful. She gets this look about her." I knew that look—stressed, drained, and twisted, a look of anguish. "Then I really got scared. 'She's dying,' I said. And the doctor gives me the 'Now, John, let's not exaggerate, shall we' routine, all confidence and reassurance. I could have killed him. Then he ushers me out into the arms of the ever-lovin' press, saying there is nothing I can do, so I might as well go home, not even showing me to the back door so I won't get mobbed with 'How's she doin'? How ya feel?' Fuckin' horrific."

"John, I have to ask. What did you tell the press?"

"I don't know, something clever. Buy a paper. I tell you what I didn't tell them. I didn't tell them what I wanted to. At least I had enough wits about me not to do that again. I wasn't ready. All those months and I wasn't ready. The way Yoko looked, the kid . . . I wasn't ready."

"But," I tried to be cheerful, "the baby's okay and Yoko's

okay." I knew because of the barrage of calls she had made to me since the birth.

"Yeah, they're okay. I'm not so hot."

"Well, you suffered all the other symptoms, right down to the labor pains—"

"That was my *kidneys,* Charles."

"Right," I didn't believe him. "Perhaps what you are feeling now is your version of postpartum tristesse."

"What?"

"Postpregnancy depression."

"Could be . . ." He seemed to be considering the possibility. "How are you fixed for depression cures?"

"Exercise."

"I get enough of that climbing the walls. Okay, maybe I should take a walk in the park."

"A walk in Central Park at three in the morning doesn't qualify as exercise, John. Suicide maybe, but definitely not exercise."

"Right, I forgot the time . . . ah . . . feel like reading some cards?" It was a request I was used to from many clients. Late at night during a crisis, the need to talk is often expressed in the request for a reading. John's questions were thoughtful. Paramount was his concern about Yoko and his new son, whom he perpetually referred to as "the baby" or "the kid."

"I thought you had settled on a name." I had done literally hundreds of readings on possible names for the expected child. Yoko had needed a name that would be numerologically impeccable.

"Yeah, we decided on Sean. It means John in Irish or Gaelic or something."

"I know." At this stage I knew the meanings of just about every name ever conceived.

"Yoko wanted to name him John, but as I already got a son

named John—John Julian—I thought having two sons with the same name a bit redundant. And Taro, that's his middle name. That's for you, like the cards."

"Not quite."

"No, you're right. It's John in Japanese or something, but I thought the similarity was fun."

"So if he has a name, two in fact, how come you don't use them?"

"Because I don't feel like he's real yet. I mean, they showed me a baby, but it could have been any baby. They all look alike. I just want to get them home. Then I'll get it straight."

"Well, if that is all you want, why not make a homecoming party, just for exercise? You could combine your birthday and Sean's and Yoko's homecoming into one major event."

"That's great!" His voice brightened noticeably. "We'll have an official family reception! King greets heir, queen returns to lair. You could perform the official baptism and seal his name on with a little ceremony."

"I think you'll be happier if you do that yourself."

"You're probably right. But you're wrong about my birthday. This is going to be just for Yoko and Sean. I already got my birthday present, the best. I got Sean."

The next several days were filled with John's excited preparations. He had begun to collect all the fan mail that had arrived to wish him and Yoko the best for their new son. Sean, not yet two weeks old, was already receiving his share of letters, telegrams, and presents. All these John carefully collected and placed in separate piles. He read each one, removing the hate letters and crank gifts. Wisely he made sure Yoko's stack was the largest. To it he added expensive little gifts of his own. Knowing his wife's weakness for jewelry, he included many pleasant, bejeweled trifles to capture her fancy.

When he wasn't plotting his party, he would visit them.

Each day reassured him that both their conditions were stable. His resentment of the doctor faded as his confidence grew. It was a confidence that his wife did not share.

"I think his head's too small," she complained. "I don't think he could have the right-sized brain in a little head like that. Babies are supposed to have *big* heads, you know, and there *was* something wrong with him at birth." Her calls from the hospital had grown incessant with her returning strength.

"Whadda ya mean, 'too small'? Doesn't it fit his neck?"

"Stop that, Charlie, this is serious. I think I should have another doctor look at him."

"Please, not *another* doctor!"

"Well this one isn't going to give me a straight answer. It's his work. He's going to say everything is fine and send me home with a baby like this."

"Yeah, they're all like that. They don't want to admit there's any problem till after the warranty's run out."

"I know," she answered quite seriously. "That's why I think another doctor. Dr. Lee maybe. What do you think?" Dr. Lee (as I'll call him) was a Korean herbalist who flitted in and out of Yoko's life.

"What do you suspect an herbalist prescribes for shrunken heads, mind expansion?"

"Stop trying to be funny. You predicted a normal baby. I've seen him, and I'm afraid he's not normal. You said that this doctor was a good one, and I don't think he is. That's why I need Dr. Lee."

I spread and read the cards, and it seemed that Dr. Lee would do no harm, aside from being an excuse for Yoko not to listen to her current physician, but she wouldn't have done that anyway. Dr. Lee's advice was mostly practical and I thought it better that the counsel she got was common sense instead of the nonsense she might think up herself.

Despite her protests, Yoko was released from the hospital in due course. Even the good Dr. Lee said that it was high time she came home and began a proper diet to lose the excess weight she had gained during her pregnancy.

Yoko's "brush with death" had convinced her that she was frail and in need of the constant attention that only a hospital could provide. John foolishly promised her that he would take care of "everything," not realizing what "everything" would entail. Upon Yoko's return to the Dakota after nearly two weeks in the hospital, the household was thrown into turmoil. While she remained bedridden, John scurried from kitchen to nursery to bedroom trying to fulfill the roles of husband, father, and nurse. I too was busy, reading cards for Yoko on the new nanny, the baby's health, and, of course, John. The nanny was a good one and the baby appeared to be fine, but with John it was a different matter. I didn't need tarot cards to tell me how John was feeling. He took care of that himself.

"How goes the home front?" I asked as I walked into the kitchen on the third day of Yoko's return. I had just finished a reading of several hours for Yoko in the bedroom and now it was Dad's turn. As I entered I noted his posture. The effort of taking care of "everything" appeared to be telling heavily on him. He was slumped down as far as possible in his white director's chair, his feet straight out in front of him, ankles uncrossed. By his appearance I surmised that this was one of his humorless days.

"Don't you know?" He snapped. "Rotten! God, I hate this —every time I plan something it never works out. Do you know how frustrating, how bloody boring that can be? Step and fuckin' fetchit, that's what I is."

I had just got Yoko's version of the homecoming: how John had ignored her and was currently tormenting her by taking advantage of her rare show of weakness.

"From the moment she got back, limoed from the hospital and claiming she needed an ambulance, she's been in bed. She calls me on the phone for coffee. I take her coffee. 'Oh! no,' she says, 'caffeine's no good for me. You know that. Why didn't you bring me tea?' So back I go for tea. Then, well! I'd forgotten the fruit, hadn't I? Then while I'm getting the fruit, she calls again to 'suggest' some noodles to keep up her strength, and royal jelly because it's got some magic elixir in it. Well, by the time I get all that together the tea's cold."

"What happened to Mrs. Jones? I thought she was going to take care of that sort of thing at least during the day shift."

"Mrs. Jones got the sack, as they say. First thing. Couldn't be trusted, you know. She stole things. Her last heist, it seems, were Yoko's 'favorite cashmere sweaters.'"

"A snug fit for Mrs. Jones." She would have easily made five of Yoko.

"Well, Charles, *according to you,* she stole them because she was put up to it by a no-account lover who has moved in with her and poisoned her mind against us. The booty is to be sold at certain less reputable pawnshops." He eyed me carefully.

"It's good I talk to you or I'd never know what I say."

"That's what you get for working in the mysteries, m'boy." He paused, looking down at the table. "I did what you said, the homecoming and all. I did it with a vengeance, but it didn't work. I wanted to create a little magic, something special for us. Do you know what the first thing she did was? She walked, or should I say limped, in the front door and handed Sean over to the new nanny, deposits him as it were, just like that. So much for the child. Well, I rescued him and told Yoko that I had a little surprise for her in the playroom." The playroom was formerly the den and originally the formal dining room off the kitchen. Under Yoko's direction it had been converted to a playroom by being emptied of all its contents and painted white again. The result was a playroom large enough for the Giants to play in. "So we make the ceremonious little march down the hall, me with Sean in one arm and her nibs on the other, and this dwarf nanny scampering up the rear. We go into the playroom where I had everything laid out, letters, presents, everything. 'Ta da!' I say, and she says, 'What's this?' So I sit her down in a proper throne I had placed there especially for the new mother and sit down on the floor beside her. I start to tell her about all the telegrams *we* got and how proud everyone was of *her* and the baby, but she couldn't have cared less, like it was expected. I sure as hell didn't expect a response like that. All she can do is tell me about her concert in Japan. That was more than a year ago. You've heard the story."

I nodded, having indeed heard the story. It was back in my early days with Yoko. She had gotten the opportunity to do a tour in Japan during August of 1974. It could not have come at a better time for her. She and John had been estranged for nearly a year. John was coming to New York to record *Walls and Bridges* and to testify at another Immigration hearing. She confessed concern that if he attracted press attention, which he was sure to do, then the press might accent the fact that they were separated. It was her hope that if the papers mentioned her, it would simply be to note that she was busy performing.

The "Japanese tour," as she called it, took on a special significance to her. She told me afterward that she was greeted by street demonstrations. One demonstrator carried a placard that struck her as particularly poignant. She said it read, "Yoko Ono, is she a saint or a devil?" She made no secret of her pleasure at receiving so much attention in her own right without being forced to stand in the shadow of her megacelebrity husband.

The high point of the tour, she said, was a performance in Hiroshima. As the show took place close to the thirty-ninth anniversary of the tragic atomic bombing of that city, her mind was naturally full of thoughts of the victims. She recounted to me that as she stood onstage singing, she looked up to the balcony and saw what she believed to be the spirits of the children who died in the atomic blast and from the radiation that followed as well as the spirits of the unborn children who would be marred for generations to come as a result of genetic disruption. These spirit children cheered her, she said, reminding her of her mission to bring peace to the world.

Now, more than a year later, John was not in the least sympathetic to Yoko's story. "I guess that's one excuse for empty seats," he said contemptuously. "Souled out, no doubt. She says this is the fulfillment of that mission. The union of east and west, a child of the children of peace. Christ! The kid isn't even a month old and he's already slated to save the wicked ol' world. So I told her, 'You might wait till he's out of diapers and into nursery school!' Well, that scorched Mommie's sensibilities, so she gathers up her jewels and poof! she's off to the bedroom and that's where she's stayed."

"The lady is not easy to please."

"It's not her," he said sadly, "it's me. I don't know how to do things to make her happy. I've spent so much time doing things for people to (big secret!) really please myself, I've forgotten how to give."

"You fake it well."

"Right, 'fake it!' That's exactly what I do. I'm trying to make her happy because that would make me happy. Terrific."

"It's not a bad motive," I maintained.

"And it's not a good one either. The whole problem is that I'm not happy myself. I try to make her happy becuase I think that that will make for a happy family, and that will work for me. But it's gotta come from inside me first. It's gotta be mine *before* I can share it."

In the weeks that followed, a new order began to establish itself in the Lennons' life. The nanny tended to the child in his newly renovated nursery, which John had arranged to have painted blue after learning that the baby was a boy. Yoko rapidly regained her strength and quickly shed her excess weight with the skillful assistance of Dr. Lee. Gofers got things, psychics read, and in general life at the Dakota began to hum like a well-oiled machine.

The single exception to all this order and calm was John. In some ways the pregnancy had served him as a distraction from the pressing inner question of his work. He had not written a song in fifteen months now, and this creative paralysis tormented him. Yoko was growing increasingly involved in the business end of John's life and had less and less time to console him. John openly resented his wife's growing interest in a subject other than himself, no matter how closely related to him that subject was, and expressed his feelings with stinging hostility. In self-defense Yoko seemed to withdraw, hoping that by giving him time and space he would resolve his inner conflict. But it was apparently company that John required, not space, for it was in search of company that he began disappearing sporadically for several hours at a stretch during the evenings to carouse with cronies or ladies of the night. When not so engaged he moped around the house, finding fault with almost everything and collecting newspaper clippings on Sean's birth.

A few days before Thanksgiving 1975, I found him sitting in the kitchen with a pile of these articles telling of Sean, Yoko, and the proud father. I had come to give him his reading, but he had no questions that afternoon, only comments as he thumbed through his stack of papers.

"Well, it's done," he said morosely, "Our nine-day-wonder ceases to amaze. I suppose it couldn't last, but it was nice while it did."

"You could have made more press if you'd wanted."

"Ah, not true, Charles. The press is a strange beast and I have spent the better part of my adult life learning its habits. It comes sniffing and yipping up to your door begging for yummies, but if you offer it the wrong treat, it will turn on you.

"It's all right to say 'Peace' but don't compare yourself to God. I know. I've tried both. It's all right to brawl in public, but just be sure not to punch any reporters when you do. I gotta be careful. I stepped on the press beast's tail on the West Coast last year. Result: Instead of being a zany rock star out on a lark, I was a ludicrous fool. For a while I didn't think anyone loved me, *really*. This year I got three nice spots. Hosting the Grammy Awards; that was nice, musician honors his peers. Then the Lew Grade special; that was also nice. Now Sean, and they're being very nice about this too. I don't want to blow it. I just wish I had more of it, but that I can't have unless I have something to say, which I don't."

"How about 'father and son seen in park,' that sort of thing?"

"Not wise, wizard. First of all that sort of thing doesn't work for someone in my position. The public expects me to be *doing* something, and strolling with the baby, playing family man, isn't *something*. Even if they did take the copy, it is really more Sean's press than mine. There's going to be enough competition later on, we don't have to rush it.

"Look at these," he waved the clippings. "I mean, it's great that the press beast loves the baby, but I used to be in the papers every day. Now, three shots in a year. I feel as though the factory closed and I got laid off."

"Do I detect a note of jealousy?"

"You detect a whole symphony of it, Charles. Look at this one, the whole story of how Sean's birth saved John from deportation. The government gives me a break because the wife's knocked up. That doesn't sound like I played a very important role, does it? Whatever whoever was going to say about the album got swallowed up by the baby, and perhaps that's just as well."

Just two weeks after Sean's birth, John had released his

album *Shaved Fish.* The public response to it had been cool. A compilation piece, *Shaved Fish* contained no new material and John admitted that he intended it as a device to keep his name in the marketplace while he was waiting for his muse to return. Along with *Rock 'n' Roll,* this piece made two Lennon albums for the year 1975, but neither of them had what the record business or the public wanted: new Lennon songs. Placed on the market with minimal promotional support, *Shaved Fish* was not selling well, as the all-important first month's sales receipts showed. For the press, the story of Sean was better copy.

"There'll be no hits this year," John continued sadly. "I'm lucky the press beast didn't start howling 'Lennon's had it.' Lucky for me I can still make babies. Maybe I should do it again."

"I don't think that's really the best idea."

"Neither do I, actually." He paused, looking back to his collection of clippings. "Can you see it? Sean's first long pants, Sean in school, Sean will be so famous no one will remember who his father was."

"That's a little hard to believe."

"Wait and see. The press beast is a weird critter and the public loves babies." He paused resentfully. "When Julian was born, all they loved was me."

· 5 ·

TROUBLES,
TRAUMAS, AND TRYSTS

As the holiday season of 1975 came into full swing, John's increasingly frequent disappearances began to worry Yoko, and she attempted to accompany him whenever he left the apartment. In the preceding weeks, John had repeatedly complained that he wanted more attention from her, but now that he was getting it, he reacted by abusing her publicly. By the second week in December this proclivity had precipitated a family crisis.

I was reading for John in the Black Room, to which Yoko had exiled him in response to his behavior. He appeared to be in high spirits, but I wasn't convinced. Ordinarily, John's love of sunlight caused him to sit nearest the window with the strongest light. But it was past noon and the Black Room's window, which faced east, had already lost its light. Under normal circumstances this would have been sufficient motive for him to betake himself to another room where the light remained strong, there to bask catlike in its rays. Not today, however. I concluded that he was chiefly concerned with avoiding Yoko by hiding in the Black Room, which was his domain. Here he could feel safe, since he could be sure that after a fight she would not search him out.

John sat in one of the black lacquer chairs, while I had pulled the other one up to the glass-topped desk to read his cards. Though I had asked him what happened, I hadn't expected the detailed account he gave.

" 'D'ya know what you are?' I shouted. 'You're no fun! You know that, don't you? No fun at all!' So's the whole room could hear me," cackled John, relating his version of the previous night's dispute with Yoko at Ashley's, a popular downtown watering hole. "Then I say softly, just for her, 'You with that great moping face of yours. God knows, I don't need you hangin' around all the time.' I could tell that I was getting to her. She craves attention so much I thought that I'd give her a good dose. So I say, playing to the room, 'She probably just wants to keep an eye on me. Keep me out of trouble.' They laughed at that one." Then, mimicking Yoko's reedy voice, " 'Oh, no, no, no, just a little joke.' And I shout, 'Joke, me arse!' The room was loving it. She hangs her head down all embarrassment and indecision, so I give her a big smile and say through my teeth, like this, 'Had enough?' " He paused to savor the recollection.

"Don't you think you were being a bit cruel?"

"Sure I was! I can be cruel, you know. She deserves it. Following me around everywhere, watching me—and not appreciatively either!"

"She's not an audience, John, she's your wife."

"In concept and contracts only, Charles, so much the pity. We wander around in this cooperative asylum of ours, the paranoid and the petered out. Nothing to do and no reason for doing it. And all the time she's watching and waiting. Waiting for me to get another grand rush, to write another 'Imagine.' That's what she wants, you know. She wants me to record something so she can do her stuff. She won't do it with me. She can't do it without me. And I ain't doing it at all. If you had to live like this, you'd find out how cruel you could get. And you'd call it justified and enjoy it, just like I do."

"You're not feeling productive, so you attack her?"

"I don't attack. I retaliate. She torments me and I punish her for it. She can't let go of me and she knows that makes me crazy. She can't let me have anything of my own. So I go out to get away. But she has to drag along because she's afraid that I'll get so far I won't come back. Then it's John and Yoko and the whole act. You know, 'the perfect couple.' So I turn the tables. I pick a nice decadent celebrity bar like Ashley's and let her have it. Believe me, I *know* the right buttons to push. If I wanted to I could make it a lot worse, a *lot* worse."

"And what does she do?"

"What can she do? Stay and take it or leave. She left." He was reminded of the scene he had created. "It was perfect!" he snickered. "I waited till she got right to the door and then I hollered, 'Don't forget to say good night, *dear.* ' And the crowd swings its collective head around in time to see her famous hair disappear out into the street. 'Where's the press when you need 'em?' I shout and everyone chuckles. They love it, you know. A rare performance, a celebrity spat. People in bars love that sort of thing. 'Gawd,' I moan, 'I'm gonna get it when I get home.' Then I waited a few minutes and left, but nobody noticed, the show was over."

"Left for where?" I knew from Yoko that he hadn't come in until seven-thirty that morning.

"Didn't care, outta there. I'd been drinkin'. I wanted to get out before the depression kicked in. I get soooo depressed when I drink."

"Then why do it?"

"Because I get sooo depressed when I don't. I just like to walk around, get lost so I can find myself in different places. A whorehouse usually, like last night, get laid, nothing special. Just go around, anywhere but home."

"You could go visit friends."

"I don't *have* friends, Charles! That's the whole point. *We* have friends. So I go out and rent a friend, nothing wrong with that. Once a month, that's not so bad. It's my full-moon reaction, except it never happens on the full moon." We sat for a while saying nothing while he drew jagged little squiggles on an official-looking envelope.

"Do you know what's wrong?" he asked at length. "The whole problem is that she lets me get away with it. She talks all this 'women's rights,' which I *do* believe in whether *you* believe me or not, but then she never does anything. We don't fight. We cold-war. I want a wife who shows she cares, who'll stop me. When I pull shit like this I expect a wife to bash me fuckin' head in. But nooo, nothing ever happens. We just sit around waiting for the next *emergency* to give us an excuse to talk to each other again. Then we pretend that nothing's happened."

"So? Tell her."

"I'm sick of making up *all* the rules *all* the time. You tell her." And I did.

The rift between the couple grew as the holidays passed and the New Year of 1976 rang in. John wanted Yoko to take a stand and restrain him from destroying his dream of a happy home. But Yoko wanted invisible power, free of responsibility. Their differences frequently exploded into flames.

"He screamed at me!" exclaimed Yoko as I sat by her bed reading cards one crisp January afternoon. "I hadn't done anything and he screamed at me!" Her voice was more full of wonder than outrage. "I just went into the kitchen for breakfast, like I do, and he was already sitting there going through the mail. He does that all the time now, you know; he has to be the first to see the mail. And I got coffee and sat down. He didn't look up or say anything at first, so I thought I'd better be careful. I was being very quiet, but watching him, you know. And then he started screaming, 'What the fuck's your problem?' and he was so loud he made me spill my coffee. I think Masako [Sean's nanny] must have seen because when I looked up she was turning to leave. I had to call her back and give her directions in Japanese, things to do, you know, because she had seen John yelling at me and I wanted to let her know that I was still in authority over *her* no matter what my husband did to me. I told her to get some things and sent her out, but that only made John angrier. 'Too many secrets!' he yelled, 'I've got to take a course in Japanese just to find out what's going on in my own house!' I had already forgotten what I had asked Masako to do, so I told him that I had sent her for my cigarettes. Then he jumps up and grabs the cigarettes that were on the table and throws them at me. Then he starts saying that he doesn't mind being lied to so much as he hates being lied to so badly, and I had to say that it was my bag I had really wanted and that Masako knows that my cigarettes are always in my bag. Then he said that he knew that I hadn't asked for my purse. I don't know if he just knew or he could tell from what I said. You don't think he can understand Japanese, do you? That would be terrible! He said that I was too stupid to see that that wasn't even the lie he was talking about. I tried to think of which lie he meant and I couldn't because I was so scared—he can be violent. His face was this far away and he was very white and shaking and screaming, screaming at me, about how all I ever wanted was limelight and attention and that I wouldn't ever have gotten any if it wasn't for him. That's not true! But he said now he wasn't getting the public attention and that I was turning on him. And I'm not, you know *that*. He said all I do is sit around and let some other woman mind my baby and that with breasts like mine I should at least feed the baby, but I can't because it would hurt me if I tried. He said all I ever did was spend money and if I didn't stop there wouldn't be any left to spend. You don't think that's true, do you? Well, he was screaming so loud the baby started to cry and Masako brought him in— she always does that when the baby cries. She says she does it because the baby wants his mother, but I think it's just to get rid of him and let me know how hard she has to work. When John saw them he pointed and screamed 'There's your bag!' because that's what I said Masako had gone for, and then he left, just marched out, and I called you. I need to know why he attacked me like that. I always know if something is bothering him. Masako or you or somebody tells me and that way I can know how to handle him. But this time there was no warning. What do you think it was?" She fidgeted with her cigarettes while I studied the cards.

"Money. It's about money and the career that is supposed to bring him money."

"That's ridiculous. We have enough money; we're not rich, but we have enough for our needs . . . don't we?"

"I think he's thinking about the future."

"Well, the future will be okay. We'll just get money from somewhere else, that's all. No, you'd better read again on this one. I think it has to be sex."

But sex was not the issue in this latest Lennon outburst, as he confided later that same afternoon when I met him in the kitchen to read the cards and play the role of liaison.

"Well, there you are, Charles. I thought dear Yoko was going to punish me and not let you read." He was in his usual postargument mood of good cheer.

"No, she's punishing me instead."

"I suppose you've heard, I've been a bad lad again?"

"Not again—still."

"Come on, I wasn't too hard on her. You know what I said?"

"In detail! So spare me having to hear it again. What I would like to hear is why."

"It's the same 'why' as always. She sits around watching me, waiting, expecting that any minute I'll turn into a monster and devour her. I think it only considerate to give her what she asks for every once in a while." I waited and watched him Yoko-like. "Why do I get the feeling that you don't believe me."

"You're psychic."

"Try this one then. I have nothing to do and she's fully employed helping me do it. I'm used to being active in the extreme and idleness gets on my nerves. Every once in a while I strike out, lose my temper, or to be more accurate, I find it. I'm a very violent man. Leading a peaceful life is a bit of a strain. I used to go out and punch the glass out of phone booths or get in a fight. Now, I'm older and not nearly so brave or stupid. You know I never used to think about the damage I could do to myself when I'd put my fist through glass; I could have been a musical man with mechanical hands. I'm not willing to risk it anymore. So I strike out at a safe target, my wife. She won't strike back."

"In case you're wondering, John, I don't believe that one either."

"Really? What does the wicked witch of Central Park West say my motive is?"

"Money."

"Right you are." He dug into his back pocket and pulled out a much-abused letter covered with green ink scribbles. "Look what the mailman brought me today."

"Is this what you've been getting up every morning to wait for?"

"The very same. A little more Capitol punishment." Capitol was John's U.S. record distributor. This extraordinary letter accused John quite baldly of refusing to write hits for them and asked in peremptory tones when he was going to get back to turning out gold records on a regular basis. "They've always been like this, you know. I've made it large and I'm still not worth the patience or the gamble of a little calculated inaction. I put out two LPs in '75. No gold but two LPs just the same. That's a lot, but it wasn't *new* material. Now they want to know what I've been doing and when I'll have a little something else for them. I haven't written a thing in more than a year. Nothing. Not a bridge, not a verse, not even a line. I dug out old stuff, but I realized that I didn't use it then for the same reason I can't use it now: It's no fuckin' good. If I don't come up with something, then all I got is royalties to live on, and they'll get smaller and smaller every year and the money will be worth less and less. Where does that leave me?"

"With enough money, if you're wise."

"It's not the money, Charles, it's the doing of the thing. Sure the money's nice, but it's just a symbol. The only proof I ever get that I'm all right, doing well, is the money. I'll make less this year than last, so I'm not as good as I was last year. The world checks my receipts and says 'Lennon's had it.' The only way out is to quit and I *can't* do *that!* What am I going to do if I'm not doing music? Other performers get away with it. They can cut a record and disappear for a year or two or five. Then presto, they're back on the scene with a new sound and nobody complains. Stevie Wonder does it, so does David Bowie, but not John Lennon. I got to put out one or two albums a year with at least one hit single or they say, 'Lennon's finished, all burned out.' Well they're the bastards that burned me."

"Then strike back at *them.*"

"Listen! Don't ever think you can attack a record company and get away with it. They own the business now. People like me gave it to them. They used to have to come to us because

70

we were the business. Not just the Beatles, the artists, all of us. But not anymore. It's a business now and business is no fun. They snap their fingers and we'd fuckin' better deliver or they've got someone else who can. They can just take your tape and leave it on the shelf or put it out with no push and let it die, picking up fan sales but not making new fans. The only reason I did it all in the first place is that it was fun and I didn't want to work."

"And how does Yoko fit into all this?"

"Yoko is my wife. She's also my liability, as wives always are. I'm afraid that if she doesn't change and we don't change, then she's going to be a liability that I can't afford anymore. She accelerates my failure, and I hate her for that."

"Accelerates failure?"

"This, Charles, is one of those times when a family is supposed to stick together. I do what I can to that end, but I need assistance. I came back for that. Family. I knew what was on the horizon, I've been through this before. I know what it's like to lose the muse, it's happened before. This is the time to count other assets, so I can say to myself, 'It doesn't matter about the music. Look at all the other things in my life!' I look around, Charles, and day by day it's taking less and less time to count my blessings. She's supposed to *be there* for me, she's supposed to be strong when I can't be. Instead she hides. She only wants me when I've got it all together. I have to be perfect for her or stay away. Well, I'm never perfect."

"No one is."

"Tell her that."

"I do."

"Then you can't be doing too good a job because she's still not being there!"

"What do you mean by 'being there' for you, being sexual for you?"

"It sure as hell helps. I want a woman who honestly loves

to love me, not just physically, but that is certainly an important part of it. But the problem is that I'm failing and she accelerates that. I get failure in the mails, I get it in the mirror, all I get is failure.

"I want a little of 'It's all right, dear, never mind, it'll be all right,' hugs and kisses all around. But that's not what's happening. So every once in a while, and, yes, more often than not lately, I try to shock her out of that ice-palace attitude of hers into a little human reality."

"By attacking?"

"It's all attacking to her. First I ask, and that's an affront. Then I joke because I'd rather laugh than plead, and that's an insult. Then I give her hell, as you are well aware. The result is always the same no matter what I do. So what's the difference? Finally I go out and there's at least a little sense of accomplishment in that.

"I can do it for myself now, you know, like a kid at potty. I used to require assistance, had to have someone negotiate the arrangements because I'd never gotten a hotel room by myself, let alone set the price and bought a lady or ladies, as the case might be. So I've cracked the code of that proud old gentleman's mystique. I can go to the whorehouse like a big boy. There's precious little satisfaction in that, but precious little is precious compared to no satisfaction at all."

"And it has the added advantage of humiliating Yoko."

"Charles, at this point, you must know everything humiliates Yoko. It used to be that she did, really did things for me. A million years ago when we first met, that's all it ever was: She did for me, I did for her. We did together. That's gone, just like everything else. It's a joke, a real Joko. She used to worry that the only reason I wanted her around was for sex, that I didn't realize that she had a mind or talent, which was hard to miss because she reminded me so often. She gave me what I needed then. She paid attention to me, not to the Beatle—

everyone was doing that. I needed something personal. I needed to be one of a kind, not one of the four. She supplied that and I reciprocated. I felt then that I could do anything, and if it didn't work when I tried a little something like peace on earth or humane revolution, it really didn't matter because in the last analysis I had one person who believed in me. That's all you ever need, you know. That's why families still work. That's why people still fall in love and do all those things that they've always done. That's, in fact, why I came back here. I realized that I couldn't go on starting over, changing the players and playing the same ol' game. I came back to make it work and it's not working. And at this point I don't really feel that it's all my fault. Family, that means more than one. Now, Sean's a little young for me to go counting on him to help me, so that leaves you-know-who. And I want you-know-who to love, honor, and tell me that I'm a big strong man so that I can go out there and be a big strong man instead of some fuckin' neurotic who's always wondering what he did wrong. It's a sick feeling to think that if there isn't music, there's nothing. After all this time there should be something, shouldn't there?"

"Yeah . . . one would think so. Are you asking me how you should be able to find that 'something' in yourself?"

"Spare me. I'm sick of finding things in myself. If I have to find everything inside me, then what's the use of having other people in my life? Not that there is an army of them these days."

"Do you think Yoko can find what you're looking for, for you?"

"She can at least help."

"She's not your mother."

"Oh, right, you're getting that routine from her. That's because I call her 'Mommie.' Well, she is Mommie and I'm Daddy, and Sean is the baby, and that's how it is. That doesn't mean I want her to be *my* mother. Sure I want my mommie. I did the therapies and all that. I screamed and cried 'Mommie's dead, I miss her,' but that isn't what I want my wife to be, a mother to me, at least not all the time, and I'm not her dad! Okay?"

The pattern was invariable. John would attack, revel in his cruelty more to justify it than because it gave him any actual pleasure. Then guilt would shoot him down. He would try to make up by showering her with attention and presents. She accepted his generosity but not his advances. In time frustration would send him out on the prowl again. And when that happened I was sure to hear about it. My phone rang a few nights later interrupting the latest of the "Late Show" reruns (a passion of mine). It was Yoko.

"Charlie, this is an emergency, very important. John just called."

"From where?" I stretched and groaned and pulled out the cards for another predawn session.

"I don't know, he just called and said that he was somewhere and he didn't know where it was but that he was tripping and watching these three lesbians making it and that he hoped they would make it with him next but more than that he wanted me to come and get him, but I don't know where he is, he just hung up!" I could imagine the wicked smile on John's face. "Where do you think he is? What should I do? This could be very dangerous, you know! I want you to pray for him."

So I did. "Dear Lord, as long as she's going to be crazy and I'm not going to get any sleep, at least let John have a good time."

· 6 ·

GETTING DOWN
TO BUSINESS

"**B**op bip ado, I'm changing you/Bee bop adee, you're changing me . . ."

John's voice filtered into the kitchen. He was engaging in his new pastime, tending to the baby, while Yoko and I read on what was quickly becoming our sole subject: business.

"What will Hilary [Hilary Gerrard, Ringo's representative to the Beatles' recording company, Apple] think? I think Lee [Lee Eastman, Paul McCartney's father-in-law and basic money mind] is going to be the real problem. He always is, but if we can get Hilary and Brooth [George Harrison's man] behind me we should be able to persuade Lee."

"Hilary's a fence-sitter. It's Lee you need. If the two of you unite, the others will follow."

"How do we do that?"

How indeed? Apple was constructed of four equal shares and required unanimous approval from all four voters before any decision could be made. The original idea had been that all four Beatles were equal and should always agree, which in those days they often did. But those days had passed and now the four seldom spoke. Each had a representative and each representative had an alternate, each alternate an assistant, and so on. Hence the meetings became congeries of some of rock's better business minds, each out to justify his salary by out-maneuvering the others. Since nobody ever agreed on anything, no decisions were ever made, and Apple had been effectively paralyzed for years now. All this was presided over by Neil Aspinal, onetime road manager for the Beatles, whom the four, in a fit of sentimentality, had promoted to the position of president of Apple. Well-meaning but unassertive, Neil interpreted his role as one of carrying out whatever decisions the four shareholders agreed upon. This gave him little to do.

For more than a year now, beginning a few months before her reunion with John, Yoko had become increasingly involved in the Beatles' business. And so had I.

Yoko's road to becoming a noted businesswoman had begun in the twisty thickets of the record industry, where creativity and finances wage constant war. In late October 1973, when the Lennons' fifteen-month estrangement began, John had just finished recording *Mind Games.* He and Yoko had agreed that when he had finished his album, it would be her turn to record, with John acting as her producer. Before that could happen, however, John went out for a paper one night and didn't return for over a year.

In December of 1973, Yoko heard that John was recording again, working with the well-known producer Phil Spector on the first recording sessions of John's intended valentine album to the United States, *Rock 'n' Roll.* Despite her strong desire to get on with her own recording project, she told me that she thought it wisest for her to maintain her distance. John was her

economic lifeline and the key to her musical career. She feared
that if she did anything to offend him, she could suffer for it
financially. She had learned that *Mind Games* had not sold well.
But as she said, she also knew that John was managing his own
business through his own manager and that neither of them
would be likely to welcome her intrusion. So she chose to be
patient and wait for John's return.

That resolve faded when she learned that early in 1974 John
had stopped recording *Rock 'n' Roll* and had headed for Los
Angeles, where he intended to produce Harry Nilsson's *Pussy
Cats.* The prospect of the three-thousand-mile separation convinced Yoko that if she were going to record at all in the
foreseeable future, she could no longer wait for John to return
but would instead have to act on her own. So she gathered a
group of musicians and began work on a new album.

It was at this point that she ran into difficulties having her
work produced and released. So long as she and John were
together, her records had always been released together with
his. Apparently their business advisers considered it more
profitable to release their records separately than to have them
sing together on the same album. The advisers even encouraged Yoko to work more on her own, which she did not mind,
for one of the things she wanted above all was an independent
career.

During the Lennons' separation, however, the industry
wasn't even willing to press Yoko's tapes into records. In time,
she told me, she came to view this wall of indifference as a
conspiracy on the part of the industry to ignore her and her
work. Throughout the rest of 1974, she hired a long succession
of attorneys, searching for one who could breach the wall that
she felt stymied her as an artist. Each attorney in turn had
taken her money and devoted himself to legal "research." Results, however, had been few. Meanwhile, the legal bills continued.

It was in the midst of this impasse that I first met Yoko on

May 14, 1974. For some months her questions of the cards were purely personal and had nothing to do with money or business affairs. But one day in the second week of December 1974, while John was vacationing in Florida with May, Yoko and I began to discuss business. It began simply enough:

"I don't know why he needs so much money," she complained of the latest lawyer. "I don't think it's fair for him to charge me like this. It's not as though I'm rich, you know." (In his absence, John had set up economic arrangements for Yoko that included an account of three hundred thousand dollars, to be replenished whenever it ran low.) "I only have my three hundred thousand, you know, and these bills will eat that right up. Why does he need so much?"

I considered the cards and made a lucky guess. "He's building a condo in Florida." Yoko startled her lawyer when she confronted him with this bit of information. To her delight, he kept asking her how she had known. She never told him.

My deepening involvement in the Lennons' tangled financial affairs began during Christmas of 1974 while John was in Florida with May Pang. Lee Eastman chose this time to increase the pressure on John to sign a two-hundred-page contract that would finally dissolve the Beatles. Lee wanted this because he controlled, through Paul, the rights to many of the Beatles' great songs, and if the Beatles were dissolved, these would increase in value much as an artist's canvases increase in value when he dies, on the premise that there won't be any more coming. But there was a lot more tucked away in this massive document, as I discovered when I studied and read each of its countless provisions. Notable among these were several that would have severely curtailed John's income by encumbering foreign funds, which constituted nearly his entire revenue. Because of this, I advised Yoko against his signing, and Yoko relayed the information to John in Florida. Lee, however, countered that John would be "in trouble with the taxman" if he didn't sign. He knew that John had an inordinate fear of such authority figures and that the threat of the "taxman" was one that could motivate him to do almost anything. He signed. As I had predicted, it did not turn out to be a wise decision. Lee had convinced John that no one cared about the Beatles anymore, and John was foolish enough to believe it. In doing so, he forfeited literally millions in subsequent Beatles-related concerts and events.

The first business maneuver the Lennons ever executed solely under the direction of tarot cards was in the spring of 1975 after John's return from what he had begun to call his "eighteen-month lost weekend" (it was actually only fifteen).

It all started during one of the many readings I did for John in the White Room during the first weeks after we learned of Yoko's pregnancy. John, anxious to reorder his existence, had been asking a series of questions about several people in his life. It was then that the subject of his manager came up.

"I want to get rid of my manager," John announced. "Every time I turn around, he's costing me more money. I thought managers were supposed to make money."

"What are the details of your contract with him?" I sorted the cards.

"I don't think there is one. He's not really a manager in the proper sense of the word. He's a lawyer. I just call him my manager because he manages the accounts and all the legal stuff. I don't really need a manager, do I? I'm not making money like I used to. I feel as though I could do better without the expense of a full-time attorney.

"I never had much luck with managers. A million years ago, after Brian [the Beatles' first manager] died we all decided that we would be our own managers. We thought we knew as much about the business as anyone else. After all, we helped make rock and roll a major industry. We were wrong. There were a million projects and they all seemed like good ideas, but we were wrong about that too. I lost confidence that I could handle things and I decided I wanted an expert. So we got Allen Klein. He had managed the Rolling Stones, so we assumed he had to be top-notch. I made him my personal manager and I supported him for the position of manager for the group. But Paul wanted his father-in-law, Lee Eastman, to manage us, and that just added breadth to the schism that was already splitting us up. Since Brian died things have gone from bad to nowhere, and that in short is where I am today."

"So now you want another manager?" I queried.

"What for? Besides, there are maybe ten people in the world who could really manage my career (if you want to call what's left a career) and I don't trust any of 'em. No, I just want to get rid of this one."

"Why not just let him go?"

"Charles, it's not as easy as all that. He's got all the records, all the files, all the contracts. If there's a problem—and there is always a problem!—how am I to know what I signed and what I didn't? I don't have any records. I always let someone else handle that. If I ask for them back, then right away I get a slowdown, possibly a lawsuit, and in the meantime he can copy everything and do a lot of damage."

"What kind of damage?"

"Never you mind, dem's my secrets, boy, and I'll thank you to keep your nose out of 'em."

"As you will—listen," I said after considering the cards, "the first thing you have to do is get mad, not just put out or worried. You are afraid of litigation or being the victim of an exposé of one kind or another and that fear paralyzes you. So you need to get so angry that it shoves you into action. Once you've done that, what I suggest is that you raid his supply dump."

"Getting military, are we, Charles?"

"Yes, for a moment. His ammunition is all that information he has about you in his files. Now, have you considered what *your* ammunition is?"

"I don't have any ammunition in this situation!"

"Sure you do! You have money and fame and you are more important in the industry than he is. His only real power in the business is his association with you. Once you take that away, by reclaiming your files and firing him, anything he says becomes nothing more than the words of an unemployed malcontent." I was pointing to specific cards as I talked so that John would know that I was getting all this from the spread I had laid and not just making it up. He had confidence in the tarot and I believed it was important that the message of his own strength in the situation come through to him clearly. "Any statement he makes to the industry will only have the power you give it. If you deny what he says, you give it force and he remains powerful. But if you say, 'What do you expect? He couldn't make the grade so he hates the school,' the industry will listen to you. He screwed up, you let him go, and he's pissed. That's what people will think."

"Sounds good. So how do I get his files?"

"*Your* files! Go to his office, bright and cheery. Tell him you've got big plans, real big. Say you're superstitious and you don't want to talk about them till you have everything worked out in your head, but you need to look through the files. He'll let you in. Once there, make a phone call to the 'assistants' that you have waiting downstairs or across the street or wherever. Make sure you have several, preferably my size. They arrive and ask to see you. You announce that working in the office makes you nervous and you want to study the papers over at your leisure, at home. You send your commandos out with the loot, you hand him his pink slip with sufficient money that he can't scream that you owe him, and that's it."

"Really?"

"You got the files, the money, the reputation, and he's got zip. All he can do is be cordial and say you're a crazy rock star or that he had a better option. What else can he do?"

"I'll have to think about that." And he did. In May of 1975, John, accompanied by Yoko and some helpers, executed the plan.

Firing his manager without notice might not have been the kindest thing to do, but given the circumstances, it was the only one that was going to work. And it was absolutely essential that it work. Given their sense of powerlessness in business situations, John and Yoko needed a large, solid dose of success in such matters if they were ever to organize their financial affairs effectively.

For the remainder of the spring and throughout the summer of 1975, while Yoko's pregnancy progressed, John, Yoko, and I methodically reviewed every facet of their business affairs. On inspection, it seemed advisable to make a number of changes. Some were needed simply because the Lennons' relationship with certain firms (their accountants, for example) had deteriorated to the point where the Lennons' interests were no longer being properly served. So the accountants were replaced with another, more conservative, firm. Other such changes were made to introduce some order and clarity into the couple's murky finances.

As the summer drew to a close, we were faced with a new problem. If John no longer had a manager, who was going to represent him at the upcoming Apple meeting that fall? I had hoped that John would represent himself, because I thought that it would help his finances if he was seen to be taking an active interest in his own affairs. I also thought that it would serve as a focus for his energies and a distraction for his spirits while he remained artistically unproductive. But each time I suggested the idea to him, he rejected it. So in late August, we decided that Yoko would act as his representative.

"I don't want to go and I *won't,*" insisted John as he paced the kitchen floor that August night. "So you can just open up your cards and find another answer. I've stopped going to meetings and pretending to know what's going on, collecting solicitous smiles and pats on the back while they're screwing the shit out of me. No thanks! *You* go!"

"I don't think you want a card reader acting as your representative."

"All right, Yoko can go."

"You really should go with her so the others can see that you are putting your support behind her."

"I'll pin a note to her shirt. 'Dad gives permission.' How's that?"

"It's going to take a little more than that. This is your business, John, and if you don't take care of it, it won't take care of you."

"It's taken care of me, all right. Business and businessmen have cost me ninety percent of what I've ever made. Well, I've tried doing it myself and I've tried letting other people do it, and the result is the same. I lose money. If Yoko wants to handle it, that's her prerogative or yours, as the case may be. It can't get any worse, so I'm not really risking anything, am I? But don't think you are going to sucker me into business meetings by telling me that all I'm really doing is holding Yoko's hand."

"Well, someone has to go. I don't really think that Yoko is the best of choices, but at the moment she is our only choice."

"Send the accountant. He speaks their language."

"That isn't such a smart idea. You need someone in there who has no other motive than your interest."

"So! Now my accountant has motives, has he?"

"The longer he takes doing your business, the more he charges. The more complicated he can make matters for you, the more profitable it is for him."

"So, what now? Do we fire the accountant too?"

"No, but Yoko was at least around when Apple was put together and she is the only person you have available who has any motive for solving problems rather than prolonging them."

"All right, I said we'd send her. I think that it might be rather fun to see her tangle with all those guys. I feel sorry for them really. And it would give me a little more freedom. Tell her it's okay with me if that's what she wants."

"You tell her."

"Well, yes, *sir!* Will there be anything else, sir?"

"Yes, there will. You can't just pin a note to her shirt, you know. The others at Apple have to see you supporting her so that they know that this is a serious selection on your part and not a joke."

"Now you're back to sending me off to the meeting too, aren't you? You've got a stubborn streak in you, Charles, but then so do I. You'll just have to come up with some other way for me to show support."

"Then write a letter."

"I *hate* writing letters! *You* write it or have Yoko write it and I'll sign."

Yoko was not at all reluctant to attend Apple meetings. After some training and preparation, she conducted an experimental series of interviews with the other Beatles' representatives and found that these legal eagles had their weak points.

"It's all father-fear," I kept drumming into her. "Both you and John suffer from it. John's dad wasn't there, your father was always away. Didn't you tell me that when he'd come home you were expected to put on little shows for him to win his approval? Well, this is the same thing. You see these men dressed in their three-piece suits just like your father and you revert to your childish pattern of thinking that you have to win their favor. That's simply not the case. *They're* the ones who have to win *yours!* So, when someone comes for an interview, throw them off base. Make them take their shoes off, meet them in the bedroom, tell them that it's a difficult pregnancy and you can't leave bed. Every once in a while during the conversation, grab your stomach and say the baby kicked. Be sure that you seat them in the hardest of chairs. They'll put up with all of it because they want something from you and they have to deal with you to get it."

From the beginning, the idea of this power appealed to Yoko. Here was a chance to perform to an audience made rapt by the prospect of bilking her of millions. It was a grand role. She was the only woman with power in Apple. She was the Joker in the deck, unpredictable and, therefore, dangerous. Her one vote, underwritten by John, could deadlock any action. By definition, she was stage center in every scene.

As Sean's birth approached, Yoko's burgeoning interest in financial matters was superseded by her concern for her coming child. After her return from the hospital, we needed every bit of the month that was left before the November Apple meeting to build up her strength and prepare her. She progressed admirably, but like any performer she got last-minute jitters just days before her Apple debut.

"It's a disaster!" she wailed. "They want to have the meeting in London, or maybe on the West Coast. I want them to have it here. Why should I have to go to London?"

"Isn't that where they usually have the meetings?"

"Yes, but I don't want it there because John won't be there. He can't leave the country because they won't let him back in. So I'll be alone. I don't think that I can go through with this if I'm alone." Her stage fright was genuine. "What can I say to them that will make them have the meeting here?"

"What about L.A.? John can go there."

"He won't! I asked him and he said that I was the one who wanted to handle the business and so I should be the one to go on the business trip. All he wants to do is stay around the house. What am I going to do? I think that John is hoping that I'll fail just so he can make fun of me. He never wants me to be successful at anything because I might look better than he does. He always encourages me and encourages me and then at the last minute he withdraws his support so I'll fall on my face and he can laugh at me."

There was more truth than fiction to what she was saying. John did have a long-established pattern of early support followed by sudden withdrawal. What he required above all was Yoko's undivided attention. So long as her ideas kept her focused on him, he would support them. But as soon as she started off on her own, John would withdraw his energy, knowing that this would force her back to him. This pattern extended to everything from travel plans to her musical career. For example, when they had first met, John had often financed Yoko's conceptual art projects. As soon as her career began to gather strength, however, his support began to dwindle. The pattern did not exclude some fairly cruel pranks. For example, in June of 1971, John and Yoko had joined Frank Zappa on-stage at New York's Fillmore East. At first, they sang together, but when Yoko crawled into a large sack and continued to sing as part of the performance, John encouraged the musicians to leave the stage, and finally he himself abandoned her. Yoko felt that he had intentionally humiliated her, and it was hard not to agree.

It looked as if the pattern would hold true in his reaction to her increasing involvement in business affairs as well. As Yoko grew more and more fascinated with the art of bluff, maneuver, and ploy, John grew more and more jealous of her increasing interest in something that wasn't him—even if that something was in his own vital interest. He began complaining that her interest was taking too much of her time and energy away from him and retaliated by starting to slip away during the evenings for several hours at a time. His refusal to accompany her to the West Coast was a further sign of his resistance. Without him, Yoko could not hope to be taken seriously at the Apple meeting. So it was important to ensure that the November Apple meeting take place in New York. We settled down to read on how to make that happen.

As I laid the cards down on their purple scarf I knew that Yoko had to succeed on her first outing. If she failed, she would not have the courage to try again. "Tell them that John is engaged with other business here in New York and feels that he would really like to attend at least some of the meetings, since he hasn't yet chosen an official representative and may choose to represent himself. If New York is impossible for the others, then the meeting will have to be delayed."

"But if I say that they will expect John to show up."

"And be greatly relieved when he doesn't." The unpredictable Lennon had done such things in the past. "You know how John gets at meetings. First he's unbearably cheerful. Then he's quiet. Then he's sullen, and then he shouts that everyone is full of bullshit and stomps out. They don't really want to see him there. But they can't refuse him either."

"But if I say that John hasn't made up his mind yet about a representative, then that will undermine my authority."

"That's not the way it works. The others will be less threatened if initially they feel your stay among them is only temporary."

"*Will* it be temporary?"

"Only if you want it to be."

"Can I really make them have the meeting here?"

"It shouldn't be too difficult. Lee is already here and the others shouldn't be too opposed to a week in New York at the company's expense. And it is certainly preferable to a delay." Yoko was settled by this thought. Her confidence was bolstered further when the others responded positively. The meeting was duly scheduled in New York. It was a small victory, but to Yoko it was the harbinger of triumphs to come.

At the big meeting the other representatives took a patronizing tone of official politeness toward Yoko, stressing to her that Apple business was too impossibly complex for her to hope to grasp. Well prepared, Yoko simply sat back and asked them to explain. Her questions to them were as endless as her questions to me. The representatives happily expatiated upon her queries.

Each of the "Apples" (as we called the representatives, alternates, lawyers, accountants, and other personnel connected with the firm) was out to win John's vote in support of his own pet projects. Thus, each set himself to woo Yoko. She loved it. She reveled in their explanations of "the way things really were" and enjoyed the way they encouraged her questions. Each in his turn flattered her intelligence and confided in her his best inside stories about the others. A lover of gossip, Yoko soon became the repository of all the dirt on everyone. She promptly related all these private little anecdotes to me, which enabled me to build up an increasingly clear picture of the Apples' interrelations and who was putting down whom for what purpose. It was, in truth, fascinating.

While the Apples fell over one another to court Yoko, the business continued to be paralyzed. The only decision the week-long meeting made was to approve the minutes of the previous meeting and thereby release the much-needed annual salary checks to shareholders. To Yoko, however, her week's survival was a great success. It supplied us with much-needed information. There were no major breakthroughs, but she was not rejected. She returned from the final day's business in triumph.

"Okay, I've got a *few* questions to ask you," she started cheerfully.

"When you say a 'few' that means a lot, right?"

"Right. Now, I want to go through everyone and see how they saw me and how they thought I did and what they are thinking about me and what they're going to say about me. It's important."

"All right, one at a time."

"First I want to see what the cards say about how I did. They didn't think a woman could sit there and have an intelligent conversation with them and ask questions. I had them practically at one another's throats. But I kept my center, and I had a string tied around my waist to help seal my aura so that they couldn't send me any negative thoughts. That's how I kept centered. Well, you helped too, of course, but you were more like a director or an acting coach. I was the star and a star has to do it all by herself, doesn't she?"

"She does, indeed."

"What do you think John thought about me? Do you think he noticed how I handled all those men?" He couldn't help it. Yoko's daily reports were related excitedly and frequently. And the fact that she appeared sincerely happy made for a noticeable improvement in the atmosphere of the family as a whole.

"Of course he noticed. He's proud of you. It's like making a hit record. It feels good for everyone who's close to you. I'm proud of you too. Just as you should be proud of yourself."

"I am. You know what I did? When the meeting was breaking up, Lee said to me that he hoped that he would see me again, and I knew from the way he said it he really meant that it wasn't guaranteed that he would see me at the next meeting, as if to say that I didn't do all that well at this one. You know how cagey he is! They call him the 'Silver Fox.' Well when he said that I just smiled and said that I was glad to hear him say that because now that we would all be working together we would be seeing a lot of each other. And then I made him hold the door for me, because I'm a lady, you know!"

Despite his actions to undermine Yoko's confidence in her Apple debut, John claimed to enjoy seeing her gain authority. Perhaps that was because once the Apple meeting was successfully accomplished Yoko had more time for him. Whatever the reason, as we sat together in the kitchen a few days after the Apple meeting John explained that, to him, the idea of a woman in power seemed quite natural.

"I've always had a woman taking care of things for me," John confided. "I can't really function without one. It started with my mom and then graduated to my auntie [John's aunt Mimi, who raised him from boyhood]. Then Cyn, and after her, Yoko, and when I was away from Yoko, May, and now Yoko again. Always a haven and a safe zone in the form of a woman. The women in my life have always had power. That's why I like them. It's like the ol' Celt tradition, the women fight the wars and the men follow. Things might work a lot better if women held the power. God knows, men have made enough of a mess of things.

"I'm just not the captain of the ship. But I don't mind being the crew. So I'm always on someone else's ship: Mimi ship, Beatle ship, Yoko ship. I dream about it like that. I'll be sailing off on this ship, thinking that it always belongs to someone else and that I really ought to get off and have my own ship, but we're at sea and I can't get off. I think, I'll just step off the side, maybe I'll get hurt, maybe I'll break my leg, or die, but I never get off that ship. If I can't even do it in a dream, why should I try it with my life? If Yoko wants to be captain that's great."

"And what will you do?"

"I'll try to figure out what it is I'm going to do. In the meantime, why do I have to do anything? I'm tired of having to be John Lennon and being pissed at the world because I'm behind schedule. I'm retired."

"You've said that before."

"And if I say it enough times maybe it will sink into my head. I keep pushing and pushing, not knowing when to stop. Well, that's over. I've stopped . . . at least for this week. For now I'm a civilian. I'll sit on my cat seat [a window seat in the bedroom overlooking Seventy-second Street] and watch people go by. Nobody knows I'm watching or if they do, I don't care. I can just sit and watch the parade of life go by instead of leading it for a change."

"And play house?" I teased.

"Who's playing? I'm getting pretty good at this, you know. I enjoy it, really. Even the diapers, although sometimes that's a bit unpleasant. But there's this little baby and he's mine and he's seeing everything from this wonderful new perspective. Probably by the time he's old enough to tell me what things look like he will have forgotten, so right now I try to pick it up by contact. I hold him, I bounce him, I look as deeply into his eyes as I can, but all I ever see is two little mes mirrored in his pupils. I don't know how long this is going to last, but right now you and Yoko are sailing the ship and Sean and I are taking the ride, and that will last as long as it does and then there'll be the next thing."

Neither John nor I realized that the "next thing" would be a year of legal struggles in which the stakes were the Lennons' future in America.

· 7 ·

GREEN CARDS
AND TAROT CARDS

"The first thing you have to do is get a proper haircut and a straight suit," I counseled John.

"I have been to court before, you know. This isn't my first time. I had to go to an Immigration hearing a year ago. I did all right. I even told them off. I said that Nixon wanted me out because of my efforts in the peace movement."

"And you believed that?"

"Sure I did and do! It's true! You said yourself that I was dangerous. The only reason I wasn't kicked out of the country a long time ago was that I fought it with enough publicity that they couldn't just whisk me off some dark night like I was an illegal alien."

"Realizing, of course, that you *were* at various points in time an illegal alien."

"Well, it's not the same thing, is it? There are priorities involved. Celebrity has its own diplomatic immunity, you know. They were afraid of what would happen if they just threw me out."

"They stopped being afraid of what would happen when they let you in. When your version of the peace movement was in full swing they didn't let you come in, did they? By the time they did you were exhausted and so was your plan for peace."

"That's true only to the extent that I didn't come here to do rallies, even though I did a few. But, all the same, they put me through hell just for being here. And I fought them. And I'll fight them again. I may not be able to win, but I won't lose."

"You'll win. There is no reason to expect you won't get your green card this time out."

"Really? Why should they change their minds?"

"They won't. You're the one who changed."

"I'm always changing. That never counted before."

"But you were always changing with a big loud voice for all to hear. This time you are quiet, and that's what they've been waiting for."

"The patient is subdued and they'll let him out of the asylum now, is that what you're saying?"

"Something like that. You're not being threatening anymore, so they don't need to keep you on such a short leash."

"You make me sound impotent."

"Not at all. You were loud, brash, and dangerous when you were giving peace a chance, so they wouldn't give you one. When you wore yourself out a little they let you in. Then when you started talking to Jerry Rubin and Abbie Hoffman and gentlemen of that ilk, they simply refused to renew your visa. That was their leash."

"It wasn't quite as simple as all that. They bugged my phone, followed me, asked questions about me, in general made my life difficult."

"If they'd asked you nicely, would you have dropped your new associations?"

"No. Why should I? It is supposed to be a free country, you know."

"Right. That's why they did it for you. Not only did you know that you were under surveillance, so did everyone you talked to and so did the press. Anyone trying to keep a low profile was hardly going to go paying calls on a fella who was putting out press releases about being followed."

"I released that so the government would get off my back."

"You might have been more effective if you'd simply cut your hair and put on a straight suit."

"Very droll. But that doesn't change the fact that I have been made a victim in this case and I have to fight that victimization or fall prey to it. Dem's the rules, m'son. And I didn't make them up. So your ideas about getting a neat haircut and dressing nice are hardly applicable. I could go in there stark naked and it would still be the same thing. It's the government that wants me out and my protection is the law, and the law is the same for the government as it is for a naked man, short-haired or long. It's a stalemate. I can't win but I won't lose either. They are never going to let me stay here carte blanche and I'm never going to leave."

"Just out of curiosity, why stay?"

"Because this is where everything is! The U.S., New York, it's the center of the world. Washington may rule the U.S., but New York rules the world. If the center were somewhere else, then I'd be somewhere else too. It's the only place that's vital enough for me, complex enough, and rich enough for me. That's why I have to stay here."

"And when the Immigration case is settled, will you stay then?"

"That is to say, if I didn't have to fight to stay here, would I? Of course . . . probably."

Immigration had been a long and often frightening struggle for John. He believed himself to be pitted against the power of the U.S. government and holding his own. This image, though arrogant, imbued the conflict for him with a nobility that was not to be found in lawsuits over mere money. Where he had refused all part in battles over finances, he was willing, even anxious, to fight this one.

As we approached yet another stage in the Immigration proceedings, Yoko was drawn into the drama. "Charlie, we must win this one. It's very important. Everyone is watching me, so it is important that they all see that I am successful. Otherwise they will see this as a sign of weakness and attack. We must be sure that we *never* lose."

"What does Immigration have to do with your business image? You're not the lawyer."

"I'm the one who has to tell the lawyer what to do. My role in this is the most important one. John is like a baby, the government and I are like the parents, and we are fighting over custody. In a case like this the baby has very little to say about what happens. It's me. I'm the one who has to know what to do."

"All right, what are you going to do?"

"That's what you have to tell me! They have been plaguing us for years. They had us followed and spied on. They even had their agents working for us inside the house, can you imagine? It was terrible. Thank God I've been able to protect John for as long as I have. It has been very difficult fighting all these years against all those men. It has had a very destructive effect on John."

"Why did you stay? I thought that you were going to live at Ascot." (The Lennons had had a mansion named Ascot in Berkshire.)

"No, we couldn't stay in England. I loved Ascot very much, but the people there are terrible. People here know Yoko and

John, but there it was just John, John, John. Do you know that when we announced our marriage the London paper printed a headline that read 'John Lennon Marries Yoko Oh! NO!'? They were awful to me there. I think it was because of the war; they're terrible bigots. I didn't want to spend any more time there than we had to. The only place left was the United States. I had lived here before and went to Sarah Lawrence and I had worked in the Village as an artist, so it was natural enough that we come here to live. That way John would be away from the others, Paul especially. They had a lot of influence over John and he needed to be free of them to develop.

"Once we were here and working and doing films it was important to stay. In some ways, all this has been very good for us, having all those men hate us, having all that attention. The government would point at us and say how bad we were and when people would look what would they see? Two people, very small, all in white, looking sad. Governments are against people, and when the people of the world saw that this gigantic government was attacking us, then we became symbols of all people. The people who saw us loved us then, both of us, Yoko *and* John.

"That's another reason why we have to win this case. If people see us winning against the government, then they will see how powerful we are, and if they think of us as powerful, then that power will actually be ours. We could use it to do a lot of good for all sorts of people. It will be in all the papers and everyone will know that I did this for John. They always think that I'm taking from John, but it's the other way around. I'm the one who's giving and he's the one who's taking. That's part of the reason I've felt so protective toward him in all this Immigration business. I was the one who got him in trouble in the first place."

"Because of the drug bust?" Immigration claimed it was refusing John the right to stay because of a London arrest record for possession of marijuana resin in 1968. As Yoko was pregnant at that time (one of several miscarriages), John had taken full responsibility so that she would not be involved.

"No, because of my peace movement. Before I met John he was not very evolved politically—"

"He still isn't."

"Well, he's certainly more developed than he used to be. I used to talk to him and explain how the world really was and try to open his eyes to the situation that surrounded him. I wanted him to see that the natural spirit of mankind does yearn for peace, but it was all disorganized and futile really. People needed a nucleus to build around and I used John to supply that. That's when it became a peace movement. But I was also exposing John to a great deal of danger and persecution. It has been difficult on his career, and these legal troubles are only a small part of it. That's why we have to win so that the world will see that even if I had to use John a little to bring peace I still protected him."

Yoko turned the bedroom into the headquarters of her one-woman war to make the world safe for John Lennon. As the apartment at the Dakota grew more crowded, John retreated to the quieter and more spacious southern shore of Long Island. He took Sean with him and brought Julian over from Britain. Yoko kept him posted with a barrage of phone calls.

"How goes the war, Charles?" he chimed into the receiver.

"No casualties so far. How goes the peace?"

"Great. It's absolutely beautiful. I've got a bit of sea and a bit of green and my sons, and every once in a while I even have my wife. You should come out here and get some of this. It's delightful."

"Maybe later."

"Well, don't be too slow. The invitation may not stay open all that long."

"It's a nice offer, but Yoko wants me here."

"Oh, don't bother with that. She's got her knickers in a twist about Immigration and there's nothing really she can do. Leon [Leon Wildes, Lennon's Immigration attorney] is handling everything. It's going to be the same ol' standoff. What can they say? I was arrested for holding hash in Ringo's apartment, which he was gracious enough to loan to Yoko and me when no one else was talking to us. It happened, I pleaded guilty, because I was, and I paid my fine. That's all there was to that. The law here says that if that's true, then I can't stay because I'm officially undesirable. The reality is that there are a lot of entertainers over here who have similar histories and there is no problem for them because no one really cares. The drug thing is an excuse. So Leon will dig up all this junk about precedents and exceptions, and then if that isn't enough, he'll bring up thirty or forty new matters that have to be examined and that will take time, and for the time it takes, I stay. Then we'll do it again in six months or a year or whatever.

"Like you say, they want me quiet and I'm being quiet. They didn't even mind when I was rowdy but nonpolitical out on the West Coast because it kept the 'bad element' away from me. I had cops and the press to keep an eye on me doin's and that scared off the underground types. So! It's a fight and this is how I'm fighting it, flat on my back enjoying the sun and my sons and the sea as far as I can see. When I have to come into the city now and then to make a statement or appear in court, that will be okay too, but there's no sense in getting excited about it."

"You were certainly excited a few weeks ago."

"Why? What do you mean? About the baby, you mean?"

"No, Immigration. You were ready for a knock-down, drag-out fight with the *federales*. You seem calmer now."

"Yeah, that. Well, I am calmer. That's why I had to get away for a while to cool out. I need a place like this, you know. Maybe we should buy it. That would be lovely. We could use the Dakota when we wanted, and the rest of the time we could spend out here."

"I think it would take a little persuading to convince Yoko of that."

"Oh, Yoko loves the city and she hates the sun and will tell me that she has to stay on top of business in ol' Manhattan, but if Lee Eastman can manage from out here, then I'm sure Yoko could too. She needs to get out of there as much as I do.

"We get so on top of each other in the Dakota. It isn't really like a ten-room apartment, you know; it's more like three rooms. Sean has his room and we have the bedroom and then there's the kitchen. We hardly ever use the others, unless we have company, which is almost never.

"There's no place I can really go in New York, especially in the summer. I go up on the roof and that's nice, but it's still pollution and all. There's the park and that's nice, but there are fifty million other people there too and that tends to limit one's privacy. So if I want to pull off my pants and run around for a while, there really isn't anywhere. Out here it's me and the sea and I love it. It lets me become human again."

"Have you been having trouble being human?"

"As a matter of fact, yes, but I thought you would have heard all about that."

"Actually, I'd heard that you've been being fairly good lately."

"Well, well, not all of my little naughtinesses find their way to your ears, do they?"

"And what little naughtinesses are these?"

"Ah, no, if you want to find out, you're going to have to hear it from Yoko, not me. But why do you think I'm out here? I'm in exile, Charles."

It wasn't until some days later that Yoko related the story —or at least her version of it—during one of the many strategy meetings concerning the Immigration case.

"I had to send him away, he was destroying everything," she began as the subject came up. "He's been wanting to get away since the early spring. He's like this every year, as soon as the sun comes out he has to be in it. L.A. just whetted his appetite for summer, and as soon as we were back he started teasing to get away and he knew that I really couldn't. There is so much business, you know, I couldn't leave, and I thought if he were out there by himself, he would get into all sorts of trouble. He does that, you know. So I said that we couldn't leave just yet, and that made him angry and he got very quiet and you know how dangerous that can be. Finally it got so bad he attacked the baby. It was terrible."

"Attacked?" John was a screamer and had a habit of yelling at Sean to stop crying, but "attack" sounded more serious.

"Yes, he kicked him. We were in the bedroom having our meditation. We were doing it almost every night because it was good for family harmony. We would sit naked in a little trian- gle, because that's the symbol of ascension, and just meditate, and if anyone had anything to say they could just say it. Well, Sean can't really say anything, but he can make little sounds and he has as much right to make those sounds as we have to talk and usually John was very good about it. But on the last night we did it Sean was crying and John hates it when the baby cries, but I felt that that was Sean's right to express himself. I mean, if John wanted to cry or I wanted to cry, then that would have been all right.

"I didn't really notice how angry the crying was making John because I was very deep into my meditation, but all at once he stood up and I opened my eyes and saw him walk toward Sean and I thought he was going to step on him, but he just brought his foot up and kicked him! It was very vicious. Then he just stood there looking stupid and the baby was screaming and I didn't know what was going to happen next. So I jumped up and grabbed Sean and took him to his room. I didn't even stop for a robe or anything, I was in such a hurry. I was afraid that he was going to kill the baby. I stayed with Masako and the baby for a little while, but then I got afraid of what John might be doing, so I thought that I had better get back and see what he was up to.

"He was still just standing there. And I thought, He's gone crazy. He's going to kill us! So I sent him to Long Island. I thought, I had better give him what he wants or he'll be too dangerous."

"But you sent Sean out there with him."

"Yes, John wanted to take him and I think Sean wanted to go too. He has Masako to look after him and I think he should be safe. As long as John gets what he wants he usually isn't too dangerous. Maybe you should read on it and see if Sean is all right out there." I cast the cards and all seemed well. "John is like that, you know. He has that side of him you never see. He kicked me before too, you know. He even kicked me once when I was pregnant with Sean. I didn't want to tell you because I thought that it would be bad for John, but you know how worried I was that there would be something wrong with the baby. Well, it was because I didn't know what kind of damage he might have done." I didn't know whether to believe her or not.

"Fortunately nothing was wrong." I was being cautious.

"Yes, thank God. I think that it was because of all the prayers and the magic, but still there might be some damage that we don't even know about, something that won't show itself until much later. Things like that can happen, you know."

Yoko's penchant for telling alarming stories about the dark side of John's nature had grown since their reunion, just as John's dream of the happy family seemed to lessen. Interestingly enough, however, John's quasi-voluntary exile had had the odd effect of stabilizing the marriage. Separated, each imagined the other as somehow more lovable. But on the weekends, when Yoko, no longer able to plead the pressures of business, grudgingly joined him, they plagued each other with petty assaults and fabricated disasters.

John's moods varied hugely, running the gamut from mischievous mirth to desolate depression. I noted that certain subjects were quietly dropped from our talks. He seldom spoke of his career now except for a particular afternoon in mid-June of 1976, during one of his infrequent visits to the Dakota. That day he did talk about his career, specifically about the most recent Capitol release.

"Did ya see this?" John paced the kitchen waving a printed ad announcing the release of the Beatles' compilation, *Rock 'n' Roll Music*.

"Can you believe it?! They gave me hell for doing this very thing last year! They even stole my title. They didn't record, remix, or anything, they just grabbed a lot of our old stuff and threw it together in a new package—and a very fancy package it is, silver foil, very chichi. Last year they said an artist of my standing would be demeaned by a television commercial and this year they're putting out commercials on the telly to die!

"I guess I didn't have such a bad idea after all. All they had to do was wait till I won the Levy case for them and then run off with my idea and promote it to the nines. They probably had this thing sitting in the wings, if you'll pardon the expression, waiting all along.

"They never gave us promotion like this when we were together. Now, we're being revived and they don't mind sacrificing me or my work to do it. A little more Capitol punishment. 'Let's get rid of Lennon, he's standing in the way of the Beatles.'

"I don't have a chance! Even if I had something to release I'd be in competition with my own past. They're spending millions to create the impression of the good old days. If I come up with something new, it will clash with what they've conditioned people to expect from me, and if I do old stuff, then they will just let it die!"

"Am I to take it that you are no longer considering yourself retired from the music business?"

"Retired, hell, I'm dead! What chance do I have now? They've got me nailed in a coffin called the past. I'm a 'golden oldie' now. The only thing I can do is Beatles stuff. Travel the circuit, do Vegas, and sing the good old songs from the good old days to a bunch of good old boys who want to have a look at the Beatle. They've made me into another Elvis, and I don't even own the rights to the fuckin' songs. I'd have to get permission and pay for the privilege of doing an impersonation of myself."

"But that isn't what you want to do anyway, is it?"

"No, of course not. I want to go on developing and seeing what happens, what changes. I can't force it, so I thought if I just lay back awhile, then things might loosen up. But now, with this thing out there, and I'm sure they'll do more of this" —he waved the ad again—"it doesn't matter what I want to do. I've been done. They've only got so much money to spend on promotion on any particular artist and it's clear where they think their money should go. There's no way they can give support like that to me now. It's cheaper for them to bury me than it is to promote me. The money is in the past and now so am I."

If the dream of the happy family had served John as an escape from the painful questions of creation, then his need for that escape faded as he lost interest in his career. The attention he had lavished on Sean dwindled through the spring as legal pressures and squabbles with Yoko distracted him from the role of doting father. Although he was not contented, John resigned himself to the distance that was growing in the family.

As June turned to July, John occupied himself in his Long

Island retreat, while Yoko and I spent our days in the bedroom headquarters of the Lennons' Dakota apartment. There we went over and over all the available information and options regarding the Immigration case. As we approached the last weekend before the hearing, Yoko wanted to be sure that all possible bases were covered.

As usual, I sat on the piano bench and used John's side of the bed as a place to lay the cards. Yoko lay on her side of the bed resting on the pillows she had propped up against the church pew that served as a headboard.

Her concern that day was not only about the case but also her family life. The distance between the couple had taken some of the tension off her, but she was not looking forward to seeing John.

"I want you to read on it and tell me if I have to go out to the island this weekend," she said.

"Why would you 'have to'?"

"Because John wants me to and I don't want to aggravate him because if he gets angry with me he might leave, and I can't have that. But really there is so much to do here and I won't be able to see you or work on business if I'm out there. I think that it's really better if I stay here."

"Which do you want? That's your answer."

"Well, I don't want to go, you know that, but I don't want John to be angry with me either."

"Why don't you invite him to come and visit you here? He's had the sun and sea all week and an evening on the town might be nice for a change. That way you could see each other and you wouldn't have to leave the city."

"Are you crazy? A night on the town? You know how he gets. If we go out he'll have to drink and you know what that means. Besides, he would never do that. He loves it out there and he won't leave unless he has to. He'll come in for the Immigration hearing, but then he'll want to go right back.

"Besides, there really is too much to do. I'm like a husband who has to work all the time to make sure his family is well provided for. That's taking care of the family. It's not my fault if there is so much to do that I don't have any free time and can't play all day like John does. Things would fall apart if I wasn't taking care of them. Look at this Immigration problem. Every day it gets closer and closer and still we have no guarantee that we will win."

"What kind of guarantee do you expect? The judge will review the information placed before him. That's Leon's job. He will call for character references, and that's your job. The outcome rests with the judge."

"It's the outcome that concerns me. If the judge rules against John, we'll be ruined."

"Hardly. If the ruling is negative—and it probably won't be —then nothing really changes. John won't be taken from the court and put on a plane, you know. There will be a grace period. During that time Leon will appeal the ruling and that will take more time and then there will be another hearing and that will take even more time. During all this time the situation remains status quo. John stays here and can't go traveling out of the country, which he doesn't seem to particularly want to do anyway."

"That's not the point. We have to be sure that we are going to win. So I can't go off to the Island or anything like that, and it would just be a distraction if John were to come here. What if I tell John that I still have to wait to see if more of the invitations come in?" As part of the courtroom theatrics we had sent out requests to a number of celebrated persons from Norman Vincent Peale to Norman Mailer to act as character witnesses. Many of the letters of acceptance had already come in.

"We could still get calls. This is for John and I think he should understand. I just don't want to make him angry."

John turned out to be understanding or, to be more accurate, apathetic. If Yoko didn't want to be with him, then he didn't care to be with her. Julian and Sean provided him days of diversion, and in the evenings, if he chose, there was always a convenient roadhouse to accommodate his need for more adult conversations. He maintained his exile and Yoko withheld herself in the fortresslike Dakota until the very eve of the hearing.

That night, Yoko asked that I read for him about the case one final time. It was after sunset when I rang the bell to apartment 72. It was John who answered.

"How do I look, Charles?" He grinned sheepishly, sporting the new conservative haircut I had recommended. "Do you think this old Beatle looks respectable enough to please the court?" He was in obvious good cheer as we walked down the long hallway toward the kitchen.

"That depends. What are you going to wear with it?"

"Well, Dad, I was thinking of going in nude, painted blue, with a lily up me ass. Will that do?"

"Not bad, but you might try a dark suit instead."

"What, no polka dots? Charles, sometimes I think that you're no fun at all. But if you insist . . ."

"I do."

"Well, what does it say?" John asked happily as we drew up our chairs to the kitchen table. "Is my green card in the cards or do we carry on the good fight for yet another year?"

It was a question I had read on so many times over the last few months it was hardly useful to look again. But it never hurts to check once more, and I do love reading cards.

The spread I cast was a simple one and I used the information that had been established over previous readings to add to the interpretations of the cards in front of me. The answer certainly looked favorable.

"I think you'll get it, actually," I said at length. "The government's general pattern under this administration has been increasingly lenient. You've stacked the cards with enough celebrities to make an adverse finding an embarrassing media statement for any judge, especially if he has political ambitions. And since a major media figure, Geraldo Rivera, is one of your character witnesses, there is no way this isn't going to get into the media. I think that you will finally be able to put this thing to rest."

"Oh, good. That way I'll be able to live and work in this country. Not that I haven't *been* living and working in this country!"

"And you'll be able to leave and come back in."

"I know. It really is important to me, you know. It's been four years of struggle and I want it to be over. I'm not bitter, but I do want it finished with. It's a pity, really."

"What is?"

"Well, if the United States had done like Canada, then there wouldn't have been all this fuss. In Canada they treated me very nicely. I met the prime minister, very impressive. It was one of the most important days of my life. If they had invited me to the White House like they did George [George Harrison had visited President Ford's son] and told me where they stood and where I could or could not stand, the way Prime Minister Trudeau did, then I probably would have wound up supporting them or at least have reached a gentleman's agreement as to what I would or would not do. Instead there has been all this struggle and all this fear and it really hasn't accomplished anything."

"You could have volunteered your support."

"I never thought of it, so much the pity. Besides, I think that it would have looked a bit suspicious if I did it that way. They would have wondered what I was really about. But none of that really matters now, does it? All water under the bridge, as they say. Now my only concern is that I will be putting one problem to rest and raising up a harvest of new ones."

"How so?"

"All these impressive supporters you and Yoko have mustered on my behalf. They're doing this for me as a favor, and favors are like debts—they have to be paid back one day. All this might prove more expensive than I am willing to pay. What price favors, Charles?"

"I don't think you'll have to worry about that, John." And he didn't. None of the many famous individuals involved (including sculptor Isamu Noguchi, author Norman Mailer, Cardinal Cushing, and newscaster Geraldo Rivera) ever asked for the return of this gift of support.

On the following day, July 27, 1976, John received his green card and his long battle with the United States government came to a close.

· 8 ·

WITCH-HUNTING

I was living in New York's Gramercy Park Hotel in late February of 1977 when Yoko called to invite me to go witch-hunting. I had just given up my Fifth Avenue apartment and had gone on a two-week vacation, a real one this time, with only three emergency calls from Yoko, and the only vacation I was to know in my six years of service with the Lennons.

On my return, Yoko had insisted that I take a modest suite of rooms at the Gramercy Park for two months at her expense while I relocated. A year of highly successful business readings had greatly improved my value in her eyes and my retainer had grown accordingly.

My days at the hotel were clearly marked by Yoko's idiosyncratic sense of humor. The day I checked in, I was asked to produce identification as "Charles Swan" before I could claim my reservation. The identification I chose was to have the startled desk clerk call Yoko Ono to confirm that the giant standing before him was the right man. Next, it emerged that there was another Charles Swan living at the hotel, a fact discovered only after the appropriate confusion and embarrassment over misdirected mail and telephone calls. Then there was the peculiar decor of this "landmark" hotel, perhaps best described as Woolworth's-Meets-Rococo, which formed a singular backdrop for my readings for other clients. Through it all, I could hear Yoko's laughter.

I was in these curious confines the evening that Yoko telephoned me with her invitation.

"Now, Charlie, you have to pack some very light things and some very heavy things too, and you'll need your passport and shots I suppose, and hurry because we have to leave before the Japanese month changes."

"Leave for where?"

"Cartagena. That's in Colombia. Dan wants to show me his castle. He has a beautiful castle there that he's restored and I want to meet his witch."

"Dan" was Dan G. (not his real name), an exotic denizen of New York's chic and seductive art scene who was of late more and more in Yoko's thoughts. Dan, sinuous as an eel, charming as an otter, had shown himself adept at acquiring the "very, very best" of anything from diamonds to Inaugural Ball invitations—for a price.

"Meet his what?"

"His witch. Dan has a witch and she's supposed to be wonderful. Dan says she can do anything and I want to meet her and you have to come because how am I supposed to know if she is a real witch or not? So hurry and get everything and call me back."

"Is John going?"

"No, no, of course not. It's a bad direction for him to go in this month. That's why we have to leave so quickly before the month changes."

"One more thing. If we're going to Cartagena, why do I need to pack heavy clothes?"

"Because we have to travel southwest to get there and we can't travel northeast to return because that's a bad direction, so we have to go to Alaska, then we can come back southeast to New York. See?"

I didn't, but I thought it better not to say so. Secretly I was intrigued with the thought of meeting this would-be witch. In my years with the Lennons I had concentrated almost totally on my roles as marriage counselor and business advisor. The chance to do a little research in my first love, the occult, promised to be a pleasant diversion.

"What do you think she'll be like?" queried Yoko a few days later once our plane was safely in the air on its way to Cartagena.

"Who? Nora the witch? I don't know. If she's a real one, I suppose she'll be like most witches, friendly, a little musty, and full of tricks and mystery."

"But do you think she can do what she says or what Dan says she can? I made a list of things I need and it's very important that she be able to do them all. I promised John and he'll be very disappointed if we don't get all our wishes. There's no telling what he might do."

"Come on now, Yoko. If magic was what you really wanted, there is enough of that in Manhattan for anything you might require. John agreed to this trip as a reward for you, to indulge a little eccentricity because you've been working so hard, and, incidentally, to get a little time on his own."

"Don't you believe in witches?"

"Of course I do! Some of my best friends are witches. But I repeat, you don't have to travel so far afield to find one."

"Well, Dan says Nora is a very special witch, very, very

powerful, and I don't think that there is anyone in New York like her. I want you to check and see if she can do everything for me."

And so I cast the cards at thirty thousand feet. "No one has the power to do everything for you. There are people with particular crafts and skills who can act as a catalyst for change in your life, but you, my dear, are the one who has to do the changing. Besides, you know Dan. Whatever he has he says it's the 'very, very best!' That's just his sense of self-promotion."

"Do you see that in the cards or are you just saying it because you are jealous of Nora's power?"

"The cards say, 'Enjoy this little trip as a vacation and that way you will receive the most benefit from it.' "

"I think you're jealous."

We left the plane and cleared Customs to be met by a pair of cocaine cowboys who flashed excited recognition at Yoko.

"Did Dan send you?" Yoko was disappointed that her pet procurer wasn't there to greet her personally.

"Yeah, Dan. That's right, Dan. Just get in the car and we'll take you to the film festival," they chirped.

"What film festival?"

"It's okay, Dan sent us. Get in the car, get in the car." This seemed not the best of ideas. I stepped in front of the open door, loomed a bit, grinned maliciously, and said, "Hi. I'm the bodyguard and what the fuck do you think you're doing?"

Dan himself chose this moment to appear.

"Oh hello, Yoko! It's so good to see you. Did they give you a bad time in Customs? Here, let my man get the bags. How are you? And let's see, you must be Charlie. Nice to meet you. Excuse us please, excuse, excuse." And so with one hand on Yoko's elbow and the other lightly brushing the air, Dan extracted us from the crush with no more explanation than "They're trying to get everyone to that awful film festival." He ushered us to "the only air-conditioned car in all of Colombia.

Absolutely the *only* one! I had the most difficult time getting it.
I think the president or someone wanted it. Cost a fortune."
We climbed in the back of the pink, blue, and white rusted
1956 Chevy and rolled down the windows.

"Air conditioning's on the fritz again, absolutely no one here
knows how to fix it. Absolutely no one!" We tooled along for
hours, occasionally stopping for refreshments or at the insis-
tence of machine-gun-toting soldiers. "There's so much con-
traband traffic down here. They have to be sure they get their
bribes." Finally we arrived at Dan's castle, which was actually
a villa sandwiched into a crowded street.

"Well, here we are, home sweet home. I had it restored
myself. Everything from the original. Terribly expensive, but
it's worth it, of course. This door," he began as he rang the bell,
"is over four hundred years old; the brass fittings came from
a Spanish galleon."

"Really?" I was impressed.

"Oh, *I* don't know." He flashed his engaging smile. Once
inside we were given the fifty-cent tour, which wound through
a labyrinth of cell-like rooms decorated with cobwebs and
packing crates. Dan chortled on about the house's splendifer-
ous past, accompanied by the drone of humming insects and
punctuated by the entrance of the occasional lizard, monkey,
or bloated toad. Dan had somewhat exaggerated the progress
of the renovation. We finally came to rest in the second-story
"salon," which was "just the place to have drinks before dinner. Do you know that I had to evict six families, all living in
this one room? Imagine, just to be able to have a salon." Yoko
was duly impressed.

Drinks, a raw local rum smothered in fruit juices, were
served by Ernesto, youthful head of the squad of ever-present
barefoot servants ("Labor here is so inexpensive!"), while Dan
engaged Yoko in the congenial art of conversation.

"You really should think about a little real estate here, Yoko.

It can be so lovely, and everything, absolutely everything, is available if you have the money. I'm thinking of renting, or should I say loaning? this place out to 'friends' while I'm away. It can practically pay for itself. Why, did you know . . . ?" And so on and so forth.

A sudden bustle among the servants and the screech of a parrot announced the arrival of Nora. Dan dashed off to meet this mystic personage while I retired to change into more appropriate garb for meeting witches. It had been agreed that I was to interview Nora before she met Yoko to assess her occult credentials and report back to Yoko if she was "a real one." I knew from previous experience that in a place like Cartagena, witches, or *brujas* as they are called, are more than spiritual advisors. They are genuine economic and political powers as well. A *bruja*'s magic is supported by an elaborate network that supplies her with information, contacts, and muscle, not unlike a Capo Mafioso. Little happens in a *bruja*'s domain without her knowledge or well-paid-for blessing. This Dan had learned when problems with his laborers brought the renovation of his "castle" to a standstill. On the recommendation of a friend, he summoned Nora. She announced that there was no problem with the workers; the troubles were due to a dangerous spirit. For a stately fee she exorcised this shade, and the work proceeded on schedule. No one argues with a *bruja*.

With care I bedecked myself with the many charms, baubles, and insignia of office that I had collected over the years. It was important that Nora know that while I was not disrespectful, neither was I a novice in her murky world of magic.

With measured step, I jangled and clattered along the blue gravel pathway that led through the house's central garden. Squatting in the courtyard, regal and ancient, was Nora the noble hag. I estimated that she was somewhere between fifty and a thousand years old. She had two keen eyes, three good teeth, and an aura of rangy strength that radiated from her lanky torso and limbs. She watched my approach with unblinking but not unkindly eyes, looking every inch a *bruja.*

"Hello, gentleman," she called in a warm Jamaican voice.

"I've brought a present," I smiled, already liking her. A gift is a traditional sign of respect. I produced a shoebox and placed it at her feet, then squatted down beside her. She studied the box with curious eyes and then, extending one huge, flat, callused foot, nudged it a little.

"Snake?" she seemed doubtful of my intentions. Smiling, I shook my head. "Open it." With a showman's care I extracted from the wrappings the image of Saint Lazarus, a popular saint in Hispanic occult traditions who is held to be the keeper of all gates. Nora looked disappointed, as if she might have preferred a snake. Then, skewering me with her glittering eyes, she snapped, "How many magics do you know with a toad?" The abrupt question held both a challenge and a tease of mystery.

"Seven."

"*I* know seventy-five." I believed her. "How do you make a love charm with a toad?"

Amphibian philters are not my forte, but I recalled something I had read. "First you wash him, then sew shut his eyes and mouth. When he's died and been dried, paint this"—I drew a symbol with my finger in the dust—"in red on his back and place him secretly in the house of the one you wish to fall in love." There's more to it, but that's the nutshell version.

"Good," she nodded. "Now, how do you cure fever with a toad?"

"I don't."

"I'll show you." And she did. Sharing a professional secret was a sign of her acceptance and trust. I listened with due respect. "I could teach you many things," she told me as she concluded the lesson. "You could stay here with me and I would show you what the Indians showed me and other things too. You could learn a great deal."

"No doubt."

"Do you have a house?"

"No."

"No house." She seemed displeased. "Where do you live?"

"In a rented apartment."

"You have no property, nothing of your own which is of value?"

"The things I value are not material things." I suspected that she was already dividing up my bankbook with the *bruja*'s practiced eye for a buck.

"If you have nothing, then you have nothing to keep you. Stay with me and I will rid you of foolish notions and teach you how to get things of value."

"I have my work and that's of value to me, that keeps me."

"Hmmmm, maybe you have foolish notions, maybe you do not. How do you drive out wicked spirits?" We sat together in the gathering darkness talking shop, exchanging rituals and recipes in half-sentences as witches do. Without ever putting it into words we agreed that she was to take the dominant role in our relationship. She was the expert. My position was rather like that of a bright foreign exchange student from an under-privileged nation. We silently agreed not to challenge each other, but a bit of playful sparring was allowed. For me it was rather like being a kitten sparring with a mama cat.

At length it was time to get Yoko and tell her the woman waiting for her in the courtyard was, for better or for worse, a bona fide witch. Minutes later, with the gravity due visiting royalty, Dan escorted Nora into the "salon."

"Hello, child," called Nora in a voice as big as the room. With a few giant strides she'd covered the distance between herself and Yoko and dropped into the sofa beside her. Yoko, who a moment before seemed on the verge of laughter at the sight of the shabbily dressed Nora, was now intimidated by her intimacy. "What do you want Nora to do for you, child?"

"Everything," answered Yoko with simple honesty. Groping

John and Yoko held a seven-day "bed-in for peace" in a Montreal hotel in May of 1969. *Wide World Photos*

Above: Julian Lennon, John and Cynthia's son, at Heathrow airport the night after John was shot in New York. *Wide World Photos*

Right: John's first wife Cynthia on the day in 1968 when she was granted a divorce from John. The divorce was granted while John was camped out on a London hospital floor to be near Yoko, who was having a miscarriage of their baby. *Wide World Photos*

Above: John and Yoko after their reunion (and his return from May Pang), arriving at the Grammy Awards dinner on March 1, 1975. *Wide World Photos*

Left: May Pang, John's mistress and companion on his fifteen-month "lost weekend" (photo taken in 1981). *Walter McBride/ Retna Ltd.*

Right: John jokes around while an airport official prepares to give him a body-check. He was leaving Tokyo International Airport after a visit to Japan with Yoko in September of 1978. *Wide World Photos*

Below: July 27, 1976: John and Yoko arrive at Immigration District Court in New York to hear that he has won his battle to remain in the United States. *Wide World Photos*

Above: A photo taken in 1977, and published with reports that John and Yoko had purchased 103 Holstein dairy cows. *Wide World Photos*

Right: An undated photo taken of John in 1980. *Wide World Photos*

Below: An undated publicity photograph taken in 1980 and distributed as part of the promotion for John and Yoko's *Double Fantasy* album. *Wide World Photos*

John and Yoko leave the Hit Factory, the recording studio in New York where they recorded *Double Fantasy* in 1980. *Wide World Photos*

Above: Paul McCartney in handcuffs after his arrest at Narita Airport outside Tokyo for possession of marijuana. *Wide World Photos*

Below: The police teletype reporting a man shot at 1 West 72nd Street—the Dakota —on December 8, 1980. *Wide World Photos*

```
PRESS 12    2345 HRS    12-8-80    20 PCT

1 W.72 ST.« REPORT OF A MAN SHOT. VICTIM REMOVED TO ROOSEVELT HOSP.

NOTHING FURTHER AT THIS TIME.

OPER UNIT- PO VAN ARSDALE

ALL KEYS

?????
```

Right: John and Yoko's son Sean, photographed outside the Dakota at a vigil marking the second anniversary of John's death. *Mark Glickman/Retna Ltd.*

Below: A photo taken of the Dakota on December 13, 1980, five days after John was shot. The flag is at half-mast in his honor. *Wide World Photos*

around in the bowels of her alligator bag she produced a list. "First of all, I have a lot of enemies and they are always trying to hurt me and curse me, so I'll need some protection from that. Maybe it would be better if you protected the whole family because it's a very dangerous situation for all of us. And you should be sure to protect me from my husband as well as my enemies because sometimes he can be dangerous too and I need to be protected from him. Then there's health. Our baby has terrible health and there is nothing the doctors can do, so they try to tell me nothing is wrong, but he does get sick sometimes and it would be good if that didn't happen. Can you do that? Good. And the other thing is career. I think you should do something for my career and my husband's career separately, and then something for our career together but not for his career with anyone else because . . . " Yoko went on and on referring to her notes and adding new things as she thought of them. Nora listened with practiced patience, nodding and smiling. Only once did she take exception to the requests.

". . . And the other thing is this thing inside me that I want you to get out," Yoko explained. "The doctor put it there, but it's foreign and it causes me pain all the time. No one believes me that it hurts, but it does and I want you to stick your hand inside me and take it out." Yoko had in mind the recently publicized practices of Filipino healers and wanted the same from Nora. The witch looked down at her own huge hand and then at Yoko suspiciously.

"You want me to stick my hand in you and grab hold on to this thing you have in there and pull it out?"

"Yes, exactly, to heal me, you understand?"

"Well, child, I can stick my hand into you all right, but I don't think that's going to heal you, I think that's going to kill you."

"Oh, you can't do that. We'll have to think of something else. Now the other thing I need is my daughter. We've been separated for years and it would be very good if I could find her, so I'll need your magic for that too and . . . " The list continued.

The days that followed were full of rituals and ceremony. There were preparatory baths to be taken to wash away all that was old. Yoko stood in a galvanized tub while Nora poured jars of water over her. Then the old witch danced a heavy-footed dance around Yoko chanting and invoking, punctuating her spells with sharp cries (of passing spirits) and birdcalls (which were pleasing to her gods). There were bitter concoctions for Yoko to drink, prayers of petition and appeasement, candles to light, combs to be used, and more. Yoko had asked for the full treatment and she was getting it.

When Nora wasn't keeping Yoko busy and I wasn't reading on how all this would turn out, Dan supplied entertainment. He chattered and flattered and took her on excursions through the small city pointing out "the very very best" of everything that he thought she should have. He even introduced her to George, his monkey.

Dan had named his monkey George. He had also named his parrot, both Siamese cats, Ernesto's dog, and any other four-footed or winged critter that entered his life George. "It's so much less complicated that way, don't you think? Now, Yoko, watch George." This particular time he meant the monkey. "Find the grapes, George, find the grapes." Sure enough, whether in pocket or covered dish, the tiny monkey found them. "Now watch this. This is our newest trick." Dan ran down the steps, leaving us to guard George. Moments later our host called out from the garden below, "Oh, Geooooorge!" Quick as a flash, the little beast jumped from the table to the railing, then *whoosh,* over the edge into the garden to land on the back of Dan's neck. "Monkey on my back, monkey on my back. Isn't he wonderful?" he called, rewarding his charge with a few grape treats.

Ernesto had warned Dan that this was not a wise thing to do, for the monkey was still very young and as he got older he would also get bigger. Much bigger. But Dan paid no attention. Some months after our trip, however, I had occasion to meet Dan again and I asked him how George the monkey was doing. The reaction was remarkable. Suddenly, furtively, Dan glanced over his shoulder, the picture of a hunted man. Ernesto's prediction had proved all too correct. George had got *much* bigger. He now weighed thirty-five pounds and had the elegantly slender Dan terrorized. Every time Dan stepped into the garden, he was taking his life in his hands. First he would hear the pitter-patter of hairy little feet above. Then silence. Cautiously, Dan would stretch his neck out as far as he could, peering upward to find George's hiding place. Nothing. Carefully he would steal to another column hoping to avoid his fate. Still nothing. But the instant he stepped out from under the protection of the archway, *eeeeeeh thwap!* Thirty-five pounds of grape-greedy monkey came careening down on poor Dan's head. He told me that he was forced to get rid of the hairy little sky-diver. He didn't mention how.

With a schedule known only to her, Nora would appear without warning and spirit Yoko away to some other part of the house.

"Now, child," she would coo, "there are many things that we must do to get you ready and we don't have too much time. We've got a witch's moon coming and we have to be ready for the sacrifice."

"What sacrifice?" Yoko was visibly alarmed.

"You've got all these things you want, don't you? Do you think that they are Nora's to give? No, don't be silly, girl. We've got to make a sacrifice with the blood of an innocent to the One who has the power. He will give you what you want, not Nora."

"But I thought that you had the magic."

"Magic isn't something that anybody *has,* magic is what passes through. Come now, you have more baths to take." So saying, Nora dragged the protesting Yoko off to work her secret charms.

"Charlie, what is she going to do?" Yoko asked hours later on the veranda. "You don't think that this is going to be dangerous, do you? She keeps talking about blood sacrifice and signing a pact. I asked her what she meant, but she keeps saying, 'all in good time.' I'm afraid of her."

"Isn't she what you wanted?"

"Well, I don't want her if she's going to hurt me."

"Call it off if she frightens you."

"I can't! I already promised to pay her and if I don't, I'm afraid she'll curse me, and if I go home after spending that much money and I don't have any magic, then John is going to kill me."

"How much did you promise her?"

"Sixty thousand."

"Pesos?"

"No, dollars."

"My God! How could you do that? A little trip for local color is one thing and a little good old-fashioned folk magic is also fine, but sixty thousand dollars? Why didn't you ask me about it? I could have negotiated for you!"

"Well, you know you're never supposed to haggle over money when it's for something religious and you did say she was a witch, so I thought that it would be better if I gave her what she asked because if I do get all those things John and I wanted, then it will be worth it. But now I think she wants me to sell my soul or something and that's very bad karma. Why don't you read and see what I should do?"

"I think all this business has affected your mind! Are you asking me to read on whether or not you should sell your soul? Or do you want to know how to get out of this without getting hurt?" Charming as Nora was, she was a *bruja* and *brujas* are notorious for dealing harshly with those who would cheat them.

"Well, I've already done a lot of stuff with her and that has to count for something, and if I do the rest, then that should count even more. And if I did the ritual but I changed some little part of it, that wouldn't actually be like doing it, would it? But Nora would think that I had done it, so she would use her power to help me and that way I should get practically everything and that would be a lot, and if it were that much, then John shouldn't mind about the money."

"I don't believe this. You believe that you're going to sign a pact with the devil, but secretly you are planning to trick him and that way you will get the wealth of the world and retain your soul?"

"Is it possible?"

"No! You can't sell your soul! You can lose touch with it, harden it, or ignore it, but you can't sell it. What you can sell in a deal like this is your sanity. Forget it! If you even half-believe that is what you're doing, get out now!"

"I can't! What if she curses me?"

"No one's going to hurt you. If you can't overcome your fear and you don't believe that you can be protected, then let her have the money. You can tell John she tricked you or tell him it's my fault or tell him whatever you like, but don't fool around with something if you think it's at the risk of your soul."

"But you said she was okay! Maybe she isn't really a witch."

"There are all kinds of witches and they practice many different things. They sacrificed animals in the Bible too, you know. The point is what you *think* you're doing. Personally I don't think that's what Nora is up to. But if *you* think so, then get out now."

"Well, if you say that you don't think she's doing anything

bad, then I guess that's okay. I wouldn't want to do anything that would be bad karma, but if she really can give me those things . . . "

"I never said she could. I said that she was a witch and she is. I said that she was a catalyst for change and she is. And I also said that you were the one who would have to do the changing."

"Why didn't you say it like that before? I wouldn't have come here on this trip if it wasn't for you. You were the one who made me do this! First you said that she had power and now you say she doesn't. Which is it?"

"Witch indeed. Yes, Nora is a woman of power. And she works in the realm of magic." I spoke slowly to make sure that what I was saying was very clear, for I had begun to wonder if Nora hadn't spiked some of her charms with a little drug. "And in magic there are many traditions, rules, and laws. The first law has to do with intention. The most important part is what you believe you are doing, what your real intent is, because that is what the outcome of any ceremony or charm or spell will be. If you believe you are healing, you will heal. If you believe you are making a fool of yourself, then that's what you will do."

"So all I have to do is believe the right thing and everything will be all right?" The argument wore on into evening and through the next day. Yoko was intent on finding a way to get the devil's power without paying him his due.

The moon turned to the last phase, the witch's moon. The time for the ritual had come. Nora arrived with a largish cardboard box in tow, filled to the brim with magical devices.

"Now come sit here by Nora, child, and you too, gentleman, and we will see what we have here." She dug down into the box and pulled a large beaded black rosary with a substantial silver cross dangling from the end. "Now this is for the little boy. You have him wear this around his neck all the time, even when he sleeps. Only let him take it off when he's bathing, because you don't want him to get it wet. Now take special care because this is his protection from all those sicknesses." Yoko accepted the charm with wonder in her eyes.

"Charlie, write these things down because I'm never going to remember."

"Oh, child, you have to pay attention!" Nora sounded hurt. She was used to having her work received with trembling hands and riveted attention. Nevertheless, I wrote down the directions for the bottles of potions and powders. I even took care to label each as she presented them. With each instruction, Yoko asked, "Can Charlie do this for me?"

"Why do you want the gentleman to do this? Don't you want to? It is for you. You should be happy to do it."

"I am, but it's all very complicated and I'm afraid that I won't do it right and I think that Charlie would do a better job."

Nora shrugged, "Makes no difference. He can do it. You can do it. Anybody can do it."

At length all the bottles and boxes, beads and leaves, were labeled and accounted for.

"Now," said Nora, "you, child, must go and rest, and later I will call you and we will do what must be done. The gentleman and I will sit here and talk a little to pass the time." Yoko slipped into her room. Nora pulled a bench and sat down with her back against the door. "We have to keep watch and be sure she is protected," she explained.

"Not only that, we have to see she doesn't run away."

"How's that? Oh, you are joking with me. But you may not be so far from wrong. I don't think she wants to do this after all."

"Then it would be wrong to have her do something she was against." I watched the old witch with care.

"Oh, it is a little devil in her that makes her want to run off. She has a little devil in her. You must have seen him." Now the old witch was watching me.

"Why don't you cast this spirit out?"

"Now I didn't say he was any spirit, did I? I said he was a devil, a little devil who is always hungry, always greedy for more and more, and the more you give him the hungrier he gets. That's a wicked little devil to have inside you."

"And what do you do for such devils?"

"Oh, Nora is a wicked old woman. I give that devil all he wants and more. I think that I can make him swell up so much he will burst and die. Then the lady will be free of all her hunger, all her enemies, all her sicknesses. They are all caused by that one devil. So I'll kill him with kindness, which is a very good way to kill a devil."

"I thought maybe you were trying to scare him to death."

"You do have very foolish notions sometimes. That kind of little devil will always be scared, scared he won't get everything he wants, but that won't kill him. That kind of little devil can stand anything just to get a little more. No, the thing to do is feed him more and more and more."

"That may take a lot."

"No, I don't think so much. The thing is the kind of food you give him. Tonight I will give him one little bird. That's not so much, if you think about it. That little devil could eat all the money and all the love and all the people he ever meets. I think he's even been chewing on you a little bit. But tonight I'll give him one little bird and I don't think he will want any more. If I'm right then my child inside here"—she inclined her head toward the door—"will be free and her man and her baby will be free too. That's a very good thing to do with one little bird. I could just eat that bird, but it takes an awful lot of birds to fill up Nora and only one to fill that little devil up." She paused and regarded the moon with some care. "Now, I've told you something. You tell me something. What kind of woman does that child think old Nora is?"

"I believe she thinks you're the kind of old woman who prays to the devil."

"Well, I am. Does that surprise you so much? There are good devils and bad devils, you see. Just like there are good angels and bad angels. The thing to be careful of is not devils but knowing bad from good. Does she think I have great powers?"

"Yes, of that she is convinced."

"Good. When a person believes there is great power, then they are respectful. They are respectful because they are afraid. But being afraid is not enough because when the one they fear goes away so does the fear. Fear is just a way of getting the attention. The real work is quite another matter."

"And what is that? What's the real work?"

"Oh, I thought you'd know that. The real work is killing bad little devils so that people can go off and be good or bad of their own accord. Now, I have to go and get ready. You watch down there by that door and when you see the candlelight you will know that I am working and when you see it go out you fetch my child to me." I waited and watched in the stillness. The servants had slipped into their quarters and pulled the curtains. They knew that it was unwise to watch the workings of a witch. Dan, uninitiated and uninvited, kept to his rooms. The usually busy street outside the walls was sleeping now. Even the moon had passed beyond the rooftops. All was dark and still.

At the given signal I tapped at Yoko's door. Pulling the bench away I let Yoko pass. I could feel her trembling as she gripped my arm and we descended into the garden.

Barefoot as the ritual required, we trod painfully across the gravel to an unused portion of the house where Nora chose to work her magic. We stepped through the darkened archway into the gloom within. Carefully picking our way through the rubble on the floor, we walked straight ahead into the blackness. Faint scratching sounds came from somewhere in front of us. Rats? I wished I had my shoes. A sudden flash of light and the acrid scent of sulfur filled the dank room, revealing the looming form of Nora. She held the match she'd struck aloft, then with a swirl lowered it to touch the wick of a homemade candle she had placed on her makeshift altar. Chanting her witch's jargon in deep-throated tones Nora beckoned us forward. She loomed above us, seemingly gigantic, on a dais of broken brick and mortar. The erratic shadows cast by the sputtering flame of her candle lent a fantastic backdrop to her pose. "Come, child," she cooed, "come closer." Yoko's fingertips bit into my arm, but she persevered, inching ever closer to the witch's call. Nora's velvet black skin shimmered with sweat and candlelight. Her eyes had the gleam of a snake's.

"Closer." She smiled an unnerving smile.

Yoko reached the edge of the little pile of debris that Nora had chosen for her stage. "Now, child, it is time to sign." Her eyes directed Yoko's to the altar and a fettered dove that lay beside the sputtering flame. The old witch slipped her long powerful fingers into a pocket and removed a folded piece of paper, the contract. This she opened with deliberate care and placed on the altar as if for the dove to read. Its surface was covered with a crazy-quilt pattern that I recognized as a witch's alphabet, the sort used in Elizabethan times. Again the bony fingers dipped into a pocket, this time retrieving what appeared to be a small sharpened stick. One long arm reached out and swept up the dove. Powerful fingers held back the wings and forced its tiny head downward. Nora rolled back her eyes and prayed her prayers of sacrifice. Suddenly, deftly, the hand with the stick moved and did its work. The dove had no warning and made no outcry as the instrument pierced the back of its neck and erased its brain. Slowly Nora removed the point and held the victim outward, "Sign, child, sign now."

"I want Charlie to do it."

"Sign, child!" The tone was more demanding.

"But . . . " Yoko was clearly panicking. Suddenly, she turned to me. "Have Charlie do it! Please, Charlie, I'll take care of you,

John and I will! Just do this for me. Sign it. It's all right that way too, isn't it, Nora? He can sign." Nora was no doubt used to moments of indecision at times like these, but I suspected that it was the first time she had had a request for a proxy. Afraid that she might lose the moment, she held the little corpse out toward me.

"Will you sign for her?"

"Sign your own name," Yoko whispered as I stepped past her. I spread the little contract on the crude altar and with a little difficulty, caused by the need for more 'ink,' fulfilled the ritual's demands.

"Go now," smiled Nora in satisfaction. So I turned and guided Yoko back into the light. She turned to look back once, but Nora chose that exact moment to extinguish the candle. The witch, the sacrificial victim, and the contract all vanished into the blackness. All that was left was the low-tone chant as the witch finished her prayers.

"That was very brave of you, Charlie. Thank you. I'm sure that you will be all right. You have lots of protections and things. John and I will take care of you for this. You had to do it. I couldn't. I just couldn't. That was very brave signing your name like that."

"My name? Why Yoko, I didn't sign *my* name!"

"But you must have! You had to! Otherwise I won't get the things I wished for! You must have signed your name or . . . Whose name was it? Charlie, you didn't! Not *my* name! Not mine!" I turned away so that she couldn't see me smiling. I decided that I would wait awhile before I answered that particular question.

· 9 ·

JAPAN-NIECES

Obedient to the curious rigors of Yoko's Japanese numerological and directional theories, we returned to New York City from Cartagena by way of Los Angeles and Fairbanks, Alaska. Yoko plunged happily back into Apple's intrigues and dealings. Her status vastly enhanced by her skillful negotiations in a dispute with Allen Klein the previous winter, she found herself assuming a position of some prominence in the eyes of her fellow Apples. If not quite their leader, she had become at least a potential rallying point for unified action—something Apple had never been able to achieve in the past.

Yoko took considerable satisfaction from her new leadership role and saw both it and John's support of it as omens of future success. She firmly believed that both were due at least in part to Nora's magic.

Her deepening involvement with Apple affairs left less and less time in her day for John. He, on the other hand, had little else but time. Inevitably, the stage was set for further conflict.

As the spring arrived, John, heliotropic to the core, yearned impatiently to luxuriate in the sun. He chafed increasingly at his confinement within the Dakota apartment's all-white walls and waited impatiently for the first opportunity to escape. Yoko, however, was far too engrossed in affairs of business to leave the Dakota, at least for the moment. She met John's growing edginess with a new and atypical placidity that had come upon her during her days with Nora, the *bruja*. John found this an unexpected side to her character with which he was neither familiar nor comfortable.

Early one evening in late April, as John and I sat in our accustomed kitchen places, reading cards and talking, he made his discontent emphatically clear. He was telling me how he had baited Yoko in the hopes of drawing her away from the too-consuming demands of business and back to being the other, more familiar Yoko that he loved.

"So I says to her, 'It's love *and* money, you know!' " he said hotly. " 'You can't go hiding behind your piles of paper work all day and all night too! You can't go crawling off to "important meetings" and discussing fifty-billion-dollar deals and leave me here with the kid all day and expect everything to be all right, because it's *not* all right! It's not right at all!' That should get a rise out of her, right? But nooooooo. She just sits there all patience and compassion while I rant and rave myself into exhaustion. She's not angry, she's not hurt or embarrassed, I'm not even sure she's *there!* What am I supposed to do with that?"

"What do you want to do?"

"I want to slap her silly compassionate face right off! But I can't do that. Not that I haven't done it before, but no more. That's right out now. But a little yelling *would* be nice."

"How about getting a referee? Some hundred-dollar-an-hour doctor to help you set guidelines for a fair fight and establish an arena where the two of you can let it out in a reasonable fashion?"

"That's terrific. Then he goes off and makes a bundle writing a book about the inner workings of our neuroses. Anyway, I've tried all that. It never works. The added element of a third person changes everything. It's like having sex with an audience. It's not the same as making love, is it? It's showtime. And that's how it would be if someone, anyone, was watching me fight. Showtime. I'd be worrying if my insults were sharp enough or my quips clever enough. I *do* have a reputation to uphold!

"And even if I *could* keep from role-playing, we'd still have the dear wife to contend with, you know. She's been to South America, which is apparently analogous to having been to the mountain, and now she's full of witchcrap and magicks. She doesn't have any hostility, no pent-up little angers to release. Not on me. Not on anyone."

"That's a little hard to believe."

"Well, believe it or don't, I don't really care what you believe. What I *do* care about is that the one outlet that I had has been taken from me, and that is no fun.

"I'm not really mad at her, you know. I want to yell at *her* because *I'm* still popular, and I can't do anything about it. Sound funny? Look!" He held up an envelope. "This is from Francis Coppola. He wants me to do a score for a film he's working on. He says, 'I'm living in a volcano and it's wonderful. Wish you were here. Want to work on a movie?' Here's another one. Frank Perry wants a little Lennon touch on his *Time and Time Again*. It's a time-travel movie. Just my thing, right? But I don't have any music in me. Here's a guy who wants an interview, but I don't have anything to say. I got three offers here to perform, one to produce, and a million letters that just want to know how I'm doin'. That's popularity. And

I don't have anything to give them, so I have to write back nice polite letters saying 'Thanks but no thanks' because on the off chance I ever *do* get out of this slump or block or whatever it is, if I ever *do* get the muse back, then I'm gonna need all these people.

"So, you know what I say? I tell them that bit you and Yoko thought up for the Immigration press last year. I tell them that I'm fully employed minding the baby and playing househusband. Now that lie *is* getting a little stale. People have to wonder, don't they? I'm a bit surprised no one has caught on yet. 'He's got a maid, and a nanny, and a cook, and gofers, I wonder what it is that keeps him so busy?' But the public will believe what the public wants to believe. So I'm a househusband. And it galls the hell out of me to turn down offers that I'm dying to accept and am incapable of fulfilling.

"So here I am with a bellyful of gall. What do I do? I try the usual, which is to give the wife a little hell, but that's no good because she understands everything now. I go off to get drunk, but that's no good because half the fun of going out is that little thrill of wondering how far I can go before I've gone too far. Will she take me back? Will she kill me? Well there's no thrill now. She'll always take me back because she understands everything. I don't want to be understood, predicted, anticipated, tolerated, and accepted. I want something a little more loving than a passive cloud of compassion that *understands* me.

"So you know what we do now? I blow off steam. And then we hypnotize me. That's right. A little technique all her own that she calls 'ten to one' because she counts backward from ten to one while I lie with my head in her lap. She pets me and counts and all my tensions and all those nasty ol' poisons drain away and everything is supposed to be all better again. I yell and get understood. I relax and get stroked. Now there's conditioning for you! I usually fall asleep. This is not a way of life, Charles; it's the high road to atrophy."

"And it still leaves you with the need to find a new outlet.

It sounds to me like you'd better get out of your shell far enough to form a friendship or two before isolation and compassion completely drain you."

"Agreed. I need friends. But I've never really known how to do that. I spend time with people and if they're nice enough, then I spend a lot of time with them and that's okay, but it's just spending time. It's not an emotion or love, it's a pleasantry. I've tried. I had a friend last year. We went out, drank, talked. I looked forward to it because it was pleasant. Then I had an opportunity to be a real friend. I don't mean in the way I usually wind up being a friend, not by financing a business or underwriting a loan. No money figured into it at all. My drinking partner got sick. Very sick. He went to the hospital and I went to see him. That's when I had a chance to be a friend. I had a chance to stand by him while the doctors cut out pieces of him because the sickness was cancer, and they weren't getting it all. They were going to cut him to pieces and I should have been there, but I wasn't. Do you know why? Because it was easier for me not to. I didn't want to watch. I didn't want to think about it. So I stayed away, and now I only think about it once in a while. I don't even know if he died or not. That's how I am.

"So forming a genuine friendship is a little difficult for me. Most of the people in my life have been placed there by fate or career. If I get along with them I call them friends. I'm pretty open. I say what I think to just about everyone because I don't care enough about them for it to really matter. If they go along with what I think, then that makes the quote friendship unquote a little easier. If they don't go along with me then I leave 'em.

"Still, I suppose, there are a lot of people who could be friends to me. But the question is, could *I* be a friend to *them?* I tend to doubt it. If I'm going to find an outlet, I have to look somewhere other than friends.

"So that brings us to the problem of 'getting out of my shell,' as you put it. I've got a summer full of diversions planned, or should I say Yoko has. We'll go to Japan. Visit the relatives. I'll get to test out my nine or ten words of Japanese, see the hot springs, visit temples. Yoko wants to go to the ancestral home in Japan, and now that I can come and go as I please, we'll do that; but I got a feeling that it is really going to be more trouble than it's worth. If her relationship with her sister and what she says about her mother are any indication, then I don't think it will be all that special. Quite the reverse actually.

"Nevertheless, I suppose I'll have to go. It is at least a way of communicating with the wife, which, although it's getting increasingly difficult, seems the worthwhile thing to do. She's inexorably narrowed the field in which I can react to her, you know. That is to some degree your fault. Business, business, business. In actuality it's gotten her real acceptance and success. They said in the paper that the Klein negotiation was 'Kissinger-like,' and she loved that. They aren't making fun of her now. And that *is* what I want, for her to be happy. To that end, Charles, I want your advice. She's running everything now anyway, so I want to know should I make it official. Not just show my support but declare her my official rep and give her the power of attorney, the works. This world of business may take her away from me, but part of loving is letting go. I want to know if it will make her happy."

"No."

"Aren't you going to read the cards?"

"Sure, if you like, but I think you're making a mistake. You are giving yourself away because you don't value yourself sufficiently to recognize the power you have and the damage you could do."

"I thought you'd be in favor of this idea. I thought it would give me an opportunity to look at her and say, 'Well, at least she's got something she wanted.' She'd be happy and you could stop playing double agent between the two of us every time there's a difference of business opinion. What's wrong with that?"

This time I did use the cards. "Naming her as representative is a good idea. She has been playing the part long enough and well enough that it won't seem as though you're doing it just because you really don't want to do it yourself and don't trust anyone enough to do it for you. I should also point out that right now the added support and authority will be very useful to her.

"The power of attorney is quite another matter. One of the reasons she has done well thus far is you."

"Why me? I haven't done anything really."

"You don't have to. You are the control. You are King John the not-always-benevolent monarch. Yoko has to watch out for you and appease you. You can withdraw your support from her at any time and leave her powerless. So you can keep her in line."

"I'm not sure I like what you're saying. I could withdraw a power of attorney, too, couldn't I?"

"If she has the right to sign your name, then she doesn't need to get your permission for anything. By the time you decide to rescind that power the things that she signs would be in effect and legal."

"This is my wife we're talking about."

"Your wife and your representative, but she's also Yoko. She's proud and ambitious. You won't be doing either one of you a favor by abdicating the responsibilities of your own life. Don't get me wrong. She has done and is doing an excellent job. But if *you* don't control her, who does? Not me."

"I just thought it would be a nice gesture. What could she do?"

"She would have complete control over you. Now when was the last time you were happy being completely controlled?"

"I see your point. You always say that you work for her. You realize that you just passed up a great opportunity to serve her."

"Not if you think about it, though I'm sure she wouldn't see it that way! Tell you what, if you don't tell her, I won't."

"Ah, another clandestine agreement? Do you have these with Yoko too?"

"Of course!"

True to his word, John officially proclaimed Yoko his representative in time for the spring Apple meeting in May of 1977. To his delight, Yoko was genuinely pleased to have the prefix "acting" removed from her title.

The Dakota was filled with chaotic excitement during the last days of May 1977. All energy was focused on the Lennons' impending trip to Japan. The apartment's main hallway served as the staging area for the expedition and had become a clutter of cases and crates and cardboard containers with Yoko dashing up and down its length pulling from this rack of clothes or that stack of books the necessities or near-necessities intended to ensure a well-provisioned journey.

John and I sat in the White Room away from all this activity. We were not reading. It was just after ten in the evening and the preparations were still going full tilt. My job was to be on call in case any item for packing might require being read on to ascertain its importance to the success of the venture. In contrast to Yoko's intense excitement, John seemed subdued.

"I don't want to go," he complained as we sat there. "I know I promised and all that, but I really don't want to go. Poor Sean, the burden is really on him. Sean has to go, otherwise I'm denying him his heritage. But if I let him go without going with him, that might be traumatic for him. That means that before all this is over I'm going to wind up resenting Sean, who is actually more of a victim than I am."

"You could always resent Yoko."

"Charles, I *do* always resent Yoko—and then I feel terrible about it. No, what I'd *really* like to know is what her motive is in all of this. Does she really want to see her family? Or is it that she wants her family to see her? You know, to show Mama-san that little Yoko black sheep has done good too."

"Come on now. You've gone to a lot of trouble preparing for this excursion. Diet changes, history lessons, even courses in Japanese to lessen the culture shock. So what's all this? Last-minute doubts, nothing more."

"There have been times, Charles, when you have been more observant. I went through all that for reasons other than preparation. To start with, I thought that if I got into the culture a bit I could pretend that I was excited about the trip and I'd get other people up for it, and their energy could carry me along too. That's one of my old tricks I play on myself. But it's not working this time. You know what I want to do? I want to go sailing."

"You could go sailing in the Sea of Japan."

"It's not quite what I had in mind, but it's an idea."

"And you get to practice your Japanese."

"I studied Japanese for two reasons. One was so I would have at least a partial idea of what goes on in this house that I'm not supposed to know, which is why I know more of the language than I let on. The second reason is that I was attracted to the instructress, who was cute, and if you have noticed, I like oriental girls."

"Well, there's a good motive for going. There will certainly be a lot of oriental girls in Japan for you to flirt with."

"It's not quite the same, is it? One here or there is a novelty. An entire country full of them is quite another matter. It might ruin my taste for them altogether. But the real problem is that I don't speak the language well enough to get around by myself. That means that I am going to be more or less dependent on Yoko. I'm not all that sure that I want to spend several months having to ask my wife for everything. That can be limiting, you know."

"I'm sure it won't be that bad."

"You're very positive about this trip, aren't you? Very chipper and bright about me going away. Why?"

"Because of what you already said, that you are committed and that you have to go. So as long as you have to, I thought I'd try to support a positive attitude."

"Oh, now that sounds wonderful. Humor the kid so he'll take his medicine. That's really very reassuring, Charles. I wish you hadn't bothered to explain."

"You did ask."

"You must like that excuse, you use it quite a bit. Now be useful and tell me something that will help me change my head around about this so I won't be a total drag and ruin the whole thing. If it goes well maybe I can just get through it and that will be the end of that. If not, I've got a feeling that I'll never hear the end of it. So open up the cards and tell me what you see, seer. Or is it saw, seer? Or seer saws? Or is it saucier if it's sorcerer?"

"What you have before you is a journey and we've talked before about the journey that you have to take within yourself. Well, this physical journey you are taking to a strange land can be used as a symbol of that inner journey. Relate one to the other and you will be doing them both."

"I like that. I travel with my body but in my head. That does give it a little purpose, adds a bit of order and romance to this whole thing. I'll try it, but you're going to have to show me how."

While John was engaged in these metaphysical preparations for the trip, Yoko set about making preparations of quite another kind.

On the following day, she and I sat in the kitchen musing

over the dozens of little pieces of paper on which she had written the intended itinerary.

"Now, read *very* carefully," she began. "This plan has to be perfect, because I want to be sure that we always get to stay in the imperial suite at the Akura Hotel in Tokyo. Now that suite isn't going to be available all summer, you know. Sometimes it's booked years in advance. They're willing to give it to us all the times that they don't have it reserved for someone else, but that means that we are going to have to find other places to stay when it's being used. I've worked out a schedule so that we'll be out of town and John won't notice that we don't always have it."

"I don't think hotel rooms are John's major concern."

"They're not his concern at all! He'd never bother thinking about this. That's why I have to. He'd stay anywhere, but I want this trip to be very special because if he has an especially good time, he might start writing and it would be very good if we did some recording. I've already researched and there are good studios available and John's numbers look very good right now, so we have to plan everything perfectly."

"Perfect is not easy."

"I *know!* That's why we have to do so much work to get ready. Now John and Sean have to leave five days before I do because that's a better time for them in the numbers and they have to fly to Europe first because they can't go west, so we'll send them east."

"Who takes care of Sean during the trip?"

"Oh, Masako is going with them. It's not a good direction for her, but I think that servants take on their employer's numbers, don't you?"

"I don't know anything about your number system."

"Oh, you should, I'll teach you. Now, when they arrive they'll want to rest, so that's what they'll do while they wait for me. When I get there, we'll have three more days in the

Akura before we lose the room. So I thought that that would be a good time to visit the Shinto shrine in the south. I want John to get as much culture as possible because if he really falls in love with Japan—it really is a beautiful country—then there's a very good chance that he'll not only start writing again but also want to buy some land there. He's always saying how he 'needs a little green' and it would be perfect if we could spend every summer in Japan.

"Now, do we do the Shinto shrine or not? South would be a good direction just then, but if it doesn't look good there are a few other choices, like there's this guy who's starting a new religion and we might learn a lot from him if we were initiated."

So with repeated spreads and carefully charted numbers we clocked practically every moment of the intended five-month trip.

"Yoko, has it occurred to you that you haven't made any provisions for alternative plans?"

"Why should I? We're reading on everything and I've checked it in the numbers. What could go wrong?"

Answer: lots.

The first thing that went wrong was that John decided traveling nonstop to Japan was a bit much, so he got off somewhere along the way and took a hotel for the night. The Akura decided that the party for the imperial suite was not going to show, so they gave the rooms to someone else. When the Lennon party arrived there was no room at the inn. Even Sean's suite was filled with a substitute guest. So John, Sean, and Masako all spent the night in an 'ordinary room.' They didn't seem to mind, but the hotel frowned on such behavior and Yoko screamed.

"Now, look, we have a major problem," said Yoko, as she entered the Black Room, where I had been encamped since John's departure and would remain until his return.

"Not an emergency?"

"Stop that. John changed the schedule and now everything is out of line. We have to change a lot of reservations and make some new plans. I've been on the phone all night and the hotel said that they would find other accommodations for us, but we don't get the imperial suite for three weeks, and in the meantime we have to make a room change about every other day. Now, I don't think John is going to like that because it will mean a lot of packing and unpacking, and so it's going to be a real problem. I want to know how John is going to react to all this."

"Don't you think he would be happier if what he had was the most convenient instead of the best? This is supposed to be a vacation."

"That's not the way it works. We're also going to have a problem about luggage. I wasn't careful enough about what I let John take with him, and it's not the right sort of thing. He needs all sorts that he didn't bother to take with him and I looked through what he has here and nothing will do. So we have to go shopping for the family and we'll send the things over by air express. Now I want you to stay here in the Dakota and I'll call you and tell you what we need as we need it and you send that over to us."

"Don't you think you're going a bit overboard?"

"No, not at all. We've never been to Japan together, you know, and the Japanese are always taking pictures, and we'll be such a novelty they'll be sending them in to papers all over the place. How would it look if we were to have the same things on in two different pictures? Now we'll have to change rooms a lot and we can't go carrying all that stuff around with us. It looks very bad for celebrities to have a lot of luggage. So you have to send us things as we need them. But before you can send them we have to buy them, right? So we have to go shopping."

"We?"

"Of course! You don't expect me to go out alone, do you? I always go with John, but he's not here, so I have to go with you."

So we went shopping for four solid days. At long, long last, when her numbers were right, Yoko left for the plane. Once she was in the air I breathed a sigh of relief, thinking that this should be a quiet summer. Wrong again. A few days after she left, Yoko called me at the Dakota from Tokyo to tell me just how wrong.

"Charlie, it's a disaster."

"What is?"

"Everything. Nothing is working out the way it should. There was supposed to be a little press conference when I arrived, so we could tell everyone why we had come and what we were working on. I didn't want to tell John because I wanted to surprise him. I wanted him to think that it was like the old days and that the press would just naturally appear wherever we were. I thought that that would make him feel good and maybe more creative, you know, but now the press is here and he doesn't want to see them. It would have been all right if they had just shown up on their own the way John thinks they have, but I invited them and I can't just send them away now because they'll write terrible things about us. And I can't tell John that I invited them because he will be angry, and I can't just see them alone because I promised them a big story with John."

"What big story?"

"About our musical. I thought if John saw a favorable press reaction to the idea, it might encourage him to actually do it. He gets very committed to things that are written about him. Now it's all going to be ruined because John doesn't want to see any reporters, and the fact that they're around has him so upset that he doesn't want to leave the room. But we have to leave the room because today is one of the days when we have to change rooms and I'm afraid that a reporter might see us. What am I going to do?"

"Call room service and tell them to send up drinks and food for the press. Tell John that the press was called by relatives as a surprise for him and it would be an insult if you didn't accept the gesture. Tell the press that the reason for the conference is so they can ask all the questions they want at once, and then you will be free to go about the city without always having to be on guard. Tell them that you both love Tokyo and you want to be able to enjoy it as if it were your home."

"Will that work?"

"Damned if I know, but it's better than nothing."

"Will John actually do all that without embarrassing me in front of everyone?"

"John's too smart to disappoint a roomful of reporters and too kind to humiliate you in front of them."

Considering the unfavorable conditions, the conference went fairly well. John said nice things about Japan and its people. Yoko talked about their plans for a musical and John did not contradict her, though he did mention that it was a very long-term project and that at the moment he was engaged full time as a househusband. The press was polite but lukewarm. Fortunately for domestic tranquillity John spoke more Japanese than he could read and was therefore not aware of just how lukewarm their reception was. This was only the first of a comedy of errors that plagued them throughout the summer. Night after night, the phone would ring on the special number that had been reserved for tarot calls. Yoko had set up a schedule whereby she was free for readings during the mid- to late Japanese afternoon, which meant, of course, the middle of the New York night. I had taken to sleeping on the kitchen sofa because I couldn't hear the special tarot line ringing in the Black Room, where my official billet was. I could always count on my nightly call because it is one of the inviolable official rules that anything as laboriously planned as this trip would immediately begin to go wrong. As for example:

"Charlie, all the clothes you sent us were wrong."

"I sent you the ones you asked for."

"But they're not the right ones. I don't think we have anything that's right for us here. I think we'd better send everything back to you and then we'll have to get all new things. The problem is that John doesn't want to go out. Usually he likes to go shopping and they do have the finest stores here, but he's depressed and doesn't want to leave the room at all. He doesn't even want to go to the Shinto shrine, and that's a disaster because we don't have any rooms booked after tomorrow. We can't move to another hotel because how would that look? We can't stay here either. John says they can throw him out if they want to and I think he means it. I think there's going to be trouble." And there was, as I learned several nights later when the usual call came. This time it was from John.

"Charles," he said tiredly, "just how much of a part did you play in all this?"

"All what?"

"All this 'let's make John a Japanese' campaign."

"I think the idea was to get you to like the place."

"It isn't working. I don't like the place. I don't like the constant confusion. I don't like the idea of being force-fed something and then told how much I like it. It stinks and I want to come home. Now apparently the numbers are all wrong for that. According to the almighty numbers we have to stay here for at least three and a half months. Now if I stay here three and a half months, I'm going to go crazy. Knowing this, I said to the wife, 'Why does everything have to be by the numbers? We have a fine upstanding giant of a tarot reader in our house. Why don't we just call him and find out if the cards have another solution for our little dilemma?' Now why don't you open your cards and tell me what will happen to me and to my dear wife and my child and the rest of this entourage if we do pull up stakes and come home now?"

"Well . . ." I considered carefully, "Yoko will be bitterly disappointed, of course."

"Yoko is going to be disappointed with anything that happens because whether we stay or go I have no intention of playing this little game anymore. I know enough about her number system to know that if we stay somewhere three and a half months, that is supposed to establish a base for us, and to Yoko that means buying a house and moving here permanently. You haven't happened to hear anything about a plan like that, have you?"

"I think it was only supposed to be for the summers."

"Ah ha! I thought as much. Now go ahead and tell me what happens if we come back now."

"There's not much to tell you, John, that you don't already know. It will upset Yoko and she'll upset you, and that doesn't look too pleasant, but it's no disaster."

"And what happens if I come back and leave her here?"

"I don't think that will happen because I don't think Yoko will let you go alone."

"Good. So, what can you do about finding a house on Long Island for the rest of the summer? If not there, maybe one of the Caribbean islands or the mountains or anywhere but here?"

There were no calls for an unprecedented two weeks. When communications were finally reestablished it was Yoko, not John, who was doing the talking.

"You have to help me find my mother. She knew we were coming to see her because I called her during the spring. She knows that we're here because the press keeps telling everyone where we are and what we are doing. But Mother hasn't called us. I think it's very strange and I want to know what she's up to."

"What about John?"

"What about him?"

"I haven't heard from you in two weeks and I was just wondering how you all are and what's been going on."

"We're fine. Now tell me about my mother."

"If you haven't tried to reach her, I think you've probably offended her. She's just as stubborn as you are. So if you don't call she won't either, and you won't see each other."

"Are you sure? Never mind, you're probably right. She's like that, you know, very proud. She always wants me to play the dutiful daughter with her. It's ridiculous. She wants me to come to her. I do! I travel all the way around the world, but she doesn't come here to meet me. It's insulting. I suppose I do have to call her though, for John and Sean at least."

"And for you?"

"This isn't for me. This is for the baby and her, really. She hasn't been the nicest of mothers to me, you know. I thought that possibly seeing Sean and seeing how well I've done with John might just change her mind toward me. Everything that I have so far in a material way comes from John and that's not good. So I need to impress on Mother that she has a Western family too and that she has a responsibility to them. My sister married a Westerner. Mother accepts him, and he's not as rich as John. I think when Mother sees how well I'm doing she'll want to make things up with me."

"Well, if that's what you want then I suggest you call her." This Yoko did and was back on the line with me in two hours.

"Do you know what she's done? She told me that she didn't realize that I had actually arrived because she hadn't heard from me. She said that she kept her plans open for as long as she could, but when summer came she had to accept some pressing offers for summer social engagements, and now she won't have time to see us until August. Can you imagine?

"She's just doing this so I will lose face with John. She's always been like that, doing anything she could to demean me. I told her that the only reason why John had left off his very busy schedule was to be able to meet his Japanese family and that it was very rude of her not to respect the sacrifice he made. So she told me that she hadn't realized that the burdens of traveling were so difficult for us because my sister seems to travel so freely whenever she wants—that's not true, you know. She said she was under the impression that John was so successful that he didn't have to work and so hadn't considered that he would have any schedule problems. Can you believe her? Then she offers us an alternative. She said that as long as he traveled all this way to meet his family, it was only fair that he should do so. So she's sending my brother Kaye's [her nickname for Keisuke] children. She said they would help keep Sean company and John would enjoy the company of his little Japanese nieces until August when she could join us because her social engagements were confirmed and she couldn't change them. What are we going to do? I don't want Kaye's kids with us. The youngest is ten. That's too old to play with Sean, and we are going to have to find them rooms here at the hotel and that's going to be very, very expensive if it is even possible at all. She's just doing this to punish me and I must say she's doing a very good job. What am I going to do?"

"Tell Mama-san that you don't want Kaye's children because you are on vacation and borderline adolescents aren't your idea of a good time."

"I can't do that. This is her way of punishing me. If I don't accept this, then whatever she comes up with next will only be worse."

"Are you sure all this is worth it?"

"Of course it is. This is a matter of heritage. Sean is half Japanese, you know, and he has a right to the heritage from this side of his family. I want to be sure that his name is placed on the family register. My mother is the family matriarch and the only one who can do that. I want to be sure that he gets his inheritance, not just the jewels and land but the tradition part of his inheritance as well. That's important. So I have to do this. I've already told her I would. Now, how am I going to tell John?"

"How is John?" My last communication with him followed by two weeks of silence gave me the impression that all was not well.

"He's fine . . . all right, but he's being very difficult. He doesn't want to do anything, and you know how he is when he doesn't want to participate. I finally got him to come out of the hotel a few nights ago for dinner, but he started in at the restaurant and we had to get out of there. You know how he does it. In a loud voice he starts saying things. He said that he was beginning to see why people said that 'they all look alike' because they do all look alike. And asking if the proper term was 'gook' or 'nip' or what. We had to get out of there right away. That's how John gets his way. He says he doesn't want to do something and I encourage him. He'll finally say yes, but then he ruins everything just to get even with me. I hope nothing comes out in the press about this."

"Well, if he wants to stay in the hotel that much, why not let him stay in the hotel?"

"You don't understand. Everyone is watching us over here and it looks very bad if we never go out. People will think that we are having problems or something. So, we have to go out. But then if John is going to act like this, I don't know what will happen. Now with Kaye's children coming it can only get worse. How are we going to handle the nieces?"

"Get John a bicycle."

"What?"

"He feels pent up. There is nothing he can do, nowhere he can go without you and Sean and Masako and the houseboy. His freedom is being curtailed. So get him a bike and let him explore a little."

"But he'll get into trouble!"

"He's already getting into trouble. Let him have a little freedom and I think his mood will improve. I'm sure of it. As for the nieces, tell Mama-san that although you'd love to have them close to you, there really aren't any rooms left at the hotel, so you will supply them with rooms in another place. Then hire a chaperon to look after them, and that way you can deal with them only when you want to. In the meantime, John can always hop on his bike and vanish if he chooses."

"Okay, I'll try."

Yoko did try, but perhaps a bit too vigorously. According to John, she embroidered rather freely upon the advice I had given, as he did not hesitate to inform me in his next call.

"Well, Charles, I'd like to thank you for all the help you haven't been to me."

"Ah, John, back from the dead?"

"No, I'd say on my way actually."

"The metaphysical journey is running into snags, is it?"

"No. I'm on a metaphysical journey all right. This is King John's descent into the underworld. Complete with little Japan-nieces to torment me. And that idea of yours for family outings on the bikes was a real beauty. I have a bike; Yoko has one; Nanny's too old, so it's the houseboy with a sidecar no less for Sean; and, of course, the little Japan-nieces. A nice inconspicuous way to travel about and see the sights. We're a fuckin' parade. I don't know what you were taking when you thought up that one."

"I don't know what could have possessed me."

"Neither do I! There is absolutely no freedom for me here. Everyone recognizes Yoko, of course, because she takes such care not to disguise herself and pauses to pose at positively every street corner. They all have cameras over here, you know, and everyone has to have a picture of the Beatle on his bike. I'm a tourist attraction. Every hick from the sticks is in with his kids in tow checking out the sights and I'm one of them."

"I take it that you decided not to come home."

"You can take it anyway you like. It's been decided for me. We have to wait for Mama-san because that's the whole point of the trip, and if we were to leave and come back, there's no guarantee that she'll bother with us then. Now we have the responsibility of the Japan-nieces. Their parents have gone off on vacation—lucky them—so we can't pack them off home.

"We're trapped. Those kids are like spoiled piranhas. Every, positively every, shop we pass has something in it that they want and so we stop. They grab what they want and the clerk grabs Yoko and out comes the American Express card—universal language, you know—and in an hour our little caravan is so loaded down that we have to go back and unload and then start out for more. Mama-san has apparently told them that their round-eyed uncle is very rich and nothing pleases him more than getting little gifts for little girls. I tell 'em, 'Cut that out. You don't need all that crap.' And all I get are smiles as if I were putting on some clown show and 'So sorry.' They don't or won't speak English, you know."

"Didn't Yoko get a chaperon?"

"There aren't any that we can really trust with such *important* little charges."

"Call the hotel manager. Tell him what you need and have him handle it."

"Do they do that?"

"How many suites are you renting right now?"

149

"Three."

"They do that. Just tell them that you are very concerned for the safety of your girls in this great megalopolis of theirs and you want to be sure that they are well looked after while you go about your important business. They'll send you someone."

"Will Yoko go for that?"

"Well, if she doesn't, the next time you're out on your bike, just turn a hard right and get out of there. That ought to convey the message clearly enough."

"You were never married, were you, Charles?"

"Divorced."

"That figures."

I continued to get regular reports in the form of frequent phone calls from Yoko and occasionally John. He gained a little freedom from the crunch of the family, but it was not enough. The hotel became oppressive for him. The constant room changes did not help his mood. Little excursions taken when rooms were not available were no solution. All the reservations for these had been made with the original party in mind and now the enlarged entourage was obliged to pack into closer quarters.

John found it increasingly difficult to adjust to his new surroundings. At each turn he seemed to be grasping for another excuse to abandon the trip. He was never shy about relating these. "I haven't been rude to anyone for a week. I've been tempted, but I've been strong. Like, there was this guy on the corner the other day. He looked just like a postcard samurai. Well, I was relieved to see him actually. I'd done all this history and cultural preparation and this was the first guy I'd seen who didn't look like he was either working in a Benihana's or coming home from Madison Avenue. So I strolls up to him and says in me best Japanese, 'Hello there' and give him a little bow because he was older and therefore venerable. For all I knew he might have been a bum, but I thought it would be a kick to meet a Japanese for a change. So the guy looks at me very carefully like he's trying to remember something and I thought that it was my pronunciation or something, so I had another go. Then he makes like he's playing a guitar and grins at me and says, "Beatle . . . Beatle, yes?' So I says, 'No . . . Rolling Stone,' and walked off."

10

PLAYING DEAD

A s the summer of 1977 progressed, the visit to Japan
was beset by more and more difficulties. John's response was
to become steadily more withdrawn. In her nightly phone calls,
Yoko recounted his growing lethargy and lack of interest.
Eventually he stopped participating in family activities altogether, creating a family crisis that lasted for weeks. The first
news of this came to me in a call from Yoko late one night in
mid-August.

"Charlie! I think John's gone crazy!" she began.

"So? What else is new?"

"I'm not joking! He's acting incredibly strangely. He's never
been like this before. I think he's having a breakdown or something. You have to do something. I'm afraid for Sean and
Kaye's children, everyone."

"Yoko, you always think John has gone crazy. According to you, he's being crazy when he goes out or stays in or gets drunk or not; he's being crazy if he's loud and crazy when he's quiet. Now you call me up from halfway around the world at, what is it? four in the morning, to announce that he's gone crazy again. So I say, what else is new? Which kind of crazy has he gone this time?"

"A new kind. I've never seen him act like this before. He doesn't talk to anyone, he doesn't seem to hear anyone talking to him. Sometimes he just stands in the corner and moans. It's terrible. I knew he didn't like it here. I knew he wanted to get out, but I kept hoping that if we just waited a little longer he would get used to things here. I think the pressure was too much for him. He doesn't have a very strong mind, you know. I think he's snapped."

"Yoko, I've read on John's sanity more than any other client, including a few in institutions. Maybe he's not the one with the problem. Perhaps the thing to do is take a look at where you are and reconsider the situation from that perspective."

"No, I know what my problems are. You don't think I know myself, but I do. Freud said that insanity was having a problem and not being able to control it. Well, I control mine. I've created a very special world to do just that. I grew up in a family where my father wasn't there and my mother was a monster. My country was destroyed by war. My feelings and my work have never been respected, and people think that all I've ever done is marry John Lennon and spend his money. When you have a life like that you have to protect yourself, and I've done a good job of it. I know I have problems and I know I will never be able to solve them. I have learned how to live with them and live successfully. There is nothing you can tell me about it because it's been my life's work to learn about myself and survive as myself.

"John is a different person with different problems. He can't handle his. He has always had a mommie or a manager or a Yoko to take care of him. That's how *he's* survived, by the good graces of other people. *I* have survived despite the hatred of others. So I don't need advice about me, I need advice about my husband, who's acting like a catatonic. I need to know if he's faking as some kind of cruel joke or if it's the real thing."

Thus began a series of abrupt and confusing communications from Yoko regarding John. I tried to be reassuring, but her fears were not to be laid to rest. John was her world, and now, seemingly, he had passed beyond her control. The terror this inspired in her was real.

It wasn't until several days, or should I say nights, of her calls that I heard from John.

"Hello, Charles? Listen, there are some things I have to ask you . . ."

"I've got a couple of questions for you too. What have you been doing?"

"I've been dead, Charles. I still am as a matter of fact. I suppose I will be till I'm reborn. You may consider this a communication from the spirit world."

"You've got Yoko scared to the point of incoherence. Why are you doing this?"

"Why? You ask me why I'm dead? Because I've been killed! Yoko killed me, this place killed me, the damned Japan-nieces killed me. I knew it was killin' me, but I never expected that the obvious would happen. Now that it has, I'm rather relieved. Being dead is not really so bad. Dying's the thing, Charles. Take my advice and get through the dying part as quickly as possible. Then you're dead and everything is all right."

"What are you talking about?" I'd begun to wonder if Yoko hadn't diagnosed his condition correctly after all.

"I'll tell you what I'm talking about. I order coffee from the nanny, right? What do I get? Tea! Why? Because Yoko told her that coffee was bad for me and when I ask for it she should bring me tea instead. I ask for cigarettes and nobody will get them because Yoko tells them not to. She smokes like a chimney, of course, but cigarettes are bad for me, so I don't get them. If I get a pack for myself they disappear. Here's the rich rock star and he has to hide and hoard his smokes like an inmate. I say to Yoko that the Japan-nieces are spending too much money and she says she will talk to them, and they spend more. They try to hide it from me. I tell them I'm on to them, in their own language, mind you, but they don't understand. Yoko says that it's because they only speak very high Japanese. Total bullshit! I say that I want to get out into the country for a little fresh air and freedom. So what happens? Mama-san offers us her house, which is the ancestral home, but she sold it, you see, to Kaye. So we have to rent the damn place at ten times what it's worth to make sure that Kaye is taken care of.

"Meanwhile Kaye's on vacation and we're minding the kids for him. Am I getting through to you, Charles? I say, I want to get out of this place and Yoko says the numbers won't let us. So I'm living my life according to numbers in some book that I can't even read. So I think to myself, This is killin' me. Then I realize, I talk and people don't hear me, they tiptoe around as if they were afraid of something. I'm right there, but they act like they can't see me. The situation isn't killing me at all. It's killed me. I'm dead. And you know, it ain't bad!"

"Just how long have you been dead now?" I still wasn't sure that the man I was talking to was altogether sane, but it had shades of the wicked Lennon sense of humor.

"A week, ten days, maybe more. We dead have no use for time, you know. We have no need of it. Just like we have no need for writing songs or telling our wives that we want to go home or being upset about money. No, we dead are a simple lot. Nothing to do all day long except spook around the house, haunt the family, moan and groan, pop out from behind doorways and scream BOO at the children, that sort of thing. It's really rather refreshing. You should try it sometime."

"Sometime no doubt I will. But tell me, oh wandering shade, how is it you can talk to me and not the family?"

"That's simple. You're a magician, aren't you? This sort of thing is right up your alley. You'd hardly be a self-respecting wizard if you couldn't talk to the dead."

"Actually, we self-respecting wizards talk to the dead for the sole purpose of putting their troubled souls to rest. So what can I do for you?" He was all right. He was just *playing* dead.

"What you can do for me is a couple of things. First of all there are some letters I am going to send to the Dakota. Now they are going to be from me to me. I want you to collect them and keep them out of sight, and I *distinctly* don't want you to read them. It's an experiment. A sort of time machine to tell me where I've been once I get to where I'm going. Very personal, so hands off, okay?"

"Okay."

"Good. Next thing is I want you to get me information about colors. I want to know what colors do in the occult. You know, like green is for harmony and healing?"

"Yeah, and red is for passion, and yellow consciousness. What do you need that for?"

"That, Charles, is my little secret, which I may let you in on or not. We dead are a mysterious lot, you know. I want as many colors and what they stand for, or do, or whatever, as you can find. Now, I don't want you to call me because I won't come to the phone. Everyone is out right now, wondering about dear ol' Dad, so it's okay, but I still don't have that much time to myself, so you'll have to wait till I call you. Understood?"

"Understood. Do you mind if I let Yoko in on your game?"

"Don't you dare! I'm having too much fun, and the only part that makes it fun is they don't know whether to take me seriously or not. Well, they weren't taking me seriously before I died. Perhaps they will now. Promise me you won't let on."

"I promise." I broke that promise on the next call from Yoko.

"All right then, if he isn't crazy he has to be terribly depressed. And we have to do something about that."

"Yeah, I'd say that when a man withdraws from his family and his work and everything else, you could say he's depressed; but just at the moment he seems to be enjoying being depressed, so I wouldn't complicate things further by helping him."

"I have to help him. My mother's coming and if he's going to act like this she's going to think he's crazy. John's never met Mother and she's a very strong woman, very Japanese. She doesn't think white people are as good as Orientals. In fact, she doesn't think Orientals are as good as Japanese. If John gives her any excuse, she can cut Sean off from everything, and that was really the whole point of this trip. Then we'll all have to come home and be miserable, and that isn't going to help the family, is it? We have to come up with something to help John before Mother gets here. First of all there's Dan."

"How is Dan going to help?"

"Well, I think one of the major reasons why John is so depressed is that he misses his own people, and Dan said he was going to be passing through this area about now. That way he and John could get together and go to whorehouses and drink, and John would feel as though he were at home and that would help him a lot."

"I don't think that's going to do it. I think what he needs is for you and the rest of your party to start paying attention to him and treating him like an adult."

"We do! We take care of him. We make sure he gets everything he needs. We keep him away from things that are bad for him. We pay a great deal of attention to him."

"That's how you pay attention to a child. Imagine how frustrated *you* would become if people kept stealing your cigarettes because they thought they were bad for you and controlled your diet and did to you the rest of the things you've been doing to John."

"Not *to* him! *For* him! John has always had people to take care of him, he needs that! If I didn't make sure that these things were done for him, he would ruin himself."

"Well, it's time you stopped doing everything for him because that loss of freedom is what the problem is."

"Charlie, that's not the problem. You have to look in the cards for that. You just think that that's what the problem is because John told you that it was, but don't you see the pattern? He told *you*, not me, his wife, not Nanny. He told you because you are the same race as John is and he's experiencing culture shock. He wants a white face around that he can look at once in a while; that's why I think Dan would be good."

"Okay, I'm looking at cards now and it certainly doesn't seem as though Dan is any kind of answer for you."

"Why?"

"Because being the same race is about the only thing John and Dan have in common. Dan is a natural promoter. As such, he's going to promote things, and the things he promotes are expensive. John is already worried about how much money is being spent, and well he should be. Dan is hardly going to put him at his ease."

"Do you think Dan could talk John into buying real estate here?"

"That isn't going to help anything."

"All right, how about Elliot?" (Elliot Mintz, whom Yoko referred to as "a friend of the family.")

"Elliot isn't much more like John than Dan is. These people are the ones *you* want to spend time with, not John. If you want to please him, then you are going to have to think of things he likes."

"That's what I *have* been doing! John likes Elliot. They used to go around to places together. Besides, I think it has to be

Elliot because there isn't anyone else except you, and I need you where you are.

"You know, Charlie, sometimes it's like I have two children. I have Sean and Nanny takes care of him, and that should leave me free, but it doesn't because there's John. And I have to be a nanny to him. Getting Elliot over here is like having to hire a baby-sitter. I suppose it can't be helped. I want you to call the travel agent and make all the arrangements for Elliot."

While the arrangements for Elliot were being made, John put in another visitation from his self-imposed land of the dead.

"Did you get the information on the colors for me?"

"Yep! Do you want it now?"

"Yeah, everyone's out shopping, so I should have plenty of time." I read off the list of information that he desired.

"Are you going to tell me now what this is for or are you still being mysterious?"

"I should make you read on it and tell me, but you get enough of that from Yoko. What I have in mind is a project, a creative project. Just because I can't write doesn't mean that I can't be creative in other ways. I studied art, you know. I was rather good at it, but then music came along and everything in my life stopped.

"My problem in those days was that I knew enough to know that I didn't know about art. I didn't know that much about music. So in music I just did whatever felt like a good idea, and if I liked the way it sounded I kept it in and if I didn't I threw it out. I was incredibly free and I loved that feeling. Like I'd hold my guitar up against the monitor and it would squeal and shriek with feedback. That didn't bother me. I thought, Hey, this is another sound I can make with this thing! It was interesting, so I used it. Like any new thing I went a bit too far, but there are groups now who are using it. Of course, they're using it as a spice and I used it for the main course, but that's okay. I was learning.

"That's why I think I never learned to play guitar the way

some others did. I didn't want to know what I couldn't do. But
in art they had already gotten to me, already taught me what
I couldn't do. That way, the only thing I could do was what
had already been done, and that's not art, it's imitation. Yoko
did stuff that hadn't been done. That's why it was art—it was
new, novel. Well, that's what I'm going to do now. I did everything in music. Now I'm going to take what I've learned and
apply it to visual art. Instead of canvas or paper I'm going to
make boxes with light. 'Paint Boxes' is what I'll call them.
They'll be big enough to get inside and the person inside will
be surrounded by color, or maybe colors. Well, you said that
the different colors created different moods and reactions, and
that makes sense, so boxes will affect people's moods. That
way I have employed color and form in a new way to create
an aesthetically pleasing piece that will affect the mood of the
viewer, which is art, right?"

"Right."

"It's a new beginning, Charles. I was mourning the loss of
my muse and then I started to feel that life wasn't worth living.
I knew that couldn't be right. There had to be something and
there is—a different kind of creation for me. But you got to
promise me that you won't tell Yoko about this because you
know how she is. She'll get all encouraging and reinforcing
telling me that it's beautiful and amazing and in no time I'll feel
that it isn't worth shit. I want to keep it to myself for a while
and let it build up force before I share it. So promise, okay?"

I promised that I would add this to the store of secrets that
I kept for him, and it was a promise that I kept.

While his plan to start a new career in art imbued John with
new energy, Yoko was busy with other problems.

"Charlie! You lost Elliot!"

"I what?"

"Lost him, that's what you did! You were responsible for all
his travel plans. I told you he was to have the best. That means

that there should have been someone there to hold his hand every step of the way. But you obviously didn't do that. Now he's lost and we don't know where to look for him."

"I had a car take him to the airport. The plane landed at Tokyo. I had a car take him to the train station and one to meet him at Kanazawa. What could go wrong?"

"Did you have someone put him on the train?"

"No." I was beginning to feel singularly stupid. "He had a ticket reserved, he was at the train station. How hard could it be? He goes to information, gives his name, gets directions, and that's that. Right?"

"We got a call from the chauffeur who was waiting at Kanazawa station. The last train from Tokyo is in and there was no Elliot. He's lost."

"Yoko, he's a grown man. Surely he's responsible enough to call you if he ran into any trouble?"

"If he were responsible he wouldn't have dropped everything he was doing to come to see us, would he? He'd be busy with his own life, wouldn't he?"

"You've got a point there."

"I don't have a point. I have a problem! I promised John that I would have Elliot here for him. He has been looking forward to that. Now you've lost him and that means when he gets here he will be in a terrible mood. We even moved back into the hotel here so John could feel a little freer. Now look what you've done. How am I going to handle this?"

On the spot for losing a friend, I cast the cards and read with care. "Well, it's a little difficult to say where he is, but I'm sure he will be with you soon."

"How soon? Come on, this is important."

"By morning."

"All right, I'm trusting you on this. I'm going to tell John that Elliot has been delayed and that we should just go to sleep and that everything will be all right by morning. Not that he will react to that. But I'm sure he can really hear me. You'd just better be right. I'll call you tomorrow." And she did.

"All right, he's here, but John isn't responding very well. Elliot is in a terrible mood. That's your fault, but I cheered him up because I told him that I would hold a mortgage on his house for him. His house is sliding down a hill or something and he needs money, so that's thirty thousand I had to spend, but he's feeling a little better because now he doesn't have to worry about his house. Now the problem is John. I keep telling Elliot to suggest to John that they go out somewhere, but John isn't having any part of it because we're in the city again. Not that Kanazawa is that large of a city, but it isn't the country and John is angry again, I think. I'm making plans for all of us to go back to Kaye's house. That means that we will have to find something to do with Kaye's children. It really is a mess."

Fortunately or not, nothing had to be done with the Japannieces because no sooner had the family arrived at the family home than Yoko heard from her mother. She was free. She was in Tokyo. If Yoko wanted to see her, then she would have to come to Tokyo. And so once more the little troupe, including Elliot and the still-noncommunicative John, packed up everything that hadn't been shipped home by air express and headed for Tokyo.

"Hello, Charlie? Now listen, this is not an emergency. It's not even important, so you don't have to make fun of me. It's just a little matter of John doing everything he can to humiliate me and insult me and ruin any chance Sean has to inherit anything from my family. That's all. And I want to know what to do about it."

"What's he doing?"

"He's being the sweetest, kindest, most solicitous ass he can be to my mother. We have to get out of here right away."

"You mean he's talking again?"

"Nonstop! He's fawning all over her. We're the ones who are

celebrities, and he's acting as if he were escorting a queen! He flatters her constantly. He has to stop at every little shop and ask her if she wants anything, and he's doing it in Japanese, so I can't stop him. He's playing right into her hands. He tells her stories! He stands whenever she comes into the room! She has to eat every meal with us! It's disgusting!"

"It sounds like he's trying to be nice to her."

"That's the whole point! I've told him what kind of person she is. I've told him how he should act. My mother thinks that white people are little more than albino monkeys. To my mother John is the monkey who married her daughter."

"Your sister married an Occidental. Mama-san must be used to it by now."

"Setsuko married a diplomat and that's important. John is only an entertainer. The only thing he has to his credit as far as she can see is money. A great deal of money. All summer she has been testing us, forcing us to spend more and more money, just to see if we had it. Now she shows up because it's clear to her that we do have it. So she wants it. And John is giving it to her."

"Is that bad?"

"That's terrible! You know how my mother will see that? She'll think that John is trying to buy her attention. She will think that John sees her as a very high and important person, and that is why he is showering her with gifts and attention. That only reinforces her opinion that she is important and I am not. I'm never going to be able to get anything out of her now! She'll just expect that she should get everything and we should get nothing. It's very unfair. John is just doing this to humiliate me."

"What do you want him to do?"

"He should be very polite but very distant with her. He should treat her like an old fool whom he patiently tolerates. I've told him this. That way she will feel that even if he is a monkey, he's a very important monkey. Now she just thinks I married a rich fool. She even says so. She tells me that he's very boorish with his wealth. She's even working on Masako. She told her that she was an excellent serving girl and that it is a pity that she has to work for a family like us. Mother has even offered Masako a position taking care of Kaye's children!"

"How do you know this?"

"Masako told me and she told me that Mother is laughing behind John's back in front of the other servants. She does that with me too. She says that I always was a strange girl and that she is not surprised that I married so many times and so badly. She calls me a silly girl."

"And do you remind her that you are married to John because you love him, while she married your father because her proud and ancient family needed money?"

"Charlie, things are bad enough! I can't say something like that to Mother! No, I have to get out of here and fast. That way I can sort of stand her up. I can say that we'd love to play at entertaining her, but we have important matters in the States that require our attention. We have many parties and affairs to attend. That will make her see that we are more important than she is. That is the only way you can cope with a person like my mother."

"So you want to come home?"

"Yes!"

We selected a day and Yoko winged her way home five days ahead of John, just as she had left five days after him at the beginning of the summer. She needed to take care of months of work in hours.

John, however, chose to stay in Tokyo with Mama-san.

"Does Yoko know where you are?" I asked him over the phone as we made last-minute plans for the return trip.

"No, I thought I would make it a little surprise for her. I

know how anxious she was to impress her mother, so I thought I'd really do a job on her. You know, I could have been kinder to Yoko on this trip, but as per usual I thought selfishly and just cut myself off from everyone and everything. It had some good effects because it led me to some decisions about myself that have been long overdue. I'm in a creative mood again and that has certainly been worthwhile. So what if it isn't music? If I'm an artist I can work in more than one medium. That has been the most important thing that has happened to me in years, since Sean actually. I'm a new man. I can pay my family back now for what I put them through. I've already started with Mama-san."

"And just how did you do that, John?" Considering Yoko's opinions, I almost dreaded the answer.

"Well, I took her around, didn't I? Showed her the sights. I know Yoko has troubles with her. Who doesn't have troubles with their parents? You should see the old lady. She's totally gray—gray hair, gray skin, gray clothes. I don't think she's smiled for fifty years. No wonder she intimidates Yoko. But I didn't let that stop me. I got real friendly with her, even hugged her once or twice. That really threw her. But there was a lot of tension in the air and I had been the cause of a lot of that tension, you know. I thought it was my duty to be nice. So these last few days we've been painting the town. And believe me it hasn't been easy. The lady is very stiff. But I figured that I owed it to Yoko to cement family relations a little bit. Yoko had to go through it with Aunt Mimi and this was my turn. Besides, after all that's happened this summer I didn't want to do anything that would humiliate Yoko."

And he meant it.

· 11 ·

TURNING OVER
A NEW LENNON

John returned from his trip to Japan in high spirits. He felt that he had rediscovered parts of himself he'd thought lost, and he was determined that nothing was going to take these refound elements of his personality away again. He related his new view of himself to me as we sat in the kitchen late one afternoon in mid-October of 1977.

"When I was in Japan," John began, "I excluded *all* the parts of me. I'd lie in bed all day, not talk, not eat, just withdraw. And a funny thing happened. I began to see all these different parts of me. I felt like a hollow temple filled with many spirits, each one passing through me, each inhabiting me for a little time and then leaving to be replaced by another. I realized then what the problem is that I have to solve. I have to be *all* of those people. But I can't be all those people all the time. And in the past whenever I became one of them, I became that thing, that person, so totally that I forgot the others. I don't know how to stop. I have no device, no magic, to keep an easy flow from one part of my personality to another. I need that because, Charles, the secret, *'the* secret' is *changing.*

"So now I walk about very carefully. I can't allow myself to get too attached to anything just yet because my atrophied personality can too easily snap back into one of my character roles and freeze me there till someone comes to save me. I have to keep reminding myself to do things differently, whatever they are, change them. Even a change from bad to worse is better than a good that doesn't change. At least, that's for right now while I limber up my personality. If I can help it nothing is going to trap me into a rigid role again. I intend to remain unchangeably changing, and nothing is going to change that."

The fates must have been listening to John because they arranged a series of tests for his new personality. The first of these was the business that he had hoped to ignore.

The tremendous expense of the Japanese trip had left the Lennons cash short. Yoko thought that the money spent on traveling could be written off on their taxes, but the accountant told her that was not possible. This meant that the Lennons were facing a heavy tax burden that could only be deflected by a serious investment into tax shelter programs. But that required cash, which they did not have. On the other hand, if they did not make such an investment, the amount owed to the government, which would have to be paid in April, would be overwhelming.

To make matters worse, it was clear that the Apples, or at least some of them, were aware of the Lennons' situation. Yoko feared that they might use this knowledge to block the release of the annual salaries by deadlocking the vote approving the minutes of the previous year's meetings. She knew that if the other Apples needed the money less than she did, they could effectively force her to agree to whatever they wanted. Her fears were well founded because that is exactly what they did.

In order to lessen the tax burden and liberate some of their cash reserve, Yoko concocted a series of plans. These extended from endorsing products and making commercials to giving her clothes to the Salvation Army. In the readings we did, these ideas did not look all that successful. But the cards suggested other solutions:

First there was the Lennons' hand-painted Rolls-Royce, which had been a gift from painter Peter Max. This was donated to the Smithsonian in Washington, D.C. Then there were elements of the Japanese trip that, despite the accountant's initial rejection, could in fact be used as deductions, particularly those that related to Yoko's research on the family estate and health. In addition to such careful tax planning, spending was cut back sharply.

Unfortunately, even under this economic pressure Yoko rejected all my suggestions that she sell some of the Egyptian art she had been collecting. Instead, she kept looking for an investment she could make with the limited dollars left at her disposal that would have both great tax advantages and the ability to generate a quick profit.

As we searched for this investment John took the economic restrictions lightly. By early November of 1977 he was making little speeches about the disadvantages of money.

"It just doesn't matter, Charles," he explained over the phone. I was trying to convince him of the seriousness of the situation, but John was having none of it. "The greatest asset I have is myself and the second greatest is my family, and possibly you're the third, but don't try to cash yourself in. Money doesn't matter, it never did. Money is just another trap.

"I was caught in that trap once. I was rich and I had to act rich, which I did. I *acted* the role. Everyone came to me for everything because of the money. I could say anything and do anything because they wanted the money. Money has remarkable powers, you know. It makes you sexy and intelligent and talented in a flash, poof! And it's a lie. If we have to sell some things, sell 'em. If we can't buy things for a while or forever, we won't. I can never really be poor again because poor was never having known what it was to be wealthy. Worse, it was the hopeless feeling that I never *would* know. So I said to myself that it didn't really matter. But I knew that it did matter to me because I hated people who had money. I thought they were stupid and even evil. Maybe that's why I've let Yoko handle things and let her spend all she wants. Maybe I thought that that way I could get rid of all that evil ol' money and the vampires it attracted. Whatever my reasoning, it really doesn't matter. I'm a multimillionaire who eats rice and fish, lives in two of his ten rooms, and enjoys the simplest things in life."

Nothing seemed to be able to faze John during the fall and winter of 1977. As financial pressures mounted, they soon began to create family tensions as well, but the usually volatile John was above it all. The only news he was willing to listen to was good news, and with one exception there was precious little of that.

The exception was the news that Yoko, through card readings, had hit upon a possible solution to the financial crunch. It involved spending money, but spending it to great advantage. The solution was for the Lennons to become farmers.

Ol' McLennon's farms, as we called them, had a fairly complex ancestry. In her search for appropriate investments, Yoko had asked for ideas and advice from Dan G., who had myriad contacts and the proved ability (in Yoko's opinion) to get the "very, very best" of anything. Yoko told Dan she was looking for tax shelters and Dan, knowing nothing about them, recommended his accountant.

His accountant, in turn, recommended cows. He sold cows, prize Holstein-Friesian breeding cattle. I recommended farms;

he sold them, too. And so, as 1977 drew to a close and the deadline of the end of the tax year approached, the Lennons decided to buy both cows *and* farms—a herd of prize Holstein-Friesian and four farms in the beautiful dairy land of Delaware County.

Since the Lennons represented a very large account, the accountant was willing to make concessions, the most important of which was to state in the contract that the Lennon farms were to be maintained as organic. Furthermore, they let *us* define what "organic" meant, since there isn't a legal definition for the word yet. By getting that agreement we were able to construct a profit-making program that would make a farming investment doubly worthwhile.

For example, by converting four farms totaling some two thousand acres to organic land, the Lennons would own the largest organic farm in the country, and it would be within easy trucking distance of New York, which is a major market for health foods. That meant that any produce we could hot-house and deliver during the off-season would undersell produce from Florida and the West Coast because we wouldn't have to pay twenty-one cents a pound air freight. Next, all four farms were rich in natural springs, and we could package and transport natural spring water for approximately thirty-four cents a gallon and sell it for over a dollar. Third, one of the farms was a functioning dairy farm. The milk it produced was being transported to New Jersey where it was being processed for sale in New York. But New York City was a hot market for *raw* milk. So we could package it as raw milk, eliminate the processing middleman, and sell it in New York at three times the price. Meanwhile, the nonprizewinning bull calves from the herd, which were being slaughtered and sold as veal, could be gelded and raised as organic beef.

The three defunct farms could be used as worm farms, which were doing rather well in those days, but even if they were merely plowed under for the next five years, that would represent "farm development" for tax purposes and the expenditures involved would be tax deductible, two for one. The expenditures would be low in any case because local agriculture schools had expressed interest in donating labor from their student bodies for the opportunity of having work-study programs.

Then there were the tax advantages provided for using alternate forms of energy, and the possibilities we had there for using hydroelectric, solar, and geothermal energy were excellent. And if all that failed, the fact that all four farms were strategically positioned with regard to major thoroughfares or bodies of water would steadily increase their real estate value, either from legalized gambling in the Catskills or simple population expansion. There was more to it than that, but that's the general idea.

Yoko, suitably impressed with this roster of lucre, forged ahead with negotiations. The final terms were agreed upon in early December of 1977. All that was lacking was John's approval, which he was hesitant to give, as it represented involvement in business.

"Farms! What the fuck do I know about farms?" he ranted as he paced the kitchen. "What are they good for? Milk and cheese! All they do is produce mucus! What do I need that for?"

I knew that it would be pointless to promote the business advantages of such an investment, so I tried another approach.

"Well, you're always saying that you need a little bit of green to get away to once in a while. Two thousand acres is quite a little bit of green."

"You aren't going to try to tell me that you cooked up this whole scheme just for me, are you? I know you, Charles, and I know it's the money angle that interests you. I've told you how I feel about the money thing. Let the government have it.

I don't need an investment, as you call it, that is going to mean more work for Yoko and more business for me."

"You surprise me. You're always so down on the military, but now you seem so anxious to support them."

"What do you mean? How do I support them?"

"Taxes. For every dollar you pay in taxes at least forty cents goes to defense. You give the government a dollar and they'll buy two bullets. So all the time you were telling the world that you were into peace, you were supplying the armies of the world with millions of rounds of ammunition. If that's what you support, fine, but if it's not, then think about the other things those dollars can do!"

That seemed to make the point with him. From there it wasn't difficult to get John at least to look at the properties in question. And once he actually saw it, the land sold itself.

John told me later that the Delaware County countryside reminded him of Canada. He could picture himself "skidooing" down the hills and playing with Sean in the snow. In the summers it would be his retreat where he could escape from the city and run around naked if he wished.

But that was not to be. From the beginning, the Lennons failed to protect their privacy. When they originally went to view the farms they traveled in two long black limos. (The second car was for Sean and his nanny so that Sean's crying would not disturb John.) That naturally attracted the attention of the locals. When the Lennons finally closed the deal with the farms, they failed to take my advice and use a fiduciary and instead signed their own names to the contract. That meant that anyone going to the county clerk's office would know how much land the Lennons had purchased and where. The manager of the farms, apparently seeking publicity, leaked the story of the buy to the press. That presented both a security problem and a vandalism liability.

The press leak, a rarity in the usually tight-lipped Lennon

operations, bothered Yoko greatly. It was the harbinger of difficulties yet to come, which would eventually force the Lennons to abandon their plans for using the farms as a personal resort. But the reports in the papers did not bother John. His spirits remained persistently buoyant.

Then, as the holidays of 1977 came, John faced a further challenge from the fates. This time the test came in a far more personal form: pure terror. I first heard of the situation during a midmorning phone call from John.

"Charles, I'm not sure we should be telling you this because we were in fact instructed not to tell anyone. However, you are the advisor and I need advice."

"Shoot."

"Your expression is singularly ill chosen because that is exactly what we are talking about. Shooting or kidnapping or worse."

"You want to explain that?"

"We, or should I say Yoko, got a call. It was from a . . . I really don't know what to call him . . . a crank . . . a crazy . . . he called himself a terrorist. He wants money and he wants it fast. The joke is that at the moment I don't have it to give him because he wants two hundred thousand dollars and I would have to do some rather fast selling to get it by the time he calls tonight."

"What did this person say?"

"Yoko spoke to him, I didn't. She's the one who should be telling you this and I suppose that she will in her own sweet time. She told the nanny first, of course, because she could tell her in Japanese and if the place were bugged then she couldn't be understood. I tell you that so you will understand the tension that has been in this household for the last several hours. Yoko is in the bedroom right now. She is too upset to talk about it. She also feels that it is dangerous to talk about it because we might be being watched or bugged.

"Anyway, she got a call last night at about ten or a little after and the voice asks for her and she does her usual Japanese accent routine and says, 'So sorry, they not here.' But the guy says he knows that it's her, and that really scares the shit out of her. He tells her to shut up and listen. He apparently had a Spanish accent, but that's only what Yoko thought and she was frightened and she really doesn't have that good an ear for accents. Anyway he says, 'We want two hundred thousand dollars or we will do something terrible to your family,' and she says, 'Who is this? Who is it on the phone please?' and he says, 'We are a group of professional terrorists. Do not call the police or the FBI. We will know if you do. Many famous people have already been contacted by our group and paid the money. The police can only protect you for so long, a week, two weeks, maybe a month, then they go away. We will watch and we will wait and we can wait for a year or two years. Then we will be back. We will kill you. Maybe we could kidnap your son. This we must do so that others will pay. We want two hundred thousand dollars. This is not a lot of money for you very rich people. We will call you tomorrow.'

"And that was it. I was in the bedroom and I didn't have any idea of what had happened. She said that she just stood there awhile in the kitchen and finally had to tell someone, so she told Masako. Then she came in to see me and one look told me something had happened. My first thought was oh God, the baby. She told me the story and I'm telling you. I want to know if it is a crank or not."

"Call the police and the FBI. If they mentioned the FBI maybe they have a reason to be afraid of them, previous pattern, arrests, that sort of thing."

"Charles, don't play Kojak with me. This program is called 'This Is Your Life,' so read those cards which you always do and tell me if this is a fake or are we in trouble."

There was no way around the interpretation of the cards in the spread.

"John, you're in trouble."

"Christ! I hoped it was a stupid prank. We get them, you know. The last remnants of the Charles Manson cult send us letters with blood on them sometimes."

"I know, I've heard."

"Sometimes I wait for 'it.' That revolutionary that we gave money to and then cut him off, Michael X. After he was executed, I thought, Oh, my God, here it comes, they'll get me for this. I was checking the halls about sixty times a day during some of those lawsuits because Yoko had me convinced that there were hitmen on their way to kill us. The logic being that a contract on us would have been cheaper than a settlement. But now it's really happening. I have to think about this. I really have to think about what I'm going to do."

"Call the cops!"

"Yoko isn't all that keen on that idea and neither am I. Somehow calling the police makes it all that much more real, that much closer."

"I'm your advisor, here's my advice: Call the police, and to make it even easier for you, if you don't, I will."

"You wouldn't . . . you really would, wouldn't you?"

"You bet! You call the cops and the FBI and then call the Pinkertons or some other agency and you get yourself a private cop in your apartment and you *listen* to what he tells you."

John called the police and the FBI and several other organizations he thought would be helpful. There was a tap put on their phones and careful instructions to keep the caller talking as long as possible. A curious group of short-haired Con Ed workers stationed themselves outside the Dakota and watched the seventh floor with unveiled intensity. The second call came.

By this time, however, John had his reactions well in hand.

Taking safety measures was one thing, but giving in to fear was quite another as he told me over the phone the following evening.

"Well, they can't be very good terrorists, I'll tell you that." John's voice held a note of triumph. "This guy didn't even mention that there is a small army hanging around outside, and if I can spot them, one would think that any self-respecting terrorist would."

"What did he say?"

"More of the same, threats and threats and leave the money in a package at the desk and their agent will pick it up and don't try to have him followed because he is only a flunky, and the real bad guys will come back and get us. The cops said give 'em newspaper, which sounds like something out of a TV rerun, and I told 'em they were the cops and they could do whatever they thought was best with my blessing. You see, I figured out what I am going to do."

"Careful. What are you planning?"

"These people are terrorists, right? Their job is to terrorize people. Well, they are doing a great job because I'm terrified and so is my family. What I would really like to do is kick the sons of bitches' teeth down their throats, but I can't do that because I don't know who and where. That's the first rule of a terrorist. Make the victim feel impotent and then he will feel vulnerable and helpless and do what he's told. Well, I am vulnerable and helpless, but I'm still not going to do what they tell me because that's the only way I have to resist, and this is the sort of thing that one ought to resist.

"What can they do to me, Charles? They can kill me, scare me, maim or brutalize my family. I do love my family more than money and more than I have words to tell. But they aren't the only ones who can do that to me. I thought I'd been fuckin' shot a thousand years ago when some religious fanatic threw firecrackers on the stage at a show. If you want to be the center of attention, then you also have to accept the responsibility of being a target. If I let these bastards do this to me, I'll be living not only in a goldfish bowl but in a cage as well, and that is *not* for me! I could get killed anytime. I don't like to say it, I don't like to think it, but that's what is real.

"So I've made up my mind. I will do the things you said. We'll get private security because that's the thing, and someone will get out of cars first and walk into rooms first because that makes sense. What I don't need is some voice from the shadows with a gun. But I am not going to give up my freedom. It's not bravery, Charles. If I live in a cage then I'm already dead. I will live my life till it ends. No one will be able to take that away. And I'm not going to pay some cowardly bastard who gets his jollies scaring my wife not to kill us.

"I should thank this terrorist really. He's given me an excellent lesson in why I really ought to live my life one day at a time and each day as the last because it just might be. Every celebrity has to deal with that.

"Now just to set your security-conscious soul at rest, Charles, I'm going to let you know that I'm getting out of town for a while. We're going down to Florida for the Christmas holidays and having Julian over and having a try at being a family. Do I surprise you?"

"Constantly, John. That's one of the things that makes the job interesting. But thank your terrorist for two things. The second is he made you conscious of security."

The Lennons prepared for their trip while police prowled the Dakota. There was a package of newspaper left. There was a man followed. The police lost the suspect, but the calls indicated that the terrorists didn't know he was followed. They offered another chance but never showed up for the package. Nor did they call again.

It was a confident John and a shattered Yoko who headed south to meet Julian. It was an outraged John who returned.

"Did I ask so much? I wanted to be myself. I was challenged to jump into the money-earner role, the savior role, and the coward role, but I resisted. I thought I had it. I thought that I could preserve myself from becoming a stereotype of me. But the greatest test is the one I failed. I failed family, Charles."

They had been home only hours, and with January outside the window, John stormed about in summer clothes.

"I've given them enough, don't you think? I could have, should have, given more of myself to Julian, but I'm trying to correct that. Then here's this fuckin' kid, my eldest, and he's looking at me all wonder and innocence and I'm trying to let down the fuckin' wall to let my son in. I tell him, 'This Christmas is going to be different. This Christmas we are going to give each other to each other for gifts. There's been enough of the material.' Now Christ, the kid is old enough to understand that. And in fact he says he understands, and maybe he did and all too well.

"Some family I'm trying to bring together. Yoko thinks Julian is trying to spy for his mother. Sean is toddling around in a daze because all the signals he's being sent are fucked up. Nanny is scared that there is an assassin behind every palm, and Julian, flesh of my flesh, bats his eyes at me and explains that it's real difficult to have such a famous father and that the only way he has to make friends is to share some of that father glory with them. He informs me that the only proof he has of my love is the material loot he can carry back, and that he doesn't even get to keep that much of it because he has to share it as payment to these friends of his. He has the nerve to ask me if the giving of our selves will preclude any other presents and then gooses my guilt god with the information that he has already secured a present for me. To top it all off he asks me if what I'm doing is an act. An act? I'm trying to be genuinely myself for the first time since I was a kid and nobody wants me! I can't fuckin' believe it! I feel pleased, honored, fulfilled, and privileged because I am finally being myself for a change, and nobody wants me!

"Well, I gave them what they wanted. I gave 'em a megamaterial gift gala and I hope it brings them great pleasure. Julian, Yoko, both seemed much relieved that I went back to being my other, older, lesser self. And if that's what they want, they can have it till the money runs out or I do with a Merry Christmas and a Happy Fuckin' New Year on top."

He tore out of the kitchen and down the hall into the bedroom. He stayed there for fifteen months.

· 12 ·

BED-IN
LOCK-OUT

When John returned in January 1978 from his emotionally shattering confrontation with his son Julian in Florida, he promptly immured himself in the bedroom. He emerged only unwillingly on rare occasions. He seemed to have lost all interest in the world around him.

Yoko struggled valiantly against John's lethargy. She filled her days with energetic activity both to keep herself distracted from John's mood and to stay out of his way. It was, she said, her hope that if given enough time and space, John would eventually snap himself out of his doldrums. Despite her efforts, the atmosphere of John's depression had its effect on her. He had undermined her confidence, and as 1978 began, so did a series of business crises that Yoko was hard pressed to confront.

The first of these was Apple. A stalemate among the Apples had prevented the release of annual salaries in January, and the delayed funds only added to the tension in the household. Then there was trouble with the farms.

As a security measure, I had recommended that two friends of mine take up residence on one of the farms as caretakers, both to keep an eye on things and to begin to set into motion the many plans we had developed to make best use of the investment. The night before they arrived, early in April, a fire on one of the farms destroyed a barn, several outbuildings, and severely damaged the main house. Yoko took this event to be an omen of doom. Instead of investigating the cause of the fire and taking further security measures, she thought it wisest to withdraw her interest. The new company she had formed, Rainbow Milk, which was intended to handle the raw milk portion of the farms project, was left idle. Reports that the Lennons' land was being used by someone without the Lennons' permission went unheeded, as did communiqués from the caretakers that there were trees being stolen from the Lennons' land.

Yoko concluded that the problems were due to the fact that north was a bad direction for the family, and resolved to do nothing about the issue until 1979. She claimed that it was a bad direction for me as well, and after I made one visit to the farms to investigate the damage caused by the fire, she expressly forbade me to go there again. Thereafter all management was handled at arm's length.

I hoped that I would be able to persuade John to take some interest and action in the farms, but it was impossible. In late April I paid him a rare visit in his bedroom hideaway. The blinds were closed and the only light came from the television screen.

"John, I want to know how you feel about the farms." He lay on his side of the bed with one arm behind his head, glasses off, studying the television, his thumb pressing steadily on the remote control so that the channels changed continuously, about twice a second. The sound was turned off.

"I don't feel anything. Not about the farms, not about you, not about Yoko, Sean, or anything else. Yoko handles business and the farms are business; that means she's handling them. Whatever she chooses to do is her problem, not mine. Does that answer your question?"

"Not really. I need to know how much you know about what has happened and how you feel about that—"

"Come on, Charles, you're a great guy and a great advisor, but a great pain in my ass at the moment. If you want my company, you can sit here and not watch TV with me, and if not, you can get out. But you are not allowed to discuss anything whatsoever reasonable or rational. Here, smoke some dope and get silly. Whatever the problem is it will either take care of itself or not. Either way it is nothing to become concerned about. So you just sit back and feel privileged that you are being granted one of my longer interviews with anyone, including the wife, and shut your logical mercenary mouth so I can hear the shows."

"But the sound is off!"

"A brilliant observation. Try hearing with your eyes. And unless you can talk some nonsense, get out. King John is tired."

"King John has apparently been tired for months now."

"And so he shall remain for months more if he chooses. King John doesn't have to do anything. I have a reputation out there that does things for me. I go out. I see shows. I molest young ladies. All this is managed by my reputation.

"Here, look at that." His eye caught a *Beatlemania* commercial on the screen. "Have you seen that show? No? You should. I did. There I was in the audience, watching me onstage. It wasn't like the old days, of course. You can hear what these guys are doing, which you never could at our concerts because of all the screaming. They've made a copy that is superior to the original. The world doesn't need me. It has clones that do a better job. I don't even have to be alive. Isn't that convenient?"

"I think it's foolish, and worse, I think that it's dangerous."

"Who asked you?"

"You did and—"

"I retract the question. Go advise Yoko. She's the one with the power now."

"Why? Because you're playing dead again?" I hoped to make him angry enough to overcome at least some of his lethargy.

"No, I'm not playing anything. You want to know about the farms? Well, I'll tell you. Everything I ever wanted has gone up in smoke one way or another. Why should the farms be any different? I say let the smoke win.

"You are the one with the ambition for the farms. Go tell Yoko that I give them to you, a royal boon. And she can have the tax advantages, or whatever they are. I couldn't care less about what happens to them or you or Yoko or anything or anyone else. I did care, and a fat lot of fuckin' good it did me. Now you can get out of here, I'm sick of looking at you. You can do whatever with the farms or any other part of the business just so long as you leave me out of it. Just get out."

And I did.

In contrast to her policy of calculated inaction concerning the farms, Yoko filled her days with other interests. Paramount among these was ancient Egyptian art. The recent money scare with Apple had made her determined to protect the family's finances with investments in antiquities, which she was sure would double in value in the immediate future. These artifacts had the advantage also of containing what she believed to be great occult power, which she felt was necessary for the family's well-being.

For more than a year Yoko had been collecting pieces from the Twenty-sixth Dynasty. Dan G. acted as her agent, and, through readings, Yoko and I structured the deals and instructed Dan how to make the most advantageous purchases.

With the exception of what Yoko referred to as "decorator pieces," which were placed in the White Room, and a few more personal totems in the bedroom, most of the collection was placed in what was now called the Pyramid Room. This room, which was situated between the White Room and the Black Room directly across from the apartment's main entrance, received its name from a copper-tubing pyramid in the center of the floor. The Lennons' "money tree," one of the prizes brought back from Cartagena, was placed inside the pyramid with the hope that the occult power of the structure would help make it grow. Originally the room had been mostly bare, but now the various art treasures filled it practically to the bursting point. The latest acquisition to arrive in late spring of 1978 was an unopened mummy case.

As Dan had informed Yoko that the mummy was that of a "woman from the East," Yoko took it to mean that these were the remains of one of her own previous incarnations. This belief made negotiations difficult, as she feared that too much haggling might cause her to lose this treasure and the magic that she believed it held.

After more than a month of dickering back and forth, the deal was finally closed, and then we had to wait for transport from the Swiss vault where the mummy was kept. But after all the waiting and effort and more than half a million dollars of expense, Yoko was far from pleased with results.

"There," Yoko pointed to the mummy case angrily. It was in early May, a few days after the prize had arrived. "Look at it!"

It was an order I cheerfully obeyed. It had been a long wait to see this prize. The sarcophagus was about four and a half feet long with semiprecious stones spotting its gold-leaf surface. The design showed a strong Persian influence.

"Is there something specific I should be looking for?"

"Yes, the face! Look at that face! If that's what the woman inside looked like, then I don't think that it could be me."

"Why not?"

"Because she's not Japanese."

"No one ever said that she was, Yoko. She was 'from the East,' and from the look of it, she was Persian."

"She doesn't look that rich either."

"She was supposed to be a merchant's wife, not the queen of Egypt."

"So you're saying that I was wrong about this being one of my previous incarnations, and that probably amuses you, doesn't it? I've spent a lot of money on this and I wanted the power that it was supposed to hold. I think that I've wasted my money."

"Fortunately, it's worth more in dollars than you paid for it even if it isn't worth it to you."

"It's not to me. What am I supposed to do with this?"

What she had done thus far was have the coffin placed on sawhorses off to one side of the Pyramid Room.

"Well, the first thing I'd do is get it insured. And then I would have some professionals get it off those sawhorses and into a plexiglass case with temperature and moisture control."

"Dan already insured it."

"Only for the time it was being transported. The way you have it set up you're asking for an accident."

"It has survived all this time. What could happen to it now?"

"That's what you said about the wooden ibis before the maid broke the beak off dusting it."

"Well, I don't want it in a case. I think that we should open it and see if there are gold and jewels inside. It's not as heavy as Dan said, but still there might be something."

"It's worth more if you don't open it."

"Well, I don't think it can be worth much the way it is now." She marched around the coffin contemptuously, dodging the other little antiquities that cluttered the room. "I don't think that we got a very good deal. It makes me look so ugly. Look at that face!"

"If you don't like it we could always sell it." I was hopeful that at last we could begin to capitalize on the collection.

"No, that's no good. I told John that I had to have it because it was me, and now I'm stuck with it. I'll tell you one thing. This is the last deal we do with Dan. I don't think he's a friend at all."

Of course, it wasn't the last deal that she made with Dan. For one thing, Dan had successfully weathered a year and a half with Yoko, and that made him practically family. Another reason for her continued dealings was that Dan could always get her what she wanted. Every time she decided that she was going to break her ties with him, he would show up with the rumor of yet another prize.

Our conversation regarding the mummy led to a subsequent reading in the kitchen. The cards could not confirm her belief that it was actually one of her previous incarnations nor guarantee that she would be able to absorb the magic she was sure the treasure held. They were, however, very positive about Dan's promise that the coffin would double in value in a few short years. As it turned out, in the fall of 1979, Citibank announced that it was starting a program of investment in Egyptian antiquities, thus forcing up the value of the Lennons' Egyptian collection.

Beneath Yoko's dissatisfaction with the mummy's appearance and its projected future value was her concern about John's reaction to the large amount of money involved. But she need not have worried on that score. John expressed no interest in money or anything else. Even the family's second trip to

Japan in the summer of 1978 failed to rouse him from his lethargy.

This second trip proved even more disastrous than the one a year earlier. John acted the recluse in Japanese hotel rooms just as he had in the Dakota, and spent all his time watching TV. Even the arrival of Yoko's mother on the scene failed to revive him. Yoko finally cut the trip short and returned to New York. On their return John retreated once more to his bedroom redoubt.

As in the previous year, Yoko returned to a mountain of paper work, but at least a downstairs office had finally been completed, and business matters were no longer conducted in the apartment. Yoko worked in "Studio One" on the first floor of the Dakota from early morning until as late as possible in the evening, more to avoid the deadeningly still aura that John had created around himself than to complete any of the numerous unattended projects. A series of new nannies replaced Masako, who had been left in Japan.

Both to maintain their public image and to try to distract John from his mood, Yoko gave Sean and him a lavish birthday celebration on October 9, 1978, at New York's well-known Tavern on the Green. At the party John went through all the motions, smiled in all the right places, and made all the expected noises. But afterward, he retreated once more to the bedroom and the TV set.

Feeling that Sean would be better off out of such a stressful environment, Yoko enrolled him in a preschool. John, who at the height of his father phase had claimed that he would never let the boy be educated by anyone other than himself, made no protest.

"If he wants to go, there is no reason why he shouldn't," he said during one of my now infrequent visits to his bedroom. He was lying on his side of the bed, seeming immobile. "It's probably the best thing for him, really. There's nothing for him to do here, and I think he's just as glad to be as far away from me as possible."

"I think that's an exaggeration. And I think you're wrong in thinking that he wants to go. He's being sent. It's as simple as that."

"Well, it's clear that he isn't comfortable around here. Have you seen the way he acts? Always so proper, a regular little gentleman. He walks around here on eggs all the time. It's strange to think that a son of mine would act like that, but there's a reason: fear. He's afraid of me, and probably with good reason. He can feel that there's something strange going on, so he is simply polite. He speaks when spoken to. He plays very quietly, and he leaves the room as quickly as he can when I come in because he can sense that there's something wrong with Daddy and he doesn't want to get hurt. I would say that shows a very healthy sense of self-preservation, but it's not a very healthy situation to live in. So school is an answer. Not a great answer, but a better alternative than staying here and being told by Nanny not to bother Daddy and being told by Mommie that Mommie is too busy."

"There are other alternatives . . ."

"Good! Go discuss them with Yoko. I don't want to hear about them. I tried the father bit and blew it. I hated the role, and then I started hating the kid because I thought that he was the one who forced me into it. Then I tried to make it up to him with presents, presents, presents, but those were really *my* offerings to the guilt god, not presents to Sean. Do us both a favor and let him get away from me."

"Perhaps you're misreading Sean's reactions."

"No, I'm not. He's reacting the way he is because he desperately wants to please. And he wants to please so much because he wants love. *I* should know about *that* one! The way he's trying to please is by being good all the time. Now, if he's trying so hard to be good, it's got to be because he thinks he

isn't. And the only way he could have come to believe that is
by having been hurt—punished and not known why. Well,
there is no 'why,' but he doesn't know that. 'Why' is because
his daddy is crazy. He's scared, Charles. I'd be scared too if I
had to live with me! I don't blame him a bit."

"Why don't you let him get to know you a little better? Then
even if he does have a crazy daddy, at least he'll know it. And
you really don't have anything better to do."

"I go through stages when I try that. Like last spring, I got
a tape of *Yellow Submarine* and we watched that together. I'd
point and say, 'That's Daddy, that's Daddy,' but I don't think
he really understood. He just sat there politely. Then I realized
that we were watching *Yellow Submarine* every day for I don't
know how many days, and all he was doing was being too
polite to say anything. He doesn't really want me around. He's
more comfortable when I'm not there. He even told me so."

"When?"

"Last spring when we were watching all that TV. Remember
when our cat Alice fell out the window? Right after that, he
asked me where she was. Well, I didn't know how to answer
him, but I knew that it was one of those questions that a kid
eventually asks and that any answer is better than no answer.
So rather than run off to consult Dr. Spock or Yoko or you, I
said what I thought would be as close to the truth as possible
without being too scary. I said, 'Alice went out the window and
the window is very high up and she fell a very long way. She
had to go away.' And he says, 'Where'd she go?' I tried to make
it as nice as possible so I said, 'She went to the Land of Death.
That's what happens when someone falls a very long way.
They go to the Land of Death and it's a place they never come
back from.' Then I told him that he shouldn't go too near the
window because I didn't want that to happen to him because
I'd never be able to see him anymore. I was probably screwing
him up royally, but it was the best I could do. So then he says

to me, 'If you went out the window, would you go away and not come back?' And I said, 'That's right,' thinking that he's getting the concept. Well, he got it all right. He thinks for a minute and then says, 'Why don't you go out the window, Daddy?' "

"Don't you think it's just possible that he was taking a little slap at Daddy to see what sort of reaction he might get?"

"I suppose tarot cards make you an expert on children too?"

"No, but a degree in art education and courses in child psychology don't hurt."

"Oh, yes, I forgot. Charles has done everything, hasn't he? Well, whatever they teach in child psychology is bullshit. And it doesn't take a psychic to figure out that the kid is telling me that he wants me to go away. And I repeat, I don't blame him."

He turned away and flipped on the TV. The interview was over.

As the winter of 1978/1979 wore on, a slow panic began to creep over Yoko. The source of this fear was John. She filled her days with manic activity as though she were afraid that if she were to stop or even slow down, the same debilitating depression that had paralyzed John would ensnare her as well. At Apple meetings her once-adroit ability to outmaneuver the other Apples evaporated. Instead, she began agreeing to everything the others wanted in the wan hope of winning their respect and approval. She feared any negative reports finding their way to John and depriving her of her only emotional stronghold by undermining her control of the business.

All through this time, in countless card readings, John was the central theme of her questions.

"I want to know what I have to be careful of with him this week."

"You've already asked me that."

"I'm sorry. Would you read on it again, please? I've forgotten what you said."

"I said that if you fear any sudden change in his behavior, then you have nothing to be concerned about. What I suggest you be concerned with is that John has entered an almost catatonic depression, and the longer he stays that way, the harder it's going to be for him to pull himself out of it."

"That's right, I remember now. But you don't understand. There's really nothing I can do. I don't want him to be like this, but I've run out of ideas. He just ignores everything I do to try and cheer him up. What else can I do?"

"I think you should get some outside help. This has been going on for more than a year. Get him a doctor."

"No, John would never agree to that. He's tried all the therapies and he thinks they're all phony. I suggested it to him the last time you told me that and he said no."

"Well, you might try talking to a doctor yourself without his permission and seeing what he says. It wouldn't be such a bad idea if you got a little help yourself."

"Why? I don't have the problem . . . do I?"

"John has the problem and you are living with him, and that is taking its toll. You might get some ideas that would be useful for John and get a clearer perception on where you're at in all this."

"I can't. It just wouldn't work. What if the doctor wanted John committed or something? I couldn't risk that. They couldn't give him better care than he gets right here. I make sure he gets everything he asks for—drink, cigarettes, grass, anything. He wouldn't get that in a hospital. They would take all those things away like I used to, and you know what that did. And if he started playing dead in a hospital they would never let him out!"

"Aren't you jumping ahead just a little? I suggested that you talk to a professional and you are already envisioning John as committed."

"Charlie, he sleeps till eleven in the morning and then he has breakfast. By two he has to have a nap. I think he's asleep till

I go upstairs about ten, but he's asleep again before midnight. All the time he's awake he chain-smokes joints. I've tried staying with him or suggesting that we go shopping or out to the country, but he always says that all he wants to do is be left alone. He says he's tired, tired of everything. There has to be something I can do. He's never been like this before and I know it can't be good. We used to be able to play off each other. We've been cruel and we've been loving, but we always supported each other with our own brand of insanity. Now it's like he isn't there at all. It doesn't matter what I do because he doesn't respond. We were always forcing each other to play different roles. That's probably not what you think a relationship should be, but John and I are very different people and we accepted those differences. I thought that we were doing it for all the right reasons, helping each other survive our insanities, but I might have been wrong. I might have really hurt him. Not the way we were always hurting each other, but really hurt him. I want to go back to the way things used to be because they were certain. I would always know that he would do what I didn't expect and he could be certain that I would always be one step ahead of him. It was very lively. Now I have nothing to measure myself against. It scares me."

"Have you said this to John, the things you're telling me now?"

"Yes. I tried everything. Now the only thing I can do is to try to keep everything going, making the business work because that keeps me busy and it keeps me away from him. He seems to want that now."

"I don't suppose you tried walking in on him and slapping him good and hard and telling him to cut the crap and get it into gear?"

"No. And I won't. What if that only makes him worse? I don't think this is a game. I don't think I can fake him out of position. I can only wait. Maybe travel. Things are such a mess here and if we got away, maybe that would help him change back. We could take a cruise around the world in a southwesterly direction. I don't think anyone has ever made a southwesterly ring before. It might have a very beneficial effect. What do you think?"

"For the last two summers now you have taken extensive trips and they haven't helped your business or your marriage. Last summer John was in this same depression and he didn't come out of it. I don't think a repeat performance is going to do either of you any good."

"But last year we just went to Japan, and I understand now that he really doesn't like Japan. And we could go on a boat this time. You know how he likes the sea. Look in the cards again and see if it will do any harm."

As the spring of 1979 wore on, I finally got another opportunity to meet with John. He was still playing the hermit, secreted away in the bedroom of apartment 72. The blinds were drawn, the TV still playing soundlessly; he lay as if he hadn't moved since our last meeting. But he had changed. There was a feeling of new energy about him, not a great deal of it, but the signs of change were definitely there.

"Remember this?" As I entered the room, John held up the pre-Columbian frog that Yoko had brought back for him nearly two years earlier from Cartagena.

"How could I forget?"

"I was rummaging around the other day and I found it. You know, it's really quite beautiful."

"Have you decided that he's your gatekeeper?"

"My what?"

"Your gatekeeper. The one who decides if he will let you pass or not from the Land of the Living to the Land of the Dead or vice versa."

"Huh . . . I don't know. I thought that he was a symbol of fertility or intelligence or something. I was just looking at it because it's lovely. Anyway, Yoko told me that it didn't do anything."

"And Yoko is of course the mistress of all your mysteries."

"What's that supposed to mean? You're in a strange mood today."

"You being the master of strange moods."

"I guess you're right about that. But what's with you today?"

"Every time I come to see you, you tell me that I'm not supposed to make any sense. I've decided to go along with you on that."

"Good! Now what's this bit about the frog?"

"You tell me, he's your frog. I don't deal in frogs, you know, only cards."

"Right, Charles the card reader. As long as you have your cards you always have an answer, don't you?"

"As long as it doesn't have to be the right answer."

"I don't know, you do pretty well. Don't you think so?" He addressed the last question to the frog and manipulated it so that it appeared to be shaking its head no.

"You see, the gatekeeper won't let you pass because you didn't give the right answer."

"I didn't give him an answer. I gave him a question. How do I give him an answer if I don't know the question?"

"It's an art. Try listening to him and see what he asks."

"Is this some kind of trick?"

"Yeah, some kind. Either that or it's an ancient tradition that I've just invented for the occasion."

"Are you trying to get something out of me about what Yoko should do with this Apple reorganization thing? You and Yoko are going to have to work that out yourselves."

"We already have," I lied.

"You have? How? Yoko didn't say anything about that."

"What do you care? That's business. Now if you were in the

Land of the Living, which you are not, then you might deserve
an answer, but I doubt it. Seeing how you're imprisoned in the
Land of the Dead, then I'm sure it could not matter less to you
what happens to Apple."

"What's the matter with you today? I'm not dead and I'm
not playing dead either."

"Yeah, right, sure, you sit there with a frog and tell me that."

"It's a game, right?"

"If you like. But of course, if you like, anything is a game."

"Okay, I'll play. I'm dead and the frog can bring me back to
life."

"Oh, no. You can't play because you don't know the rules.
Only your frog knows for sure. But I can tell you this much.
You can't be dead because if you were you would be lying
around stinking up the room even worse than you have been.
No, not dead. That's an official diagnosis. But you are trapped
in the Land of the Dead, and only that frog you have there can
get you out."

"How did I get trapped in the Land of the Dead?"

"Classically, my son, classically. You have attempted the
classic hero's journey. You, like the classic hero, were successful in your day. Like the classic hero you received the message
of the herald beckoning you on this journey. True to form you
resisted the journey and many terrible things befell you. The
Levy case, the Klein case, etc., ad infinitum. You were given
magic charms to aid you on your journey, not the least of
which you hold there in your hand. You wandered to a far-off
country and were deceived into thinking you found the truth,
and then you were carried off still alive into the realms of
Hades, like Aeneas or any of the other classic heroes. So there
you are, trapped in the secret realm of death, facing your
greatest trial. No one can help you through your labyrinth. You
must unriddle the riddle of the sphinx there, except in this case
it happens to be a frog. But frogs are very spiritual. Ask him."

"For someone who's just playing, you're hitting very close to home. That in a sense is exactly what I've done. Are you sure this is a game?"

"Baby, would I lie to you? What you got yourself there is a frog on your hands, and if you're not careful he'll hop away, and you, my dear, will be trapped forever away from the cool clear winds of day."

"I'm supposed to figure out what the frog wants? Are you sure this is a game? Maybe this is some kind of occult test . . . right?"

"This is indeed a test. You started out on an occult journey and you never came back."

"But I did come back!"

"Tell your frog, mister. I can't get you out."

"The frog, right? Yoko got this for me when she went down to sell her soul or yours or whatever. Charles, tell me something seriously. Did you ever feel that you really had done that? That you had sold your soul?"

"Seriously?" He nodded. "There have been times in my life, very bad times, when I thought I'd lost touch with that part of me that is a soul. Times when I thought that I was all on the surface and couldn't get back into the real being. But I was just confused."

"How did you make contact again?"

"Magic. I used magic. Ask the frog. He'll tell you."

"Forget the frog. There's a real reason why I'm asking. I want to know because I sometimes feel that I've sold my soul. Not in a pact with the devil and not signed with blood, but sold it just the same, or gave it away. There was a time in my life when I would have given anything to be on top, anything. Nothing stopped me. Not the deaths of friends, not the advice of people I loved, not the danger signals that flashed in front of me, like drinking too much, smoking too much, getting arrested, getting laid by women I didn't even know, getting bartered and sold by people I didn't even know. All I knew was more, more, MORE, and I got it. You understand? I got it. I was committed to getting it at any cost, but what was the cost? I've given pieces of myself to everyone and anyone all over the world. The primitives used to believe that a photograph held your soul. Do you know how many photos I've given away? Millions of record covers with my picture on them have been sold, and they're little pieces of me too. And signatures! I've seen the magic *you* can do with just someone's signature. And I've given away millions.

"I think sometimes I've fallen into the Faust trap. I wanted everything the world had to offer and I got it. I was willing to do anything and I did. And who's the devil that I sold out to? The God Almighty public! That's the god I pray to. The public is the only god with the magic I need. They used to give me love, which poured into one end of me like water and flowed out the other like music. I was a channel. But now that I am truly and totally hooked, they won't deal. They've got my soul, what else is there?"

I reached across the bed and made the frog nod its head. "That must be the right track—the frog likes it. Keep working on it and you might get out of the Land of the Dead yet."

"I told you to forget about the frog!" he snapped, tossing the little image onto the bed. Then, reconsidering, he picked it up and slipped it into his pocket. "Listen, Charles, this is my house and my room and you're visiting me, and as long as you are on my ground it's going to be on my terms. So we are going to talk about what I want to talk about. Got that?

"I'm at war here and I'm losing because I don't know how to fight, and I don't think anyone else does either, but maybe, just maybe, if I talk about it enough I can get some kind of inspiration. I've tried stilling myself, I've tried smoking, meditating, ignoring, and nothing has worked so far. So now I'll try talking."

"Those are pretty passive ways to fight a war."

"It's an interior war, Charles. This is how it's supposed to be conducted."

"Well, it hasn't seemed to do much good so far."

"What do you suggest?"

"Instead of fighting, I think you should play. You have a huge playroom here with about a ton of exercise equipment. So why not try stretching out a few of those atrophied muscles of yours and seeing what that does for your head?"

"You should talk! I don't see *you* hitting the ol' mats."

"You don't see me locking myself in the bedroom for a year either. Instead of squatting on your lily pad and waiting for some beautiful princess to kiss you and turn you back into a prince, try looking around and seeing what answer is in front of you. That's one of the rules, you know, the answer is always in front of you."

"Yeah, yeah, yeah, well if that's your offering for today then I'll consider it. That doesn't mean that I'll do it, mind you, but I'll think about it."

And apparently he did. Slowly, like a becalmed ship responding to the first long-awaited breezes, John creaked and groaned into motion. Perhaps taking his cue from the little golden frog, he began more and more to use the small trampoline in Sean's playroom. Ever so slowly, the physical exercise began breaking up his emotional paralysis. Ever so tentatively, he began to move into a brighter frame of mind. Thus began his long, halting journey back from the Land of the Dead. It was full of fits and starts, heartening progress and discouraging relapses. He was moody and unpredictable, cranky and argumentative, and those immediately surrounding him bore the brunt of his discontent. John had repeatedly built up his private myth of the Happy Family in the past. Now he was the chief agent of his own myth's erosion.

Meanwhile, Yoko planned, confirmed, canceled, and replanned the family's summer excursion. It was to be a south-westerly ring around the globe. The numbers, she insisted, said that this would enhance family happiness. John, who felt he had made great strides forward by dragging himself all the way from the bedroom to the playroom, was not ready for such an adventure. But at the same time, he felt guilty enough about his own thorny and exasperating behavior to want to acquiesce to Yoko's wishes.

The process of persuading him, however, was no small challenge. His few sallies outside the fortresslike Dakota had been mostly unpleasant. He grew surly during dinners with "friends" and snippish at clerks during shopping expeditions. I thought the flashes of Lennon ire were a welcome relief from the past year's apathy. It was not an opinion everyone shared.

"Charlie, you have to tell me what we can do to make John come on this trip. He keeps saying that we can all go without him, and you know we can't do that. And he says we should forget the whole thing, and we can't do that either."

"Why not? Is it really all that important?"

"Yes! Ever since I've been planning all this he's been showing signs of improvement. The other day we were all playing in the gym together, and we've never done that before. I know that he still has a long way to go, but I've got him started and we have to continue."

"You could continue right here. At least for a while till he's a little more ready to meet the world."

"That's exactly what we can't do. If we stay here he's going to be meeting the world, the real world, a lot sooner than he would on an ocean liner. Everything is crowding in on us here. We're getting more and more invitations and we'll have to accept some of them if we stay or we'll look like we're avoiding everyone, and that will look as though there is some terrible problem here. What we don't need now are rumors that will start people prying into what's really happening. And we can't risk going out too often because he's getting just assertive enough again to cause fights and all sorts of trouble. If that happens here in New York, it will start finding its way into the papers."

"So what about Long Island? He always likes it out there."

"No, that's no good either because that puts us in one place all the time and then people will know where to find us. We have to stay on the move, that's the only way. I have all sorts of things I have to deal with here and if I'm attending to them I can't help John too. All the Apples are saying that they want to come by and the attorney too. I can't keep saying no. And what am I supposed to do if I'm meeting with one of them down here in the office and John walks in? He's started doing that, you know. He brings Sean down for lunch and says that it's my lunch hour and I should be spending it with the family. I know he's getting better and I am grateful, but he's so unstable and unpredictable that I can't risk exposing him to anyone important right now. Apple lives on rumors, and they could start saying that John has had a breakdown or something; that would just be an encouragement for them to attack me. I can't have that! There are just too many pressures going on here. We have to get away."

"All right, all right. But if you are intent on doing this, at least try to avoid the problems of the last two years. Keep the schedule looser and make alternative plans. And for God's sake make some sort of arrangements about the business. You still haven't caught up with the backlog from last year's trip, so you can't just let things go for six months now."

"It will be okay, Charlie. I'll take care of all that. The important thing is, how are we going to convince John that he has to go on this cruise? I've told him that it's for the family, but that doesn't seem to have worked very well."

I cast several spreads and made various suggestions as to how she might communicate her need for this trip to John, but each of these she rejected as impractical. At length I said, "I think it's pretty clear at this point that I'm not going to be able to come up with an answer that you are going to find acceptable. So you might consider another tack. If you can't find a way to make John *want* to go, then just make the reservations and *take* him. Order him. He is still lackadaisical enough to be unlikely to put up any genuine resistance. So just tell him that all the plans are set and paid for and that's all there is to it."

So it was that John was carted off for yet another summer on an extensive journey that, according to the theory, was for his own good. As it turned out, it was.

· 13 ·

RING-AROUND-
THE-WORLD

Sooner or later nearly everyone close to Yoko found
themselves circumnavigating the globe on some peculiar itinerary of Yoko's devising. Said itinerary was dictated by the
numbers, a complicated numerology system of Japanese ex-
traction. Although I knew little of their theory or practice, tarot
cards being my métier, my observations had led me over time
to the conclusion that for Yoko the numbers were a device to
lend divine authority to her own personal wishes. But there
may really have been something to them. Any system is only
as effective as its practitioner. I know some pretty bad tarot
readers, too.

Some time earlier, Yoko had sent me on a curious westward
journey in which I circled the globe and returned to JFK airport
in two and a half days, all for the purpose of making me "more

worldly," a somewhat odd requirement for a spiritual advisor perhaps, but there it was. Now, the numbers required that the Lennon family accomplish a southwesterly ring around the world. Despite his initial unwillingness, John seemed in surprisingly good spirits as we came within days of the great departure.

"So tell me, Charles, why do you think this cruise is going to secure family happiness? Have you become a believer in Yoko's Japanese number theories?"

"I didn't say that the trip would bring family happiness. I said that I didn't think it would do any harm."

"You're a funny one. You believe in tarot cards and magic but draw the line at numbers."

"I never said that either. The Japanese number theory may work and it may not. I don't know that much about it."

"Oh, yeah? Then why did you go on *your* trip around the world when she said that the numbers were good?"

"The numbers, according to Yoko, said that it was a good time for me to travel in a western ring around the world because that would help me become more worldly. That was in November of '78. Do you remember what was going on then? The negotiation on the farms. I was telling her what she could and should get, and she was getting antsy and thought that the reason I was not agreeing with her was that I was 'too spiritual.' I figured I could take the trip, come back, tell her that now I was all worldly, and then get her to listen to me and drive a better bargain on the farms."

"Don't you think that was a rather expensive gesture to placate the lady? You could have just hid out in your apartment and say you went."

"You know Yoko, she would have checked."

"She did." He grinned.

"Anyway, I thought that it was an experience worth collecting. And I didn't pay for it, you did."

"How nice of me."

"And I knew that if I were obedient to the will of the numbers, I would see a salary hike as a reward."

"That's just about what I do."

"Aha, does that mean that you too are a secret doubter?"

"It has nothing to do with doubt or numbers, it's family politics. Numbers are just Yoko's safe zone in the games she and I play. If *I* want to let her know I seriously want something, I scream and yell or sulk or in general act out. Yoko won't act like that. It's against her nature. So . . . she has the numbers. If there's something *she* wants, like going to Japan every summer, she sees it in the numbers. Experience has taught me that when she does that there's no point in arguing. It *might* be hell if we go, but it will *definitely* be hell if we don't. So we go. According to the numbers, last year was the last year for the next nine we could go to Japan, but lo and behold, by traveling in a southwesterly direction on this cruise for my mental health, we'll just happen to be traveling through the land of the rising price tags once more."

"But you don't want to be there. Is that why you go into those black depressions on these little excursions?"

"That's part of it. It's the entire traveling road show that I find difficult. So I stay, hide in the hotel, and try to sleep through it. That distresses Yoko, which I'm sure you hear all about, and the land of her ancestors becomes one big unholy bore. And that, Charles, is why I go into those 'black depressions,' as you so unkindly phrased it.

"I don't need a whole road show to travel, you know. I've made one of those fabulous rings around the world on my own just like you did. Like you, I was heading perpetually west and stopping off here and there to see what there was to see. I didn't take a ton of luggage. I didn't need it. I didn't worry about being the superrich rock star because nobody recognized me. That's a little trick I've learned. It's all in the way you walk and carry yourself. Then too, I suppose not being recognized as a Beatle in Bangkok isn't all that difficult.

"I liked traveling on my own. At first it had its problems, language mostly and not really knowing what to do with myself because I didn't know the cities I was in or anyone in them. I suppose I could have always gone out and found someone because every city has that potential. But even if I didn't believe what Yoko said about the numbers, I thought that I should at least try a little self-reform, and that meant not going to the local wateringhole and picking up a local caribou or two. I had already done all that, and the thing I hadn't done was to be on my own and try to find out more about me.

"So at first I kept to my rooms. Sound familiar? I kept to my rooms and delved into my favorite subject: me. I played this game with myself in Hong Kong. I started taking off different layers of myself as if they were layers of clothing and setting them out about the room. I imagined my different subpersonalities as sort of ghostly forms. I would lie there listening to the radio and wait till one of my other selves came up and took control. Then I would project it, see it sitting in a chair or standing by the door and talking to me. There were rules to this little game. Wherever I placed one of these ghosts, that's where he had to stay. Hanging on a hook in the closet, draped over the dresser, wherever. I kept them there for days. It was like creating my own haunted house.

"Every time I had successfully peeled off another layer I would go in and take a bath. After every bath I would take another drink. The baths were to help me relax, but they were also a test. If I found I couldn't emotionally handle being in the water and had to jump right out of the tub again, then I knew that I hadn't managed to get that last layer off successfully.

"I don't mind telling you there were some very scary moments. Every little sound and shadow seemed twenty times louder and a hundred times larger. I was exposing myself and

I was afraid that someone, that invisible, unknown someone, maybe my long-absent father, would come storming into the room and catch me and I would die of fright.

"I played that game for three days before I left my rooms. I would wake up out of half-sleeps and look around to see if all my mes were still draped around where they were supposed to be, and they were. My goal was to get them all off and leave them in the room and not come back. I thought I could escape them that way, but of course it didn't work. They can walk through locked doors, you know.

"When I finally did go out it was sunrise. I started down the street with just my passport and credit cards, thinking that I had tricked those other mes and got away. It was a great feeling for a while, terrifying but great. But of course it couldn't last. They caught up with me. I'd walk around the corner and there I'd be, waiting for me. I was caught and I'd jump back inside me. So I went back for my suitcase and said to the rest of my ghosts, 'Come on,' and we all went to Bangkok."

"And that was from traveling in a western ring? You make it sound more spiritual than material."

"I don't know if it was spiritual or not. It certainly was mental. I think it had more to do with the psychological effect of being on my own than the direction I was traveling in. A stranger in any number of strange lands. Add to that the sheer impact of culture shock and future shock. 'Oh, I think I'll take a little outing and travel around the world.' That's a bit unusual, you know. There haven't been that many people in history who've done that. Until recently it took years. Me, I did it in two weeks and took my time. Do you know how quickly you can make that trip if you really hustle?"

"Fifty-two and a half hours actually."

"You're kidding! Is that how long it took you?"

"That's right."

"Charles, you're a strange man. Where did you go?"

"Well, there are two answers for that. One, I went to Tokyo, Hong Kong, New Delhi, Tehran, Frankfurt, London, and then back to New York. The other answer is that I didn't go anywhere. I changed planes in Tokyo, and after that I never got off the plane again."

"You must have gotten some looks for that."

"Not at all. I told the crew that I was a professional gambler and that I had a bet going, à la *Around the World in Eighty Days*, except this one was around the world in eighty hours. I told them that I had chosen their airline because of its efficiency and that I intended writing up the experience. Naturally they all wanted me to know their names and gave me the best of treatment. Free booze, special food, even sleeping arrangements. Hospitality at thirty thousand feet is very pleasant, considering it was over two days on an airplane."

"But why didn't you go anywhere? If I were you, I would have got off somewhere and taken a little vacation."

"Well, that wasn't possible because on the one hand Yoko insisted that I take the trip and on the other she didn't want me to be away for any period of time. She had originally suggested that I take a friend and stop off in Japan, but that had been three months earlier and I was busy with other things. I suspected also that stopping off in Japan meant checking up on her family in some way, and I wasn't interested in that."

"A wise decision. Yoko has a very efficient way of thinking. There would be no sense in having you take a vacation if you weren't combining it with a little work. I'm surprised she got you to go at all."

"It was political, just like it was with you. All of us have to do this at one point or another. You, Yoko, me, even Sean. It's all part of the indoctrination. If we make these little jaunts, then any good that befalls us later is all Yoko's doing. If that's what she needs for her confidence and I'm still getting paid for my end, it really makes very little difference to me. And I suspect if I didn't go, then she would have found some excuse to get rid of me."

"Do you think she really believes in it, the numbers I mean? She won't tell me, of course. I ask her and she always insists that it's the only way to fly, but I wonder."

"Judging from the amount of energy she puts into it, I would say that she believes."

"I thought that maybe taking these little trips was her way of getting rid of me for a while or getting away by herself. Like never being able to travel at the same time I do, so she always has time to set up last-minute arrangements or clear the decks for my return."

"As you say, Yoko has a very efficient way of thinking. Still, I think that she actually believes that these magical journeys will get her everything she wants. It's an extension of the same thinking as the South American trip to see Nora the witch."

"You're probably right, Charles, so much the pity. That means I am condemned to fly endless rings around the world because you know she is never going to get everything she wants. No one does. So the whole crew of us will be shuttled here and carted there, from hostel to Hilton and back again. Around and around we go."

"John, if it's all that predictable, and I think it is, and it's all that unpleasant, and I believe that too, then why?"

"Because she is my wife, and that means doing what she wants half the time and liking it or at least *trying* to like it even if I can't. It's like in some families the husband goes out and gets drunk with the boys and the wife has the girls over for bridge. Neither one likes what the other one does, but to make it as a family there has to be compromise. Our family just happens to be on a slightly exaggerated scale, so instead of bridge parties it's summers in Japan.

"This year I think I've done a little better. The Japanese junket will be shorter. There'll be other places, and hopefully we won't have to do the clown act everywhere we go. You know, 'Superrich Megacelebrities Seen Traveling.' "

"Do you really believe that things will be that different this time?"

"One can only hope. But even if they're not, at least I'll be able to tell myself that I've done my bit by being dragged along. That way I can be a rat with impunity, which I probably will. We'll be on shipboard for some of it and I do like the sea. It's probably the closest I will ever come to my fantasy about sailing around the world in a *Kon Tiki*-type craft. The idea of me, the sea, and the sun has definite appeal, and if I have to put up with the convenience of a luxury liner to get it, that's a concession I think I'll be able to adapt to. At least we won't have to change rooms every two days while we're sailing."

"One must be thankful for small mercies."

"It's not so bad. It's a matter of having to adapt. I've never learned to work it out with another person, mostly because I've played roles and believed that somewhere out there, there was this perfect world where everything is as it should be, and there isn't. All there is, is the way things are. People are people and that's the same as saying people are crazy, which we all are. So if a relationship is to be formed, it has to be forged with an entirely different set of rules for each couple. These are the rules that Yoko and I seem to be forming. We don't know if they'll work and we won't know till they don't, and then we'll have to change them."

"John, that sounds good, of course, but isn't it just a little dishonest? Isn't this just your same old pattern of saying that you'll change yourself to meet the circumstances, then getting angry about it? Now, in the short term, a little anger might help break through that stoned wall you've been hiding behind, but in the long run, all it ever does is make you and everyone around you unhappy."

"Sure, it's my same old act! It's my only act! It's the act that's got me through life thus far with relatively few disasters. If I'm not acting a role, then I can't control the people in my life. If I can't control them, I get hurt, and, Charles, I don't like getting hurt. Now, there are a limited number of choices available to me. I can get hurt, which is bullshit, so forget about it; I can manipulate, which I am very good at and will do; or I can discard the people in my life, which I will not do. I don't think it's so bad. You have your shell. You can do anything, say anything, be anything, as long as you have that table with the cards on it between you and the rest of the world. The cards make you appear in control because they are your private world, and to talk to you a person has to step into that world where you are in control. Well, I don't think you're in control, Charles. I think those cards are like a stick up your ass, and you pivot and spin and give that oh soooooo clever illusion of control, but an illusion is exactly what it is. So don't go casting aspersions on *my* shield till you throw away your own."

"Okay." I gathered up the cards and tossed them over my shoulder. "Let's talk about your shield."

"Very cute."

"Here's one that's even cuter. I think that the trip has nothing to do with rings around the world or the sea or being nice to Yoko, or establishing rules. I think what you're really doing is setting up Yoko to fail in business so that you'll have a good excuse to hurt her in the best way you know how. The only thing she has ever received praise or admiration for is her accomplishments as a businesswoman, and she loves it. But that also means that she now has an area of acceptance and achievement that has nothing to do with you. You are no longer her total world. Now then, if you work on her long enough, you know you will make her fail. And her failure serves your purposes, doesn't it?"

"Oh, really? How?"

"If you drive her crazy on this trip, which you know so well how to do, then she will concentrate all her attention on you, which we know you love, and not on the business, which you hate. And why? Because it takes your number-one admirer away from you, an admirer whose attention is riveted on you because it means her survival. But your business can't stand another year of this, and I'm not sure your marriage can either."

"That's a load of shit, Charles, and you know it. The business is hardly sooo complex that she can't take a vacation. She puts in twelve hours a day here, and if she didn't take some time off she'd exhaust herself. Even executives of IBM get vacations. Christ, even the president takes time off!"

"Oh, come on, John, you *know* Yoko isn't working twelve hours a day to manage your affairs. She's hiding from you because you've made it expressly clear that you don't want her around. We haven't even caught up with last year's work yet because she spends all her energy worrying about you and whatever your latest mood is."

"Come on, yourself. You're exaggerating. Whether we travel or stay at home, Yoko's on the phone with you every day several times a day taking care of business. She tells me that everything is under control and things are all running the way they're supposed to."

"She's lying."

"I think you'd better pick up those cards and stop chipping away at me like this because you're beginning to get nasty, and I can't say as I care for it. I certainly know that Yoko is far from *totally* honest with me. I know she tries to hide little failings. But what you're suggesting is that everything is going to hell, and she's telling me that it's all sunshine and roses."

"That's exactly what I'm saying. Because of the way you act she's afraid of you. I think your *real* motive is to lose all the money, and that way you'll be forced to go out and be the hero by earning more. You believe that if you can create a large enough crisis in your life, it will win back the sympathy of your muse and everything will be like the good ol' days."

"All right! All right! You've got your cards back now, so let's play nice. I'll talk to Yoko about this and see what she has to say. And whatever she says I'll believe it because I don't believe you. But because I'm a sport and despite your approach I believe your intentions are basically good; when I talk to Yoko I won't mention to her that we had this little conversation. I think she would consider you a traitor if she knew you didn't believe she was the world's best businesswoman."

"That's what the press releases say, but you're right, I don't believe them. After all, I wrote 'em."

I don't think John ever mentioned any part of our talk to Yoko. If he did, she kept it to herself. But in late spring of 1979 when they left, there were no new provisos or contingency plans for handling the business. And as predicted, things began to go wrong almost immediately.

The first thing to "go wrong," however, was actually something that began to go right: John. As their departure drew near, he had begun to take great strides toward shaking off his fifteen-month depression. Once on board the ship, the exposure to other human beings had a positive effect on him. More and more he began to respond to the people around him. Paradoxically, this seemed to distress Yoko greatly. By the end of the first week of their journey Yoko called me at my home to ask about several of John's new friends and their possible motives for associating with him.

"Yoko, you're always so willing to believe that the only reason that anyone would be friendly toward John is to get his money, and the only reason why anyone would be friendly toward you is to get to John."

"Well, it's true, isn't it? Why else would people act the way they do? I have to protect John. He's very vulnerable."

"Sure he is and so are you, but you've both been public

personalities for some period of time now. Surely you've come
to realize that there will be people who are just curious, people
who just want to get a little of the aura, the magic of being next
to a celebrity. Not all of them portend trouble. You love drawing attention to yourselves. Now that you have it, enjoy it."

"We don't draw attention to ourselves! We don't have to.
Everyone is always following us, the press, the fans, promot-
ers, everyone. That's why we have to be so very careful. People
are always trying to pretend that they are our friends, and then
they try to get us involved in some business deal. You know
John. He always says yes to everything just to keep people
happy, but then the next day he regrets it and hides. People get
very angry when he does that and then they threaten to sue
us, so we settle and give them money. That's always happening, you know."

"Yoko, that hasn't happened to you in years."

"Yes it has! I just didn't want to bother you. It happens all
the time, only you didn't know about it. That's why I need to
know about all the people John has been talking to. It's so
dangerous, there is no way to avoid people on a boat. I think
we really should finish the trip by plane. John is always going
out and wandering off. There is no way I can control him."

"Then don't try! It's clear that there is an incredibly strong
tie between the two of you that has already been forged. Let
that tie sustain you. You don't have to try to control each other
all the time. You're on vacation! Relax!"

"I can't do that. It wouldn't work. I've had to work very,
very hard to make the situation as secure as it is. I can't stop
now. Everything would fall apart if I did."

But from Yoko's point of view, things began to fall apart
anyway. John's interest in the world around him grew apace.
His mood became one of perpetual good cheer. The only thing
that seemed to escape his notice was that his wife was slowly
but ineluctably being drawn into the same dark world from

which he had so recently emerged. It was as though the inexhaustible Yoko had finally become fatigued.

Ship to ship, plane to plane, they hopscotched around the globe. Here a hotel, there a safari, each stop held another trauma—the loss of money, the need to dismiss staff—and there was always confusion over what was supposed to be the original plan. Yoko reported these regularly to me by telephone in an uncharacteristic monotone that seemed to be saying that these disasters were inevitable. Then, in the same drained voice, she would return to the subject of John.

"I need to know what he's thinking about me right now."

"Why? How is he acting?"

"Fine . . . happy. He says he's happy all the time now. But I can't tell anything from that. I want you to look and see what's going on inside his head. He's talking about going to England, and he never does that. He says that the family should all get together. It's such a change from the way he's been. I need to know if it's an act or if he's really happy, because if he is, I don't think it can be any good. Everything is going wrong and if he's happy about that, then it means that he's laughing at me, so I need to know what he's thinking."

"I think he's happy, or certainly happier than he has been." I was basing my answer on the cards in front of me. "You wanted this trip to have this effect and I guess that it's worked. That's very good for you."

"John and I have different numbers, you know. Do you think that I could have made a big mistake and gone in a direction that's good for him but a 'killer' direction for me?"

I knew I had to be careful how I answered that because it encroached on her private numbers domain. "I wouldn't think so. Probably there are simply different beneficial effects."

"Different? Like what? Explain."

"Well, for John it's been a mood elevator. For you it is most likely being a sort of enforced relaxation that gives you a chance to recharge your batteries. You know, it's been a long time since you've had a real rest."

"That's true. I suppose it could mean that."

"I'm sure it does. And now that John is stronger it means that he can take care of himself more and that's less of a burden on you."

"But you didn't tell me what he's thinking about me now."

I shuffled the cards and laid them with a deliberately loud snap that I knew she would be able to hear through the receiver. I didn't want her to have any doubts that the positive reading she was about to receive was the real thing!

"Well, let me put it this way," I started after a sufficient pause for dramatic buildup. "I'm looking at the Lovers card, the Success card, and the card of Enlightenment. I don't think you could ask for a better spread. You might want to frame it." Occasionally she had done exactly that, believing that if she framed and hung the cards from particularly favorable spreads, they would have a positive influence on the family.

"Then it's good, isn't it? That's good. That's good. Then do you think everything will be okay if I just take a little time and rest?"

"I think you'd be wasting the trip if you didn't."

"Good. But we're going to come home. I don't want to travel anymore." Within a week a high-spirited John and his very weary wife returned from what would be their last ring around the world.

· 14 ·

A HERD OF
WHITE ELEPHANTS

When the Lennons returned from their dizzying world cruise, Yoko plunged once more into schemes for disposing of cash, although she preferred in general to think of her efforts as "investments." Hitherto, these investments had consisted primarily of her purchases of Twenty-sixth Dynasty Egyptian art (whose investment value was considerably dimmed by the fact that Yoko could never be persuaded to resell anything). That fall, however, Citibank had announced that it was entering the field of Egyptian antiquities for investment purposes. On one hand, this was good news for the Lennons, as it immediately forced up the value of their own collection. But on the other hand, it meant that Yoko was no longer going to find the sort of bargains she had been picking up in the past months.

That did not deter her enthusiasm, however. If Egyptian art was a closed avenue, there were sure to be others.

"Charlie, it doesn't matter if Citibank has ruined Egyptian art for us. All we have to do is find *another* area that is going to triple in value in the next few years!"

"Triple! I thought that you were looking for things that would double in value. This isn't the world's greatest economy, you know."

"Well, that's what we have tarot cards for, isn't it? I've been thinking this might be a very good time to do that musical I've been planning. You know Lee has invested in musicals for Paul and has done very well. I think he must have more than tripled his money. If he can do it, we certainly ought to be able to. And we have a lot of advantages."

"Such as?" I braced myself.

"Well, the things that Lee invests in are unknown musicals. We would be doing our own music and everyone knows who we are. I've thought a lot about it and we could do it as 'a day in the life of Yoko and John.' That way everyone would want to see it because everyone wants to know what we've been doing. I've already written most of the songs, so there would be very little work to do. The only problem is how do we get John to go along with the idea."

"Actually, that is not the only problem. To start with, you know nothing about how to produce a show."

"That's not true! John and I have done a lot of shows together."

"Those were concerts, not Broadway productions."

"Well, they are almost the same thing. And we would keep everything very simple. We could use our own furniture for the sets and we would only need one set. That would be very inexpensive. And that's good because you know we have to be very careful about money now. And because we'd be investing our own money we wouldn't have to share the profits with anyone. All the music would be prerecorded, so we wouldn't have to pay musicians. And John and I would star in it ourselves. We wouldn't need anyone else. Everyone would want to come and see us live."

"There is of course the little drawback that John isn't writing."

"He doesn't have to! I already told you that I've already written all the music that we'll need. If any problem comes up I can always write more. I write songs very quickly, you know."

"The attraction for a show like that would be that it was John's music. He's the one who's had the superstar musical career. I don't think that you would be able to attract investors with just your music, and I don't think that John will be all that interested in working on someone else's stuff, even yours."

"You haven't been listening. We don't need investors. I know money's tight, but we have enough to do a show. Besides, if it's really all that important, I'll give John half the writing credit. That way people will come to see *him* and hear *his* music, and they will love it because they will think it's John Lennon. Then when it's all popular and on the top ten, I can tell everyone that it was really me. That way I will finally be accepted as an artist in my own right. You know, I've already written a lot of things that the fans think John did. People don't like my pieces because they think I broke up the Beatles and stole John away from all those groupies and fag industry people. They're jealous, that's all."

This was one of Yoko's classic themes. In her heart I think that she honestly believed that if it weren't for some huge conspiracy against her, she would be the queen of rock and roll. I knew that I wouldn't be able to convince her with practical arguments that her plan had major holes in it, so I had to come up with something else.

"Well, you are still putting yourself in terrible danger. Think about it! Up on that stage every night. Exposed to all those people. There is no telling what might happen. I would think about that very carefully, if I were you."

"Perhaps you're right. It could be dangerous. Perhaps that's why you were seeing all those other problems in the cards. It was really dangerous and I hadn't asked that question. The cards were saying no because they were trying to protect me, but we hadn't asked the right question, so they couldn't tell us why there was a no."

"Very clever, those tarot cards."

"What? . . . Yes, isn't it amazing? But that still leaves us with the problem of what to buy."

"If I could make a suggestion. Why don't you invest in heavy write-off tax shelters? They won't show you any return, but at least they will eliminate tax burden and free up cash flow so that you could keep up with your other investments without draining your cash the way you have been."

"Charlie, that's no good. Why should we invest in something that isn't going to make us a lot of money?"

"Things don't make money until you resell them. You never do that! The type of investments you like are still using after-tax dollars, and so the problem of cash flow is still critical."

"Well, we can deduct the Egyptian and other art pieces this year because Dan got me a dealer's license. That should take care of the taxes."

"All that does is get rid of the sales tax. And even there you are going to have a problem. It's not a business. You need to show that you have made some attempt to resell the pieces, and you haven't."

"I can't resell them! They're magical! Anyway, I don't want to talk about taxes. I want you to find an investment where we can triple our money in a year. That's what we really need."

So we read on various retail businesses, jewels, a new scientific device for killing rats, more cattle, but always we would return to Yoko's artwork.

"Okay, now you're really going to like this one. I have an

idea for a record. A series of records actually. We'll use subaudio sound waves and they will affect the listener unconsciously. We could make them happy or sad or whatever we wanted. What do you think?"

"I think we read on that one two years ago. The problems were limited technological development to reproduce subaudible sounds, inconclusive research as to the effects of those sounds, and legal problems of producing that kind of project."

"Oh, but that was a different one. You're thinking about when I was going to do records of silence where the person would put on the record and not hear anything but would be affected unconsciously by the soundwaves that we recorded. This one is different. I will sing on the records and we'll lay down a track of sounds they can't hear that will make them very happy and they will think that they are just being happy because they're listening to me. There won't be any legal problems because we won't tell anyone that that's what we're doing. I think that will be great. It's sure to make a lot of hits."

"Yeah, but can you dance to it?"

"What?"

"Look, the problems are still the same. And the most important problem is that there is no sure way of telling the effects of that sort of thing. There are people with theories, but the theories haven't been proved yet."

"That's the beautiful part of it! We would be making a great contribution to scientific research."

"The thing that's wrong with your idea is the same thing that was wrong with the idea of the sonic rat killer. If it is powerful enough to drive away the rats, then what is the effect it has on people? You want to record sounds that may affect people positively—or not. What happens if it doesn't work the way you intend? What happens if it creates cellular disruption? Affects the hearing? The sense of balance? Not to mention the possible psychological ramifications. I think that you are being less than ethical with a plan like this."

"Bad karma?"

"Okay, if that's what you want to call it."

That's what she did call it, and the subject of the record was dropped.

We began a new series of questions seeking an investment that would guarantee her a fortune. After weeks we had exhausted her list of ideas.

"Charlie, there has to be something that is a good investment."

And then I said five little words that I lived to regret.

"Well, there's always real estate."

"That's right! I'm very lucky in real estate. That apartment on the ninth floor that you said I should buy, that's gone up to six times the original price. And apartment seventy-one, you got that one for us through magic."

Yoko credited her acquisition of the eight-room apartment next to the Lennons' to a ritual I had performed at her request to cut the owners' psychic ties to the place during their absence in the summer of 1977. She eventually bought the apartment, but that was more than a year later and it was the attractive asking price more than any occult operations that had decided the issue. As a professional magician, I'm perfectly ready to take credit where it is due, but I prefer to keep the record straight.

"I love real estate. Charlie, you're amazing."

Somehow, I didn't feel amazing. I felt like I'd just put my foot in my mouth.

In early October of 1979, we began a series of daily readings —lasting months—both in person and over the phone, to study the subject of real estate.

At the next meeting I found Yoko sitting in her office on the ground floor of the Dakota. She had a foot-high stack of magazine clippings and letters that had come in response to her putting out the word that the Lennons were buying land. Each of these had to be read on carefully. It was her belief that "it's very important that we're sure to get only the best of houses."

"Best" to Yoko meant biggest and most expensive. As I was aware that the family budget was already stretched, I did my best to discourage any purchase. This involved concocting a series of acceptable excuses that ranged from termites to hauntings.

"No, Yoko, not that one either."

"But why not? I think you're just rejecting all these because you don't want us to have a little house somewhere."

"Thirty-four rooms is not a 'little house.' "

"But it's a farmhouse and we need a farm!"

"You already have four farms and you aren't developing them."

"Well, that's because things went so badly with those farms. Now we have cows up there and more in Virginia, and we really don't have any safe place to put them. I think this farm would be very nice and if things got worse we could always put all our cows there."

"Look, if you really have to have real estate, then there is only one way you are going to be able to do it successfully. First, form a company so that you don't have to use your name because that only forces the price up. Then, get yourself a good negotiator to barter for you."

"I'm going to do all the negotiating. I'm a great negotiator. Look at the Klein case and all the others. Why should I have someone else do that when I can do it better?"

"Because the minute the seller finds out that it's the Lennons, he's going to expect a lot more money and better terms. You have made too much of a show of your wealth."

"You're forgetting the fan market. There are a lot of people out there who love us and would give us a better price than they would anyone else because of who we are."

"Be that as it may, the sort of places that you are looking at are the largest and most expensive houses there are. They're called 'white elephants' and they are notoriously bad invest-ments. Their upkeep and utilities make maintaining them prohibitive. They sell at a high price, and so the chances of putting them back on the market within a year and getting triple the price are very poor."

"No, Charlie, you aren't thinking about the fans. Anyone would want to pay a fortune to have Yoko and John's house. It makes them kind of historical and that does a lot for the value."

"I really wish you'd consider buying smaller pieces of prop-erty. What they call 'B and C grade' real estate. Places that are a little run down. You install a few fixtures and carpets, that sort of thing, and rent the places out. That way when you go to make the sale you have a desirable piece of property to offer, complete with rent-paying tenants."

"Rent them! I don't want to rent them! That would make me a landlord and landlords are terrible people! That's very bad karma, you know. No! What we are going to do is buy all these wonderful old houses and renovate them so they are really beautiful, then we'll sell them. I'm sure that will work."

"If by renovation you mean painting everything white the way you always do, including the natural wood and the wall-paper, that will not increase the value of the place. It will do the opposite."

"You just say that because you don't like white and you should, you know, because white is very spiritual and psychic. I'm an artist and I know what looks good. Maybe I'll paint them all white and maybe I won't. It all depends on what I think is best at the time. You have to do these things by feel, you know."

It became clear that if Yoko weren't gratified soon in her urge to buy a house, she would buy almost anything just to prove she had the power. At least she did take the precaution of forming a company called Pentacles, "like the tarot cards, you know, I think that that will be a very magical name," and it was Pentacles that was to do the purchasing. And surprisingly enough, in the midst of the herd of white elephants there was a place that seemed a likely prospect.

"Now, Charlie, this is a place in Cold Spring Harbor, Long Island. I'm not sure that it's any good because they don't want that much money for it." Yoko disdained looking at items that were priced at less than a quarter of a million.

"Looks good to me," I commented honestly after checking the spread I had cast.

"Well, it's so cheap there has to be something wrong with it." And so we read and read and read, looking for the flaw, but none was apparent. Then we read on the owner, his finances, and the best way to make the deal. All this information was put into a plan for purchase. And three weeks later, the Lennons had acquired the Cold Spring Harbor house for a price far below what had originally been asked. I thought that this piece, along with ninety acres that they purchased for $134,000 in Livingston, N.Y., made an excellent foundation for the Lennon land cartel. I also thought that as the year was coming to a close these two were enough for a first sally into the world of real estate, at least for the year 1979. Yoko did not share that opinion.

"Okay, now in Virginia there are two places. You said that Virginia was a good place to get land, right?"

"I said a client of mine was doing very well buying and renting town houses in Virginia."

"Okay, so that means that it's a good place, then. Now we've read on these two places quite a few times and out of all the other Virginia places these appeal to me the most. They are Poplar Grove and Auburn House. They're both landmark houses and they have very beautiful gardens, so I think that they must be worth the money. I want you to tell me how much I can get them for and how to go about it."

"Don't you think that you've done enough for a while? You have made two good buys and not strained the finances too much. Both these places are much more expensive than the ones you have already purchased and you still haven't done anything with those properties. You really ought to cut back spending and develop what you have. How do you expect to afford two more houses?"

"Mortgages! That way we can buy a lot more houses and not have to spend as much money. We can spread the payments out over a long period of time."

"And that way you encumber your future finances with outgoing payments, and I doubt if that will curb your personal spending. You're already having enough trouble making the payments on the farms. You simply can't afford to do this."

"Of course we can! Apple reorganization is going to free up all that money in the Apple account and it will be given to the shareholders. Then we will have all the money we need and we'll have all these houses to live in."

"Yoko, the cards never said that the reorganization was going to take place in the foreseeable future."

"But the numbers did. This is going to be a very, very, very good year for me, and what else could that mean except that we get the money?"

"Don't you think that you had better wait till you have it before you actually put money down on these houses? You could lose them if you are wrong."

"That's just negative thinking. If I don't buy these now I won't get good buys. The numbers won't be right for land in a southern direction next year. So we have to buy all three now."

"Three? I thought that you said that there were two?"

"Two in Virginia and one in Florida. That makes three."

"By Florida I suppose you mean the Palm Beach house?"

"Oh, yes. It's beautiful, and it will be a great saving because

225

we are always going down there for Christmas and renting a place, and the rental costs are so high and we don't have anything afterward."

The Palm Beach house was the whitest elephant of them all. Originally intended as a showplace, the structure had outlived fashion. Yoko called the owner and announced who she was and that she was very interested. The price was doubled. In the to and fro of negotiations the price was slowly being whittled back toward the original. Already it was the subject of much local gossip. Certainly it was not a buy.

"We have to get that one. John will love it and it will be very good for the family."

"That makes five houses that you want to secure this year plus the apartments in the Dakota. What do you intend to do with five houses?"

"Live in them! That way the value will go up very fast."

"Won't living in five houses be a little difficult?"

"No, we'll spend our summers in Japan and a month in each of our houses. It will be beautiful."

Although I advised against it Yoko went forward with her real estate ventures. Her plans depended on the release of Apple's asset of some $40 million through reorganization, which did not happen. The added strain on the family finances left Yoko with no opportunity to recoup her strength from the previous summer's ring-around-the-world. It was a weary Yoko who made plans for the family to enjoy the Christmas holidays in the Palm Beach house.

John, who had emerged from his shell brighter and stronger than ever, was still in no mood to deal with any business, no matter how pressing. Still hesitant about attempting any confrontations, he was convinced that the only way he would find any peace was by giving others what they wanted. He considered curtailing Yoko's spending spree as tantamount to taking from her what she wanted. Thus, he delayed action until the

Christmas holidays. The Palm Beach house was rented for the holidays and John, knowing Yoko wanted him to love it, said he loved it. Yoko claimed that John "needed" the house, and subsequently purchased it for far more than it was worth. The Lennons used their new home only once, and within a year Yoko was forced to sell it at a loss to meet the demands of creditors.

15

BUSTING
OF A BEATLE

The Christmas holiday of 1979 was a happy one for John at least. His newfound energies gave him confidence in himself and a new image of who he was. He was truly alive again.

While John frolicked in his new perception, Julian, who had joined them, withered a bit under his father's brilliance, which had been liberated from the smothering pall of guilt. It is to his credit that Julian was able to adapt to yet another change in his difficult relationship with John. For Yoko, life was not so pleasant.

Since the Lennons' return from their world cruise the previous September, Yoko had seemingly closed herself off more and more from the family. Even on this vacation she was anxious to avoid family outings and surrounded herself with work. This work seemed to represent a protection for her. While John and the others enjoyed the sun, Yoko began a series of trips, commuting from Palm Beach to New York in order to be able to attend to all-important business.

John stayed in the Palm Beach house until February, luxuriating in the sun and sea, forging new ties with Julian and delighting in rediscoveries of himself. He told me that he was going to commit himself to a project of constant rebirth. He returned to New York revitalized and ready for this project with an intensity he had not shown for years. In his heart he had reached the bottom of himself and was now starting the journey back.

There was not enough room in the Dakota to contain John's new energy. So, very early in the spring of 1980, John took up residence in the Cold Spring Harbor house, while Yoko remained in the Dakota.

The Lennons were still maintaining separate living quarters and separate interests when they heard the news, late that spring, of Paul McCartney's arrest. Paul had been arrested for trying to smuggle marijuana into Japan while visiting there to perform in a concert tour. The illegal product had allegedly been discovered in his suitcase, and he was taken into custody immediately. His wife, Linda, and the rest of the company were allowed entrance without incident.

Yoko worried that the news of Paul's arrest might throw John back into the old depression. But when I talked to him over the phone one afternoon a few days after the incident, his voice held no depression, only righteous indignation and sympathy for Paul.

"It's lousy, Charles. Typical, but lousy. Some petty official probably needed a promotion and set Paul up to get it. Not that I have any great love for the man, you understand, but this sort of thing is just somebody's cheap trick. If he really wanted his smoke, you know he wouldn't have had to carry it on his person. The mere fact that he was checking in his own luggage tells you that he wasn't carrying anything. Usually all the star carries in is an overnight bag. The rest of his stuff is checked through as equipment and costumes. Paul's smart enough to know that. He's known how to handle this sort of thing for twenty years, just like I have. If you want to smoke, you say to your producer, 'Hey, where's the grass?' and poof, magically it appears. You don't have to buy it, you don't have to carry it. It's all budgeted into a show as entertainment or transportation expense. Take care of the star's head, fill his lungs, or his nose, or his veins, or whatever. No, no way do I believe that Paul was carrying. He was set up and that's the long and unfortunate short of it. Some little creep wanted to make a name for himself like all little creeps do, and he used Paul to do exactly that.

"Just how hard do you think it is for a Customs official to lay his hands on some grass? Not that hard. He had it all along under the counter or something, and the minute the Beatle steps up, it's presto! Headlines.

"Stars are victims like that, very vulnerable. The pity is that Paul wasn't expecting it. Nobody is busting stars for drugs anymore, so he didn't take precautions, you know, like having Customs waived because he's a star or something like that.

"Paul's been busted before, you know. This is only going to make life more difficult for him. Not that I care, but it's just the meanness of the thing that irks me. When I was busted, it was the same sort of crap. I was sounding off a little more than the government liked, and poof, there's a drug bust. Police dogs, cops, the works. As if I were the only kid on my block to have a little stash. But they wanted *me*, see? And they got me. The bastard who busted me couldn't have been more smug. Certainly made his day.

"Paul's getting more press out of this than he has since the sixties, which just lets you know where the press is at. They love this sort of thing. The worst part for Paul is that they've got him in jail. Do you believe that? They know how much money they're costing him. A whole fuckin' concert down the drain. Promotion wasted, transportation wasted, tickets to be returned, the whole thing's a waste. And all for what? In the world of rock and roll you won't lose any fans or sales because of a drug bust. At worst it makes you controversial, and that's a plus. So what are they holding him for? That's just the work of some power-mad little creep showing off to the world, knowing that the longer he holds Paul the longer he's important."

"For someone you claim not to care about you seem awfully upset."

"It's the injustice of the thing that upsets me. If Paul were just some nobody, the Customs agent would have pulled the grass out of his bag and said, 'Don't be stupid, son, just throw this away over there,' and that would have been the end to it. I've heard stories like that. But because he's a star he gets set up instead. That's injustice and it would bother me if it were Shirley MacLaine, Baryshnikov, or the Muppets. Maybe it affects me a little more because it's Paul and I know him and he's a musician, but I doubt it. It would bother me no matter who they got."

The papers continued to put out daily reports. The Japanese prison officials announced that they were giving Paul preferential treatment by serving him tea and biscuits instead of the usual tea and rice. A fan had attempted to hijack a plane with a toy gun so that he could go to rescue Paul. John Eastman, Paul's brother-in-law, went to Tokyo to act as legal representative. Yoko followed all this with intense interest.

During Paul's second week in prison, she and I read regularly on his moods and welfare. As we sat together in her office, she told me that she had come to see Paul's situation in a new light.

"I think the whole problem for Paul was caused by his going

in the wrong direction," she said. "I have been studying his numbers and I can see where he made his mistake.

"It's a pity, really. I like Paul! I think of him as a friend. John is the one who doesn't like Paul. Paul was always the cute one and John was jealous of that. When I first met Paul I was attracted to him. I'm like that when I really like someone. I try to get close to the guy who's close to the guy I like. That's why I was getting close to John, so I would be near Paul if he wanted to make a move. And Paul was attracted to me, I could see that. But he couldn't handle the idea of being attracted to somebody John was with because that would be a violation of the fraternity rules. I was someone else's property; that's how men think, you know. So then Paul was very frustrated because he wanted me and felt that he couldn't have me. That's why he always acted so mean to me. Men always think like that, you know. If they can't have a woman they want to punish her. But I think that he was always a little interested because of the way he looked at me. Even when he used to come here with Linda, he was always looking at me funny when he knew Linda and John couldn't see him doing it. There were other things too, like he got married because John and I did."

"I thought that he got married to Linda before you married John."

"Well he did, but he knew that John and I were planning to, so right away he married Linda so he would get the headlines first. He's like John that way, very competitive. I think that if it wasn't for me, he never would have married Linda at all. She was just a groupie, you know. I don't think they ever would have married if it wasn't for the competitive pressure between John and Paul and Paul's frustration about me. He just married her to prove that I didn't mean anything to him. I think he does still feel something about me though. Do you want to read on that and see how he's feeling about me?"

I did and it didn't look like love. Disdain, maybe, contempt certainly, but definitely not love.

"He seems to have gotten over his infatuation with you."

"Are you sure? That's very funny. Well, he hasn't seen me in such a long time, so maybe that's it. You know, a lot of the men around John have been attracted to me. Mick Jagger was. He used to come around here a lot saying that he wanted to see John and that they should be friends because people at the top should be friends. That's what he said, but I could tell from the way he looked at me that I was what he really wanted. You know, he'd always show up without a date to let me know that he was available. I never thought that he was that attractive and I had to protect my position with John.

"Mick even tried to move into this building to be closer to me, but I put a stop to that. I told the board that two rock stars in the same building would be a terrible security risk and that Mick has a terrible reputation. The real reason was that if I were that close to him, something might have happened between us and that would be a disaster for my marriage.

"I think John sensed something was going on because he and Mick had a fight, well sort of a fight. We were in the car and going to dinner and Mick was talking to me, a very intellectual conversation—he's very smart, you know. Well, John had been drinking and you know how he gets. He just shouted at Mick right at the top of his lungs, 'That's a lot of middle-class bullshit!' and Mick told the driver to pull over and he just got out. That was before he tried to get into the building, so you can see that he had to be very interested in me if he was trying to get close to me after a thing like that.

"I don't know why men think that I'm so attractive. But they all seem to. I can tell from the way they look at me—Do you think if Paul were to see me that he would be attracted again? I still like him, you know. I feel very sorry for him because

Japanese jails are not very nice places. Do you want to read and see how long Paul is going to be in there?"

"A few more days, maybe four."

The constant appearance of Paul's name in the press began to unsettle John. It recalled memories that he would have preferred to let sleep.

"You don't think they're mistreating him, do you, Charles?"

"Aside from the fact that they are holding him in a jail cell, I doubt that there is any mistreatment."

"That's good. Not that I really care, you understand, but I wouldn't want to think that they were abusing him in any way."

"You keep telling me how much you don't care. I begin to wonder if it's true."

"Of course I care! Not that I want to, but you can't know a person as long and as intimately as I've known Paul and not care. I'm pissed at him and have been for years, but that's my private war with the man. It has nothing to do with the way I feel about his having this happen to him.

"We were never really close. That may sound funny, but we were working so hard and so long that that's all we were ever doing. I thought very highly of him, of course, but ours was the sort of relationship that I imagine soldiers develop during wartime. The situation forces them together and they make the most of it, but it's all a lot easier when the other guy, Paul in this case, happens to be a nice guy.

"But we weren't close creatively. We were more opposites. Paul was safe. I wasn't. I was the radical always looking for something newer and farther out than the last time. Paul was always looking at what would sell, which was good, I suppose, because we did sell and that certainly had its advantages. The differences in our approaches kept us on top. But if it hadn't been for me, we wouldn't have got on top. I decided when I was a kid that I was going to be on the top, the veddy, veddy toppermost of the popper most, and I made it. I was the one who always gave more, did more, pushed more. I was the engine. Paul didn't have that dream. I had to instill it in him. I know you think this sounds terribly vain, but it's true and I am vain about it."

"No reason why you shouldn't be. You've done a thing very few people have. You set the goal of being the tops in your field and you made it. That's something to be vain about."

"Keep it in perspective, Charles. I did more than become tops of my field. I literally *made* that field what it is now. My goal was to be bigger than Elvis and we were. But there I do have to share the credit with Paul because if I had done it all my way, that wouldn't have happened. Paul was as responsible as anyone for that.

"The thing that held us together was that we could work together. You'd be surprised how much that matters. When things fell apart it was because I fell apart. I wasn't willing to do the extras I always did, and I resented it when Paul tried or George tried. I'm not altogether sure why I felt that way. Tired I guess. I had been putting out and putting out and things were getting higher and higher. At first I was afraid that we were never going to get there. Then I began to get afraid that it was never going to stop. Then it seemed everybody was drifting off in different directions, and that seemed to make more sense than trying to go on. All that was needed was for someone to pronounce the patient dead, but none of us really wanted to do that. Then I decided that it was my job, unpleasant as it was. I talked to Paul about it and he asked me not to announce the breakup. Asked! Hell, he begged me! I was touched because I thought that it was because he had the faith that somehow, somewhere, everything would work out and we'd do it all over again. Well, I was touched all right. Touched in the head. Paul went behind my back and made the announcement as part of a publicity campaign for a record. And for that, my dear Charles, I am never, no not ever, going to forgive him. It was like he took the Beatles away from me as part of a promotional trick."

"You know, it might not have been his idea. He could have been told to do it by Lee or practically anyone."

"I warn you, Charles, don't try to defend him. I don't care who-what-when-where-why-or-how he came to do it. He did it and he knew what he was doing. He knew that he should have come to me and he didn't. We all have limits. Paul passed mine and I just wrote him off. After that I'd see him once in a while, but whatever had held us together had died.

"I called him once though, when Yoko was pregnant. It didn't go well. There was nothing there. I had got all sentimental about the news and I wanted to share it. But Yoko was listening in on the other end and I was too uncomfortable."

"Why didn't you tell her that it was a private call?"

"Charles, don't you know that a couple as close as my dear wife and I have no private anythings? I was so uncomfortable that it made Paul uncomfortable. I was already wishing that I hadn't tried by the time I got him on the line. I felt foolish. 'Hi, it's me. How ya been? What's new? We're pregnant! How are you?' The conversation just deteriorated into, 'That's nice, okay, good-bye, see ya,' and that was that.

"Then he started coming around the Dakota when he was in town, but you know about that."

"He was using you. Seeing you not producing while he was doing Madison Square Garden helped psych him up. He needed to think that he was that much better than you to get his energy up."

"The funny part is that I let him get away with it for so long. You know, I used to dread it when he was in town, but I never had the sense to go out to the island or just not answer the door. He'd come striding in with a guitar under one arm and

Linda under the other, asking me what was new, knowing nothing was new. Then he'd always ask if I'd heard his latest, which I usually hadn't. The guitar was so we could sing together, but that was never going to happen. I'd just tell him that I was really busy being a father. He must have seen through that because he's a father many times over and that certainly doesn't tie him down. It wasn't till I told him that I was real busy and that if he wanted to see me he'd have to call first that he got the message to leave off. I have your tarot advice to thank for that."

"Think nothing of it."

"I don't. But really, that was important because it got me off the hook without losing face, as Yoko would say.

"I have to confess his success irks me, but he deserves it because he writes the sort of stuff that sells to the largest audience, the middle of the road, great midwest where hits are made. George and Ringo aren't doing as well, but they're still doing better than me. I don't feel the same way about them, you know. George could have given me a little more credit for the role I played in his career, but everyone does that. You know, we all need help getting there, but once we're there we did it all by ourselves."

"Including you?"

"Yes, I suppose that's the way it sounds, doesn't it?"

"What about Ringo? You know of all of you he was the one I really wanted to meet."

"Thanks a lot. Well, you could have made a worse choice. We were all supposed to be something different. Paul was the face, I was the smart one, George with all his mysticism was the spirit, and Ringo was the heart. I certainly don't have any hard feelings about him. Never had a reason to. But we drifted apart, anyway.

"You know, it's nice to think that we made such an impression that people still want more. That's the best way to leave things, with people wanting more. There will always be fans and they will always want more of the same thing. That's what Paul gives them, the same thing over and over. Not that I've paid that much attention, but you can't help but notice. So he keeps all that alive for the fans. I wouldn't, couldn't, do that. I'd want to do something new. Every time, something new. That means tearing down what's old and establishing the new thing, every time. That's not easy for me, and right now, it's impossible.

"You know when I first met you I was trying to hold on to all that history. I could have come out then with a lot of new stuff done the old way. It's never hard to do the thing you've already mastered, but being chained to all that history made me realize that I didn't want it. I wasn't going to become a repetition of myself. I was going to do something new or nothing at all, and as it turns out, it's nothing at all. Then all of a sudden, there's Paul. Jailed for a drug bust. That sounds like the sixties, doesn't it? It's like I'm looking at him through a time machine. I'm glad I'm not him. Not just because he's in jail—that will pass soon enough—but that whole world he's in is something I've left behind and I'm grateful. Surprisingly enough, I'm not jealous anymore."

Two days later Paul was released. The concert had been canceled and he and Linda left Japan immediately. John greeted the news with a great sigh of relief.

"I'm glad that's over. I feel like I've been keeping a vigil for him. Not that I care, you understand."

· 16 ·

CAPTAIN
COURAGEOUS

A s the news of Paul's arrest faded from the press and the summer of 1980 began in force, John returned his attention to his various projects for breaking his creative block and securing the rebirth of his muse. To this end he engaged in a series of wide-ranging experiments. First, he attempted the spiritual exercises of Saint Francis. Then it was a ten-day vow of silence. He meditated, fasted, tried his hand at yogic breathing, and even spoke of getting a sensory-deprivation tank. His reasoning: "Nothing works altogether, but everything works a little."

With Sean, Uda (the new nanny), and a gofer to keep him company, John was content to spend the summer in his Cold Spring Harbor house. Yoko, who hated the sun, preferred to stay in the Dakota. There were no plans for travel that summer. The tremendous outlay of funds required to purchase, maintain, renovate, and redecorate their five houses made extensive travel abroad impossible. But shorter trips were possible.

"What about this cruise?" chimed John over the phone one hot July afternoon. "Should I go?"

"What cruise?"

"Ha! See there? You don't know everything! You haven't heard about the cruise yet, eh? Well, according to the numbers, the thing for Sean and me to do is take a little cruise down to Bermuda. So spake the oracle of the East."

"Well, that sounds pleasant enough. A little off-season perhaps but pleasant nonetheless."

"It is, I suppose, but it worries me."

"Why?"

"Because the mode of travel is to be a little ship and a little crew, and that strikes me as a little dangerous. It started with these people I met out here and we were sitting around having a few, and the idea of sailing off to sea came up because they're into sailing. I was having them on a bit about how we should all go sailing off to the islands. It was fun to talk about. But they really got into the idea. Now they are making plans, and the wife insists that it's the thing to do. Well, I do know how to sail. I took a course in it, but I tend to feel that a trip down the eastern seacoast is a bit ambitious for a first run."

"That's a point."

"Yeah, but there's that old number thing working against me. Hitting the high seas is a long-standing fantasy of mine, but it has me worried. Being out on the water with a less-than-experienced crew seems a little too much like tempting fate.

"The part that bothers me the most is that Yoko is so insistent that it's the thing to do. I could always refuse, but if I challenged her numbers by not complying, then I'm not sure what sort of problems I'm opening up in the marriage, which has enough of them at this point."

"So go, but go by plane."

"No, I thought of that, but it seems it has to be by boat. It's all very funny, Charles. And I don't like the idea of taking Sean along. If it were just me then I might risk it. It's kind of exciting that way, but with the baby involved it's a different story. On the other hand, if I don't take Sean I'm not sure how well he'll be taken care of. And if I left him and anything did happen, I would be repeating my father's trip yet again of going off to sea and leaving a five-year-old behind. I confess it's a tangle. I seem to be in the position of losing something no matter what I do. That's not a very pleasant feeling."

"So tell her that you are going by boat and then take a plane."

"Surely you don't think such a transparent little ruse is going to fool the wife?"

"If things are like that then I suggest that you don't go. Play sick, pick a fight, get arrested, tell Yoko off, whatever you like, but don't go."

"Four guys and a girl doesn't sound like the safest of crews to take the baby on the high seas with, does it?"

"Actually, it sounds pretty stupid."

"And thoughtlessly reckless?"

"Every bit of that."

"Yet the more I think about it the more the idea of the danger of the whole thing appeals to me. It's like the deprivation tank. Danger is thrilling."

"But you decided not to do the tank."

"Well, I prefer to think that I haven't decided not to do it just yet. Now there's this other somewhat thrilling distraction to lure me with its appeal."

"And the danger for Sean, does that appeal to you as well?"

"That's right, Charles, you keep reminding me about that. Just keep hitting on that point. I keep looking for a way to change myself and there is a certain seduction about flirting with death, especially when you are standing with both feet planted firmly on dry land on a sunny day. I don't want to lose track of the fact that the whole plan is totally off the wall."

I kept reminding him, and Yoko kept urging him to go. Finally, the lure of the sea, his old fantasy, and the possibility of "real danger" won out. John and Sean, with a four-man-one-woman crew, took to the high seas in a small but seaworthy craft.

During John's absence, Yoko and I spent our days in her office reading cards. As had become typical, her questions were no longer focused on family or finances. Her only concern seemed to be what others thought of her and why.

We were so engaged one day, almost a week after John's departure, when the phone rang. As it turned out, it heralded the momentous news that John had, after six paralyzed years, broken his creative block and rediscovered his long-absent muse. But there was no way to deduce this from Yoko's behavior. She answered, then turned sideways in her chair as if to hide the phone from me. Her voice was soft and she answered in monosyllables. Finally she said, "Yes, but I'm very very busy now and very tired, so I have to go." She hung up the phone and looked over toward me with a face full of pain. For a moment she simply stared and then she began to collect herself. At length she said, "Well, I guess you will be pleased to hear that all your little fears about the safety of the family were ill founded. John and Sean are in Bermuda."

"That's terrific! Are they okay?"

"Apparently."

"Well, come on, what did he say?"

"I'm not really sure. John is all excited. He's writing or says he's writing. He just sang me a song that he wrote and now he's talking about getting all these musicians together and recording."

"That's wonderful! How did it happen? What made the change?"

"Oh, I don't know, Charlie. It isn't important, is it?"

"One of the world's foremost songwriters hasn't written in six years and all of a sudden he's unblocked and writing again? I would say that that's important!"

"That's your opinion and you don't know anything about music. I was the one who heard the song and it wasn't that good."

"Well, don't say that to him. If he's writing poorly, that's better for him and for all of you than not writing at all."

"Not really. I don't think that this will change anything. I think that he's just fooling himself again and thinks that he's made some major change like he's always doing, but nothing will come of it. Now if you are through being a John Lennon fan, can we get back to important things?"

For the rest of the next hour we batted questions back and forth. About an hour later the phone rang again. This call was longer. "He's written two more," she said after she had hung up.

"You mean since the last call?"

"Yes, he's convinced that he's gotten his muse back and he's very happy about it."

"I don't blame him! This has been a long and difficult time for John and writing again offers him a kind of hope that he will finally become creative again."

"Long and difficult for *him?* He's made it a long and difficult time for *me!* I don't see why you couldn't be a little more sympathetic to me. I'm the one who's had to struggle with everything while he was just lying around the house complaining or going out."

"Having sympathy for your situation doesn't preclude the pleasure I can take in John's success." I was not able to express the pleasure that I felt directly to John for several days. But on the following Saturday afternoon I got my chance when he called from Bermuda.

"Yoko told me that you're writing again," I said when I heard his voice. "I think that's wonderful! How did it happen?"

"I don't know, really. It's this place, I think. The music down here is terrific. It's an entirely new sound, reggae. I've never heard anything like it before."

"Reggae is hardly a new sound."

"I know that, Charles. That's not what I'm saying. Reggae has been around for years, but when I got here it was like hearing it for the first time. There are these street musicians everywhere, the place is full of music and it kind of inspired me. You have no idea what it sounds like. At least you don't know what it sounds like to me, in my head. No matter how good you are you can't hear with my ears, which is why you can't do what I do. With you it's your eyes. I can't see what you see, which is why I come to you, and you can't hear what I can hear. No one can. I have to hear it and translate it into records, and then you can hear it the way I do. All these years, it's like I've been deaf. The music was always there, but I couldn't hear it and now I can't help but hear it . . . and sing it and write it.

"I've finally got her back. It's such a pleasure. I really thought that I had lost her forever this time."

"Lost who?"

"Me muse, Charles, me muse."

"You mean Euterpe."

"What?"

"The muse of lyric poetry."

"Well, that's what you call her if you want, but I have my own name for her."

"And what's that?"

"Never you mind. This is a very private relationship and I have no intention of being even the least bit unfaithful. If I tell people her name, they might go calling her up, and if someone a little more desirable than me comes along, I will lose her again. And I never ever want to go through that again."

"I think you're probably right."

"Never righter, Charles."

"So you think that it was the change in environment and the sound of a different kind of music that finally did the trick for you?"

"No, Charles, actually I don't think that. I think that it was taking the boat trip down here. You know I was scared to death, but I've been talking about going off to sea for so long that I had to make like it was all for fun. But really I was frightened. And having Sean along only heightened my fear because I felt so responsible for his life. You know, you can play games with your own mortality a lot easier than you can with someone else's. And there have been all those dreams about stepping off the boat and I thought, Maybe this is the part where I actually do that.

"Well, we sailed into a storm. Probably it wasn't a very big storm, but from the perspective of that very small boat it looked like a big storm. And I thought, Jesus, I've bought it. This is it. I really thought that I was going to die there. Then I thought about Sean and the others, and nobody else seemed to know what to do and the boat's going uuuuuup—and splat down. And I thought, Someone really ought to do something, and then I thought, *I'm* someone! I didn't know what to do, but nobody else seemed to know either, so I took command. Me! I always tell myself that I never want to take charge and then things always work out so much better when I do! I started shouting orders about furling the sails and being sure that the baby was secure belowdecks and I took the wheel. I headed her

into the wind and held her steady. I didn't know if that was
the thing to do, but I sure as hell wasn't capable of running her
before the wind. So there I am, holding the wheel and singing
these sea chanteys at the top of my lungs. It felt wonderful! I
thought, Here it is, man. This is where you die. And I didn't
mind at all. It was so poetic. I started laughing at the poetry of
the universe.

"Well, as you can see, or at least hear, and shortly, I hope,
see, I survived. That storm is when everything changed for me.
There was no back door in that storm, no way I could say, 'I
want to stop now, please.' It was life or death.

"That's how it always was when I was most creative. Not
always in quite so literal a form, but there was always the
threat of being utterly changed. When people in general
didn't like rock and roll, I fed off that dislike and it made me
strong, and then when everyone loved rock I fed off that love
and *that* changed me. I took the image I had of myself and
destroyed it. The poor John was killed by the rich John. The
nobody John was killed by the famous John. Whatever I
thought I was, was constantly being killed by some new series of events and I realize now that I loved that. I don't
know how many times in my life I have created chaos just to
establish a new order of things. But I never admitted that to
myself before. I would say I wanted to change, but then I
would hold back, frightened that I would die. But no more,
Charles. The next time I see that specter of death, I'm not
going to hide under the covers. I'm going to grab him by both
hollow cheeks and give him a big wet kiss right on his moldy
teeth because that's the only way to go. Headed into the
wind and laughing your head off.

"You should have been there. For so long I had been con-
necting the sea with my father. But, you know, she's the
mother, not the father. She rocked this child in her sweet lovin'
arms and shook some of the nonsense out of him, I'll tell you

that. Unstuffed my ears and let me hear again. I've written fourteen songs since I got here. Soon I'll be back and back with a vengeance, my dear."

In the first week of August 1980 the Lennons were reunited and, after months of separate quarters, chose to live together again. John had returned from his heroic journey.

· 17 ·

JUST LIKE
THE BEATLES
ALL OVER AGAIN

Yoko struck a dissonant chord on the piano and cut loose with one of her famous caterwauls. It was July 1980 and we were sitting in the office in the midst of one of our many readings to select a group of her songs to be recorded for her joint project with John, the album that became *Double Fantasy*. The procedure was that she would sing each piece for me and then ask me to read the cards and predict which ones would be hits. It was a process that made for long afternoons.

She played on with teeth-grinding determination. "What do you think of that one?" she asked, her eyes bright with anticipated approbation.

"Actually, Yoko, I'm not the one to judge. I'm not all that fond of modern music. I prefer more medieval sorts of things, really." No way was I going to be caught in that trap.

"Well look in the cards and tell me if this is going to be a number-one hit."

"You asked that about the last one. They can't all be number one, can they?"

"Well, they could all be in the Top Ten. If all my songs on the album are in the Top Ten, that would leave some room for John's things too. People will buy the record because of John, you know, but it's important that they hear my work. I've been doing a lot of things for years that other people are just starting to do now and calling it new wave and punk rock. I did all that stuff years ago."

"That makes a good press release. Tell that to the agent. Pick a few popular groups and say that they were influenced by your work. That will make the readers think twice about your stuff and the groups won't deny it because it's free publicity."

"Well, it's true! Don't you think so? At least they certainly could have been influenced by me. I've played a lot bigger part in rock and roll than anyone knows."

"Now, now, don't go believing your own press releases."

"But it could have been true and we just don't know it! We have to let people know that there have always been people who loved me and that those people have always been the most advanced and far-thinking."

"No, in fact that is *not* what we have to do. The main theme to get across is that you *were,* past tense, hated for so long."

"We can't say that! That will just start that old hatred back up again."

"Not really. Hating you used to be fashionable, but that time is past. It makes interesting copy. 'Why did people hate this excellent person?' That's how you have to play it. Otherwise if you try to ignore the past, someone else will dig it up for you. It's better if you hit the issue head on. It makes you look stronger."

"I think that's going to be very tricky."

"Not so tricky. Your reputation from the old days is more of an asset than you realize. If there is a really tricky part in all this it's going to be the problem of protecting yourselves. You are going to have to change the way you've been going about things. You are exposing yourselves more to the world and you have to step up security."

It didn't take tarot cards to realize that increasing their exposure was bound to increase their vulnerability, but my anxiety was intensified by the fact that things did not look that safe in the cards either.

"Charlie, you're sweet to worry, but our fans love us and the reason why they do is that we are so accessible to them. Your idea of security is to have the bodyguard around all the time. We can't do that. What would people think? It would look as though we were afraid, and that would only invite trouble. That's why I have to keep sending the bodyguard off on those little trips. I can't have him around. Besides, he makes me nervous. You know, he sees all sorts of things around here and it would be very embarrassing if he were to go to the papers."

"When you go out you always take someone with you, don't you?"

"That's different. I'm a woman and it's very dangerous for a woman to be on her own, but when I have John with me he protects me."

"And who protects him?"

"John's a man and men don't need to be protected in the same way that a woman does. Now this isn't getting us anywhere. The problem that we have to solve is to select the songs of mine that should go onto the album that will be guaranteed to be successful. You see, John's stuff isn't all that good, and when people buy the record to hear him and they hear how much better I am, I will have an instant market for my next release. I want this record to make people think of Yoko and John, not John and Yoko. Then it will be easier to make them think of Yoko only. That's my real goal, an independent career."

"The independent career is certainly an obtainable goal. But if you are thinking that you are going to outshine John in the popular music market it simply isn't possible. He has too much of a head start."

"But I'm much better than he is! There really has to be a way. Think of John as an old star who is fading and me as the new star on the horizon. So tell me what I can do to make that song I just sang a number-one hit."

"You might consider a different arrangement."

"I can't do that! I can't change anything in my music! My songs come directly from the sky. They are given to me in one whole piece. I'm not a craftsman who chisels out a piece slowly. I am an artist."

"Listen, if Beethoven chiseled out his pieces, I'm sure you can stand to make a few changes."

"I don't care what some dead composer supposedly did. He wasn't an artist anyway. If you think that being a craftsman is art, then I shit on you because you don't know anything about art. I want you to tell me how to make these songs hits, but I am not going to change any part of them."

"Well, that leaves only promotion. If you time it right and back it with the right kind of publicity, like arranging to get some school kids to crowd around in front of the recording studio and whoop and holler a little, that will help. Start conditioning the people around you to say, 'Wow, it's just like the Beatles all over again.' And loud enough that the press can overhear. Announce that there will be a tour, a world tour, starting with the Third World, then Japan where you have some market, then Australia, Germany, London, then bring it back to the West Coast and start intensive publicity for, say, fourteen major cities, releasing the record as you go. That will certainly help. Take a videotape for promotional release later.

You should be able to sell gold before you even release to the main market of England and the U.S."

"That's going to mean a great deal of work and spending a lot of time away from home."

"The work is all part of it and you like to travel anyway."

If Yoko was shy about the amount of work involved, John was just the opposite. To him the idea of the road held a special thrill.

"I hear you are telling Yoko that we should book a two-year tour as part of the promotion."

"That's a little excessive, but I don't think it's such a bad idea."

"Tours don't make money, Charles. You know that, don't you?"

"But they make sales, and sales make money and reputation."

"Would that 'twere so simple. It's not that I mind the idea of touring. I love performing. It scares me shitless of course, but I love it. I wonder if it is going to be any different to perform again after all this time and all the changes I've been through. I suspect it won't. Half the thrill is how frightening it all is. I get so scared I get sick. Half the time I think I'm going to throw up right onstage, but if you think about it you never do and I always think I will, so I guess I have nothing to worry about."

"Well, if you do, make a point of suing the last place you ate at for food poisoning."

"You have a devious mind, Charles. No, my real concern about a tour is not whether I'll be able to make it or not because I always do and always will. That's the serious professional in me. What I'm really worried about is Yoko."

"Why? She seems to be looking forward to the tour and she certainly enjoys recording."

"There's a very big difference between recording and touring. Yoko and I have done some concerts together, but she's never really toured. I doubt if she's the type. Not to be rude, but when you tour that's all you do. It takes all your energy. Most of the time you are traveling or waiting and that's simply boring. It's all for those few short moments onstage. On a tour the star is just another piece of equipment that gets loaded and unloaded and shuttled about here and there at the convenience of the engineers. I think Yoko is going to want to be more important than that. To be frank, I'd be a lot more comfortable if she weren't going."

"Them's mighty harsh words, partner."

"It's a mighty harsh business, m'son. You can't just go out and do it when you feel like it. Because the longer you tour, the less you feel like it. I'm not at all sure that once the novelty has worn off Yoko is going to be all that interested in keeping pace. This is not just old John trying to get away from his wife. I seriously doubt if Yoko has enough respect for the audience to keep it up. All she has to do is say, 'I'm sick and I can't go on,' and there goes a whole damned tour down the tubes, and that is something no performer can afford.

"It takes more than vanity to keep you onstage, you know. It takes a kind of lust. The tour, the crowd, the demands are all like some very strict mistress that puts you through your tricks before she'll let you get it off. It hurts like hell and you love it. Or you lust it. Onstage you're not a king. Kings don't go before the crowds like that. No, onstage you're a slave who's allowed to play the king, and the thrill and freedom of that is worth it.

"I'm not sure I should risk putting Yoko through that. Not for her sake, mind you, because in some ways the object lesson would be good for her. It's the ticketholders I worry about. They're the ones who own the show and the players. If there is a king it's the crowd, and if you displease the king, then it's off with your ratings and down with your sales."

"That leaves you with rather a problem, doesn't it?"

"Not really. We've told the press we'll do a tour, but I think I'll wait on it a bit and see what the sales receipts say. If things look promising enough we might try a short one and see how that works. Ease her into it, as it were."

"That's a liability for sales, you know."

"I know, I know. But fortunately I don't have to do this for a living. I can afford to take it easy. That publicity agent you got us is getting us more coverage than believable, and we really haven't done anything yet. No, I can afford to just do a little recording and some TV promotion, like that.

"I don't have to be a superstar. I don't need all the frenzy and mania now. That's not the sort of thing I'm doing now anyway. All these songs are much more middle-of-the-road than what I used to do. They're easygoing. I sort of wanted to bring a new message to the public, at least new for me. I used to promote revolution. Now I want to promote a bit of institution, home, marriage, family. They were certainly the old standby virtues that pulled me through when I needed it. My message now is that all those corny old truths are corny but true nonetheless.

"It sounds a little sentimental, but as I approach forty I'm feeling just a bit sentimental about it all. A lot lower key. I do need the music. Not to prove I can or to compete with Paul because God knows he's way out of my league now. But I need the music because I need it. It's what feeds me and I'm dying if it's not there. Just like I've been dying all the time you've known me."

"Until now."

"Yeah, until now. Now I've got it back again and I have no intention of losing it.

"The pieces finally seem to be falling into place again, to my great relief. I'm actually in a studio and I hadn't realized how much I missed that. You know, when you've so much money that you don't have to work, you begin to realize what a privilege it is to work. I suppose that sounds funny to you, but it's not funny to me. I love working, and not being able to do my work for so long was like being in hell. I'm out of that hell now and I'm grateful, grateful to you and to everyone else who tried to get me out. And again this may sound vain, but I'm mostly grateful to myself for getting out because all the teachers and advisors in the world don't do a bit of good if you don't listen to them. I finally listened. You said that I would have to do it for myself and that seemed impossible at the time, but in the end that's exactly what happened.

"But what will I tell them I've been up to for the last half decade? And why did I stop that if it was so important to be a househusband?"

"You ought to tell them the truth. That you lost the muse and after a heroic struggle you got her back. That's a good story."

"I don't care how good it is, it's not what I'm going to tell the press until I get some reviews from the mags and the music critics. I don't want to announce that I lost the muse and then have somebody say, 'Well, you still haven't got it back, John.' I'm sticking with the househusband story and anything else I can think up until I hear some results. Later maybe I'll tell that other story because it might make good press and because it might actually be of some help to some other artist, but for now I intend to keep it quiet. There's no point advertising the bad times until you're sure they're over."

In keeping with our agreement, as the Lennons drew more and more public attention, I withdrew more and more into the background. Advertising that you listen to fortune-tellers is not the soundest business policy. But although I was no longer haunting the Dakota, there were phone calls. They came at odd times on odd subjects. For example, I was in the bathtub when Yoko called to ask me about signing a contract with Geffen Records. I had my cards close by (I *always* have my cards close by), so I read in the tub. Then there were calls from the studio

255

asking what to do with some of the songs, and the cards recommended closer synchronization between the bass drum and the bass guitar or more syncopation. As the autumn progressed, the original recording schedule had to be extended and the calls grew less frequent. I was somewhat bothered by the lack of communication, but on the other hand, it represented my first uninterrupted vacation from the Lennons in six years. In October, Yoko said that they were busy remixing and that I should just rest for a while until they were finished. The press was going well and I was busy with other clients.

I was a little surprised when John called late on a chilly October evening in 1980 and invited himself over for a drink, "or drinks depending on how the spirits strike us." It was clear when he arrived that he had gotten a head start on the drinks.

"Hello, Charles, how goes it with your mysteries? I haven't seen you in a bit and thought you disappeared. Magicians do that, you know."

"Of course we do. I've been there. You just haven't seen me. How goes it?"

"If you've been there you should know, shouldn't you? But never mind, I'll play. Things go well, Charles, extraordinarily well. In fact they couldn't be weller. I wish I could say the same for you."

"Why? Is there something wrong with my numbers?"

"Possibly. I've been getting omens about you, Charles. Signs. You do believe in omens, don't you?"

"Only the good ones."

"Well then, perhaps you won't believe in these. The wife tells me of late that she is getting stronger and stronger psychic messages. She says, 'The spirits are coming to me all the time now and they say that I'm an initiate. Isn't that amazing? We won't need all those psychics anymore because I will get all the messages.' That's a bad omen as far as you're concerned, I fear."

"And what do the spirits tell her?"

"Oh, the usual crap. Apparently the spirits are a lot more flattering than you are. The record will be a great success. Everyone will love us in general and Yoko in particular. 'But don't feel too badly, John, because they'll like you too.' It's her game, and if it makes her happy or gives her confidence, so much the better. Just so long as she doesn't go off the deep end."

"And what do you consider the deep end?"

"I don't really know. I've been so crazy I wouldn't recognize madness if it jumped out and bit me. But I was thinking just the other day about you. Do you remember about a thousand years ago, we had a conversation in the apartment and you said that there were seven things that you were supposed to get for Yoko?"

"Yes, I've been working on them."

"And succeeding. At the time I thought that you were a nice enough guy but trapped in all the glamour of being with the famous Lennons."

"I would hardly call it glamorous."

"Not to be nasty, Charles. Even you would have to admit that working with us is a little out of your ordinary realm of experience."

"With that I will agree."

"So I thought you had decided that you were the world's greatest magic-maker and you were going to save ol' Lennon from a fate worse than obscurity. But you were interesting to talk to and I thought that there was no harm in keeping you around."

"Gee, thanks."

"Come on now, I'm trying to compliment you. Then things started to change. Lawsuits. You said you were going to get rid of them and now they're gone. There were other things, too. And as I was thinking about it I realized that all seven things you promised have happened."

"Just about. All you have to do is release the record."

"That means that it's just about time the piper got paid. That is why I think the wife is getting all these messages and saying that we don't need psychics anymore. She certainly calls her medium and others but not you now. She says she's gotten messages about you and all those clandestine agreements you make with people. She's beginning to think you're dangerous. I'm telling you this by way of a warning. If the wife decides to drop you, then you can always come to me. A deal is a deal."

"Let's hope it doesn't come to that."

"Well, just in case it does. Anyway, that's what I wanted to say because I think that that's fair, so I said it."

Considering his duty done, he mused for a moment, then continued more brightly.

"Aside from that, everything is going well. I've been fiddling around playing engineer, mixing and remixing everything we've done. Actually Yoko is the one to do that. She'd surprise you with her abilities at a mixing board. Of course she prefers to be in front of the mike and not in the booth, but I can't blame her for that.

"You know how the record is set up, don't you? One of my songs, then one of hers, then mine, then hers, and so forth. That was her idea because it's supposed to make it more like dialogue, a radio play. I think the real reason is that she's afraid that if she got the B side no one would play it. I can't blame her for that either. The stage brings out the ham in all of us and I'm no exception. But it's better for her this time than it ever has been before. At least the producer doesn't throw his hands over his ears and run out of the room when she starts to sing. That makes things a bit easier. She's convinced that this is the beginning of a whole new recording career."

"And what do you think?"

"I think it wouldn't be such a bad idea. I told you I was a ham too, and I'm not all that interested in sharing the limelight with anyone. I mean, we do interviews together and I try not to step on her toes, which is fairly easy because she doesn't say all that much. I don't contradict her, and if I sense that she is getting off in the wrong direction, I gently interrupt and change the subject. So I think I've been pretty cool about it. She wants to record and why shouldn't she? What I don't need is to have her singing the same song with me because that would cramp my style. So I do my thing and she does her thing, and that way we are doing it together but separately.

"She tells me the truth and I need that, you know. Now we have a lot more people around us and they are new people, but it's the same old act. Everyone fawns and flatters and she eats that up, which is fine if that's what you like. But I need something more than that. I don't need anybody except the reviewers and the fans saying that I'm terrific. I need the people close to me to say, 'That song you're doing shits, change it!' And maybe I'll give 'em an argument and maybe not. But it forces me to reexamine what I'm doing and that's good. I can always count on Yoko for that because she has never been suckered into being impressed by me. I like it and she likes it, and now that I'm working again everything is going as smooth as glass. We're actually acting like a married couple again. Sean seems happier and I even feel as though there is a real relationship beginning to blossom with Julian. Like I said, things couldn't be weller. I only wish that it all could have happened years ago. I feel like I've lost a hunk of my life that I will never get back."

"But if you didn't lose that hunk, then you couldn't have this time now. You learned and that's what saved you and got your muse back. If this hadn't happened, then you would still be doing things the old way, and you know how successful that was."

"I know, it's that old saw that everything that happens to you goes into making you up, so if you are happy with the way you are, then you have to be grateful for all the things that have happened, good and bad."

"The funny things about all those corny old truths is that they are corny but true."

"I think I heard that somewhere before. I don't mind them being true, Charles. I just don't like it when they're painful."

"The funny thing about pain is that when it's happening it feels so real and when it's over it seems so unreal."

"You're just full of all these little bromides, aren't you?"

"It's a living."

Double Fantasy, John's last recording, was released in November and we all held our breath for the public reaction. John kept himself distracted with remixing in the studio (he had, of course, recorded far more than a single album's worth of material). On the evening of December 8, 1980, he had just finished working several hours on this project. For John that was a short day. He was used to working incredible stretches. As he was preparing to leave the studio he met a young producer named John Mathis. Mathis was a longtime admirer of John's and was thrilled at the opportunity to meet his hero. Together they chatted cheerfully about the record, about the business and the music. John was in his element, talking about his favorite thing, music, with his first love, the fan. He had just released a new record and the world was his again. Yoko on his arm, he left the studio saying that he was off for a bite to eat.

A half-hour later, John Lennon was dead.